William Barnes was born near Sturminster New-
ton, Dorset, in 1801, the son of a small farmer. He
has been called 'the greatest poet ever to have written in English dialect' and the publication of *Poems
of Rural Life in the Dorset Dialect* in 1844 brought
him national recognition. The publication of further volumes of poetry added to a list of admirers
that included Hardy, Tennyson, Browning and
Matthew Arnold. After leaving school he became
a solicitor's clerk. He later became a schoolmaster,
establishing a successful school in Dorchester
which he ran with his wife Julia. He was ordained
in 1848, becoming rector of Winterbourne Came in
1862 and remaining there until his death in 1886. As
well as a poet, he was an expert linguist familiar
with sixty languages, a skilful engraver and a com-
poser.

Chris Wrigley is Senior Lecturer in Economic and
Social History at Loughborough University. He
has written widely on the nineteenth and twentieth
centuries and his books include *David Lloyd George
and the British Labour Movement*, *A History of British
Industrial Relations* 1875–1914, and he was joint
editor of *The Working Class in Victorian England*.

William Barnes

The Dorset Poet

INTRODUCED AND SELECTED BY
CHRIS WRIGLEY

THE DOVECOTE PRESS

This selection first published in 1984 by
The Dovecote Press Ltd
Stanbridge, Wimborne, Dorset

Reprinted 1988, 1990

ISBN 0 946159 17 3

Introduction © Chris Wrigley 1984

Designed by Humphrey Stone
Printed and bound in Great Britain by
Biddles Ltd, Guildford and King's Lynn

Contents

PREFACE   xi

INTRODUCTION   I

REFERENCES TO INTRODUCTION   18

PART I: POEMS IN NATIONAL ENGLISH

White and Blue	23
Melhill Feast	23
Rustic Childhood	24
The Woodland Home	25
The Lane	26
Autumn	28
Moss	29
To a Garden – on Leaving it	31
The Bird-Boy's Dinner Token	31
Leaves	33
Rural Seclusion	33
The Home-Ground	33
The Elm in Home-Ground	35
Moonlight	36
The Eegrass	37
Memory's Stores	39
Learning	41
Athelhamton House	42
Friendly Light	45
Plorata Veris Lachrymis	45
My Dearest Julia	46
The Wind at the Door	47
See or Hear	48

The Bank Steps 48
Beechley 49
Season Tokens 50
The Church Tower 51
The News of the Day 52
Brown Bennets 53
Benighted 54
The Depopulated Village 55
Goody Tired 56
Home-Field 57
A Sabbath Lay 58

PART 2: POEMS IN DORSET DIALECT

The Spring 61
Easter Zunday 61
Easter Monday 62
Dock-Leaves 63
Woodcom' Feast 64
The Girt Woak Tree that's in the Dell 65
Vellen o' the Tree 67
Evenen Twilight 67
Evenen in the Village 68
May 69
Bob the Fiddler 70
The White Road up Athirt the Hill 71
The Woody Hollow 72
Jenny's Ribbons 73
Eclogue: The 'Lotments 74
Eclogue: A Bit o' Sly Coorten 76
Whitsuntide an' Club Walken 78
Woodley 80
The Brook that Ran by Gramfer's 81
Sweet Music in the Wind 83

Uncle an' Aunt — 83

Haven Woone's Fortune a–Twold — 85

Meaken up a Miff — 86

Hay–Meaken — 87

Hay–Carren — 88

Eclogue: The Best Man in the Vield — 89

Where we did Keep our Flagon — 90

Week's End in Zummer in the Wold Vo'k's Time — 93

The Evenen Star o' Zummer — 95

I Got Two Vields — 96

Be'mi'ster — 96

Eclogue: The Veairies — 97

A–Haulen o' the Corn — 99

Harvest Hwome: (1) — 100

Harvest Hwome: (2) — 101

A Zong ov Harvest Hwome — 102

Grenley Water — 104

Out a–Nutten — 105

Shrodon Feair: (1) — 106

Shroden Feair: (2) — 107

Martin's Tide — 108

Guy Faux's Night — 109

Eclogue: The Common a–Took in — 110

Eclogue: Two Farms in Woone — 112

Eclogue: Rusticus Res Politicas
    Animadvertens, the New Poor Laws — 115

Grammer's Shoes — 117

Zunsheen in the Winter — 118

The Settle an' the Girt Wood Vire — 119

Keepen up o' Chris'mas — 121

Zitten out the Wold Year — 122

Eclogue: Father Come Hwome — 123

Eclogue: A Ghost — 126

vii

Uncle Out o' Debt an' Out o' Danger 128
The Wold Waggon 130
The Common a-Took in 131
The Vaices that be Gone 132
Aunt's Tantrums 133
A Witch 134
Eclogue: The Times 135
Blackmwore Maidens 142
My Orcha'd in Linden Lea 143
Bishop's Caundle 143
Day's Work a-Done 145
The Waggon a-Stooded 146
Ellen Brine ov Allenburn 151
The Maid o' Newton 152
Meary's Smile 153
The Window Fream'd wi Stwone 154
The Water-Spring in the Leane 155
The Poplars 156
The Linden on the Lawn 156
Zun-zet 158
Spring 159
The Water Crowvoot 160
The Lilac 161
The Blackbird 162
Lydlinch Bells 163
The Stage Coach 164
Trees be Company 165
Jessie Lee 166
Ivy Hall 167
The Wife a-Lost 168
Herrenston 169
Pentridge by the River 171
The Turn o' the Days 172

Gammony Gay   173
Leeburn Mill   175
Woone Smile Mwore   176
Woak Hill   177
The Hedger   178
The Flood in Spring   179
Comen Hwome   180
Early Playmeate   181
Picken o'Scroff   182
Good Night   183
Went Hwone   183
Childern's Childern   184
The Rwose in the Dark   185
Zummer Winds   186
Zummer Stream   187
Lindenore   188
The Love Child   189
Times o'Year   190
Zummer an' Winter   191
To Me   191
Tokens   192
Tweil   193
Evenen Light   194
Vields by Watervalls   195
Fall Time   196
The Zilver-Weed   197
The Fancy Feair at Maiden Newton   197
I'm Out o'Door   198
Sliden   199
The Humstrum   201
Shaftesbury Feair   202
Daniel Dwithen, The Wise Chap   203
John Bloom in London   204

ix

Shop o' Meat-Weare   207
The Knowl   207
At the Door   209
Hill or Dell   210
Fellowship   210
Air an' Light   212
Meldon Hill   212
Black an' White   213
Clouds   214
The Wind a-Playen Round   214
The Parrick   215
By the Mill in Spring   216
Shellbrook   216
Rings   217
Mother o' Mothers   217
The Geate a-Vallen To   219

PART III: SELECTIONS FROM BARNES' WRITINGS

INTRODUCTION   223
Auctions   225
Gardening   226
Association   228
The Church and Culture   229
Human Progression   231
Linguiana (three parts)   232

PART IV: GLOSSARY OF DORSET WORDS

Preface

William Barnes' poetry has remained almost continually in print since his death a hundred years ago (1886). In recent years those wanting a selection of his verse have been served by a number of small selections; perhaps the best being *William Barnes: A Selection of His Poems* by Robert Nye (Oxford, Carcanet Press, 1972). Scholars have been well served by the excellent, huge, two volume edition, *The Poems of William Barnes* edited by Dr. Bernard Jones (London, Centaur Press; U.S.A., Southern Illinois University Press, 1962). However the last major selection of Barnes' poetry was Geoffrey Grigson's fine *Selected Poems of William Barnes* (London, Routledge and Kegan Paul), published in 1950. Undoubtedly there is demand now for a relatively cheap large selection of Barnes' verse – and this book is intended to meet this demand.

When Thomas Hardy agreed to make a selection of Barnes' poems in 1908 he informed his publisher that he had 'chosen those I think best as poetry, and most representative as pictures of rural life.' I have found myself following similar criteria. Usually the two criteria blend into one – but I have felt that in a large selection it would be a pity not to include, occasionally, a poem where its subject matter, a place or a custom, is of considerable interest even when its execution is less satisfactory.

Hardy in his Preface to his selection, *Select Poems of William Barnes* (1908), observed:

A selector may say: These are the pieces that please me best; but he may not be entitled to hold that they are the best in themselves and for everybody. This opens the problem of equating the personality – of adjusting the idiosyncrasy of the chooser to mean pitch. If it can be done in some degree – one may doubt it – there are to be borne in mind the continually changing tastes of the times. (p. iv).

In some cases where I have differed in my judgements from those of Hardy I have felt that it reflects, perhaps, a late twentieth century resistance to the appeal of verse about once glimpsed damsels who died tragically young. More often I have found myself in agreement with Hardy. The best of Barnes is timeless.

Much of Barnes' best poetry is that which he wrote in Dorset dialect. At first sight this may be off-putting to any reader today. In fact the meaning becomes clear if one reads them out loud, following Barnes' spelling. Barnes was a considerable craftsman when it came to writing verse, and this becomes apparent very soon to anyone reading them with a little care. One does not need a Dorset background to enjoy these poems.

The text of the poems is generally drawn from the last version Barnes made of the poems; in the case of many of the dialect poems from his 1879 collected edition. In many cases I, like all others interested in Barnes, have benefitted from Dr. Jones' scholarship. His edition of Barnes' poetry is likely to be the definitive work for a very long time.

I am also indebted to David Burnett for his care in producing this book and to Janice Lidgett for typing it.

Introduction

William Barnes (1801–1886) was a rural eminent Victorian. Like so many outstanding people of that period his interests were wide ranging and he wrote on a large number of subjects. As a poet he received national recognition with the publication of *Poems of Rural Life in the Dorset Dialect* in 1844. His admirers included Matthew Arnold, Robert Browning, Edmund Gosse, Thomas Hardy, Gerard Manley Hopkins, Francis Palgrave, Coventry Patmore, Sir Arthur Quiller Couch and Tennyson. In the later years of Barnes' life many leading literary figures made their way to Dorchester to visit him.

William Barnes was born in the Blackmore Vale at Rush-Hay, a smallholding at Bagber Common two miles west of Sturminster Newton. His father, John, was a tenant farmer who gained only part of his livelihood from his land, having to supplement his income by working part-time for the more prosperous farmers of the area. John's sister and her husband Charles Roberts farmed nearby land which ran down to the River Stour.

William Barnes' mother died when he was five. He then spent much time with his aunt and uncle. He enjoyed a happy childhood in the quiet countryside around Pentridge Farm. He was to write many poems recollecting these years at Pentridge Farm, including specific ones such as 'Pentridge By The River' and 'Uncle An' Aunt' to the more generalised such as 'The Elm In Home-Ground', 'home-ground' being the field by a farmhouse in which young children played. Indeed much of his rustic verse looks back to the countryside of his youth, to the prosperous times of British agriculture during the French Wars (of the 1790s to 1815) and to the Dorset countryside before the coming of the railway.

Barnes clung tenaciously to his memories of the good times of his youth near Sturminster Newton for the remainder of his life. In 1847, in one of the more prosperous phases of his life, Barnes bought two fields at Bagber, thereafter renting them to a local farmer. Although they had not belonged to his family in the past, Barnes clearly felt that he was keeping faith with his forefathers. In later life Barnes gained great pleasure from revisiting the places

I

of his youth. His daughter recalled one visit in the early 1840's to Ham Hill where they could overlook the Blackmore Vale:

Towns, and villages, and lonely farmsteads were dotted about, some forming a cluster of warm red or thatched roofs, others only suggested by curling smoke amongst the trees. The poet pointed out each place to his wife. 'There was the farm of my grandfather;' 'that was the house my great-grandfather possessed;' 'there was one of my favourite haunts when a boy', and so on, every place seemed to be full of story to him. [1]

Such family pilgrimages were undertaken at intervals up to 1883, when Barnes' health began to deteriorate.

However the agricultural prosperity which had underpinned his idyllic childhood by the Stour came to an end after the victory at Waterloo. Many farmers were bankrupted in the ensuing depression, including William Barnes' uncle. This family catastrophe is recalled both in some of his poems and in his short article 'Auctions', written for *The Dorset County Chronicle* in 1829 (and reprinted in Part 3 of this book). [2]

William Barnes began work before Waterloo. He had excelled at school. As a result of his abilities and his beautiful handwriting he had been taken on as a clerk by a Sturminster solicitor, Thomas Henry Dashwood, in 1814. After the death of Dashwood, Barnes, in 1818, moved on to a similar job in the old solicitor's firm of Thomas Coomb and son in Dorchester. In Sturminster and Dorchester his employers and the local clergy helped him in furthering his own education. He learnt Latin and Greek and studied drawing and music. In the next few years he published poems, a small collection in 1820 and a long poem, 'Orra: A Lapland Tale' in 1822; and he also became skilled in the arts of copper and wood engraving.

In 1823 William Barnes took a considerable gamble. He left his work in Dorchester to go to Mere in Wiltshire to take over a school. It had nearly collapsed during the illness and death of the previous master. For four years he taught in the Old Cross Loft in the Market House. In making this move Barnes was impelled by his desire to marry Julia Miles. However it is quite possible that his intellectual interests, already underway in Sturminster and Dorchester before he met her, were encouraging him to think of teaching as a career.

Julia Miles was very much the love of his life. He fell in love with her at first sight, when she and her family came off a stage coach in High Street, Dorchester. He was eighteen and she was sixteen. Soon they were going to concerts together and walking in the countryside. Her father was Supervisor of Excise. Several writers have made much of her father's opposition to their marriage; probably they have made too much of it. It would be surprising if James Miles had not been cautious about his sixteen-year old daughter marrying the first man who took a serious interest in her. There seems to be no reason to doubt his views as reported in a letter Julia wrote to William in 1823:

He told me plainly he had no objection to you in the least – but on the contrary you were a young person whom he much respected. But then he told me I must remember that when you first walked with me I was but a mere child and it was his duty as an affectionate father to make objections. But still he wished me to understand he would not be an obstacle in the way if I had placed my affections, by no means.[3]

They married in 1827, when Barnes could expand his teaching activity into running a boarding school for boys and girls (with Julia in charge of the latter part of the enterprise). Clearly theirs was a very happy marriage. Barnes was to be devastated by Julia's death in June 1852. Their meeting had stimulated his earliest verse. With her death he expressed his anguish in some of his most moving verse such as 'Plorata Veris Lachrymis' (which originally had as its first line, 'My Julia, my dearest bride'), 'My Dearest Julia' and, nine years later, 'Woak Hill'.

His years at the Chantry House, Mere, from 1827 to 1835 were among the happiest of his life. At Mere Barnes wrote poetry, enjoyed music and engraved in wood and copper. He read widely, learned more languages and began writing on philology – he wrote of English words in a series of letters to *The Dorset County Chronicle* (three of which are reprinted in Part 3 of this book) and in articles to *The Gentleman's Magazine*. He even had published booklets on government (for use in schools) and on mathematics. In addition to all else, he found immense pleasure in gardening. Gardening brought him close to God's works and provided profitable enjoyment. It suited his almost peasant outlook to be tilling the soil to supplement the family's food. He eulogised gardening and advocated the provision of allotments in one of his letters to *The Dorset County Chronicle* (see Part 3 of this book)[4], and wrote of his sorrow in leaving his garden at the Chantry House in his poem 'To A Garden – On Leaving It'.

Both William and Julia Barnes felt it was economically advisable to move to Dorchester. Barnes later recalled:

3

Mere was out of the way for pupils and I always yearned for Dorset and Dorchester; and as I had strengthened my teaching power, and was told by friends at Dorchester that there was an opening for a boarding school, I put my hopes of after life in work at that place, to which I returned in 1835, and was happy and thankful with an income on which I brought up my children.

They set up school there first in Durngate Street (1835–1837) and then in South Street. They successfully built up their school as one which aimed to specialise in preparing middle class children for the professions, the army or navy or to the universities. As one writer has observed, 'In the year of the Great Exhibition, the Rev. William Barnes's Academy was one of the largest, and potentially best-equipped, schools in Dorset for the sons of the middle-classes'. [5] This was to be its peak. In the following year Julia died. Quite probably Julia had had more business sense than her husband. Her death shook Barnes and aged him, making him less effective in running such an enterprise. Although he was helped by his older daughters, Laura and Julia, the school declined thereafter.

Earlier, Barnes had taken holy orders. He was ordained at Salisbury in February 1848 and immediately became curate at Whitcombe, a village three miles from Dorchester; he held this curacy for four years. In 1837 he had started on the lengthy course of study which would lead to a Bachelor's degree of Divinity at Cambridge University. This involved being registered for at least ten years, spending three full terms in college and satisfying the examiners in a range of tests. Barnes spent the summer terms of 1847 and 1848 and the spring term of 1850 at St. John's College. His B.D. degree was conferred on him in October of that year.

Barnes was to achieve financial security for his family through the Church, not through school teaching. His school declined steadily during the 1850s. Barnes received some relief when, on Palmerston's recommendation, the Queen granted him a Literary Pension of £30 a year in 1861. Security came, in 1862, when Captain Seymour Damer offered him the living of Winterbourne Came. Barnes lived for the remainder of his life in the fine Came Rectory, a picturesque thatched building which still survives. It is a mile out of Dorchester, by the main road to Wareham.

Barnes achieved the literary acclaim which led to the pension from the Queen through the publication of his dialect verse in book form. He had published poetry in *The Dorset County*

4

Chronicle for many years, at first in national English and later in dialect. In his *Poems of Rural Life in the Dorset Dialect* (1844) he observed, of his verse:

The author thinks his reader will find poems free of slang and nice as they are written from the associations of an early youth that was passed among rural families of a secluded part of the County, upon whose sound Christian principles, kindness and harmless cheerfulness he can still think with delight: and he hopes that if this little work should fall into the hands of a reader of that class in whose language it is written, it would not be likely to damp his love of God or hurt the tone of his moral sentiment or the dignity of his self respect; as his intention is not to show up the simplicity of rural life as an object of sport, but to utter the happy emotions with which his mind can dwell on the charms of rural nature and the better feelings and more harmless joys of the small farm house and happy cottage.

Barnes' poetry had attractions for the reading public of a country which was experiencing rapid industrialisation and urban growth. The success of John Clare's first collection, *Poems of Rural Life and Scenery* (1820), had shown there could be a market for good rustic verse. Clare had had trouble with his patron over 'improper verse' ('Dolly's Mistake' and 'My Mary') and 'radical and ungrateful sentiments'. [6] Barnes' verse mentioned the occasional illegitimate child and made some critical comments of certain changes on the land; but, as in his dissertation at the start of his first dialect volume, the tone was generally one that would meet with approval in fashionable society. By and large it fitted in well with the dominant outlook of the literary world of the time, which presumed literature should reflect the political and moral *status quo*.

Barnes' second and third dialect volumes (1859 and 1862) consolidated his reputation even if, like Clare's later volumes, they did not sell as well as the first volume. Barnes also published selections of his verse in 'common English'; though, as he correctly foretold in his preface to the 1868 collection, he did so 'not . . . without a misgiving that what I have done for a wider range of readers, may win the good opinion of fewer'. However his dialect poetry remained popular. Kegan Paul brought out in 1879 an edition of his dialect verse including nearly all the verse in the three earlier collections plus additional material. This volume, which was uniform with their edition of Tennyson's verse, was reprinted seven times up to 1905.

Barnes also published numerous other books over the years.

Some arose from his interest in comparative philology. Others, notably his *Notes on Ancient Britain and the Britons* (1858) and *Early England and the Saxon English*, arose from his interest in archaeology and early history as well as his enthusiasm for philology.[7] In 1845 he had been one of those who had been alarmed at the prospect of the coming of the railway to Dorchester devastating ancient remains. As a result of these fears the Dorset County Museum was set up, and in 1846 Barnes was one of its initial joint secretaries. He was to remain an enthusiastic supporter of the museum and of the Dorset Field Club (which was founded in 1875).

Barnes' historical books stemmed from courses of lectures. So too did his *Views of Labour and Gold* (1859), a book on political and moral economy. Indeed *Views of Labour and Gold*, which incorporated much earlier material he had written for the press, was based on the lectures he gave to adult education audiences during the 1850s. Adult education was to be one of Barnes' major enthusiasms from 1851 until he was 80 and no longer able to travel to give lectures.

Barnes remained active until 1884. In his last months, confined to the rectory and, later, to his bed, he still occasionally composed verse. In October 1885 he dictated 'The Geate a-Vallen To' to his daughter Lucy. He died a year later on 7 October 1886. The funeral, four days later, gave rise to a poetic tribute from Thomas Hardy – a tribute not just of subject but of mode of expression, Hardy using several of the metrical techniques with which Barnes experimented.

THE LAST SIGNAL

A MEMORY OF WILLIAM BARNES

Silently I footed by an uphill road
That led from my abode to a spot yew-boughed
Yellowly the sun sloped low down to westward,
And dark was the east with cloud.

Then, below the shadow of that livid, sad east
Where the light was least and a gate swung wide,
Flashed a reflection of the sun that was facing it,
Like a brief blaze on that side.

Looking hard and harder I knew what it meant –
The sudden shine sent from the livid east scene;
It meant the sun mirrored by the coffin of my friend there,
Turning to the road from his green.

6

To take his last journey forth – he who in his prime
Trudged so many a time from that gate athwart the land.
Thus a farewell to me he signalled on his grave-way,
As with a wave of his hand.

★   ★   ★

Whilst Barnes' rustic verse and the views expressed in his
dissertation at the start of his first collection of dialect verse
would not offend fashionable society, it would be harsh on
Barnes to see him as a 'Yes-man'. E. M. Forster gave this verdict
in an essay in his *Two Cheers For Democracy* (1951): 'There is no
difficult or disturbing view of society . . . . He is truly, affection-
ately a Yes-man'.

Barnes' views were much more complex than is suggested by
Forster. He could be very strong in his criticism of industrial
capitalism, where relationships could be reduced to 'the cash-
nexus' and free market forces could reign supreme. He could be
just as critical, or even more so, of changes in rural society. His
views reflected a traditional, paternalistic conservatism, which
emphasised the duties of property and idealised the social role of
the squirearchy and clergy. Usually his views were very critical
of the predominant *laissez-faire* Liberalism of his day.

His views were much coloured by his family background. His
grandfather is described as a yeoman farmer, his father a tenant
farmer and he himself, as we have seen, took great pleasure in
buying fields at Bagber. So many of his rural poems express
almost a peasant-like satisfaction in someone being free and
independent to work their own plot of land, however small. This
is expressed bluntly in poems such as 'I Got Two Vields':

> I got two vields, an' I don't cëare
> What squire mid have a bigger shëare.

and in 'The Hwomestead':

> I'm landlord o' my little farm,
> I'm king 'ithin my little plëace;
> I don't break laws, an' don't do harm,
> An' ben't afeard o' noo man's fëace.

Poems such as 'My Orcha'd In Linden Lea', probably his most
popular, express a sturdy rustic independence as well as conjuring
up idyllic rural situations which appealed to those living in the
midst of Victorian industrialisation and urbanisation. In 'Linden
Lea' he directly contrasts rustic life with town life:

7

Let other vo'k mëake money vaster
In the aïr o' dark-room'd towns,
I don't dread a peevish mëaster.

As well as his undoubted skills in versification, much of Barnes' magic is the way in which he brings us close to rustic life. The poetry displays the seasonal rhythm; indeed in his first collection of dialect verse he divided most of the contents between 'Spring', 'Summer', 'Fall', and 'Winter'. As well as depicting the work (hay making, hauling in the corn, thatching etc.) he brings alive the village pleasures; harvest home, Guy Fawkes night, the Christmas feast, and such special celebrations as those to mark the end of the Crimean War ('Bishop's Caundle'). Barnes' verse portrays a pattern of rural life which has long gone. In fact much of it had gone by Barnes' old age. Much of what he wrote recalled his bucolic boyhood in the Blackmore Vale of the first two decades of the nineteenth century, a past which was being eroded by new farming techniques and machinery and by transport improvements. Against the fading pattern of the old rustic ways, Barnes also emphasised the transient nature of human life: reflecting on people's younger days (poems such as 'Martins Tide' and 'Grammer's Shoes') and on those who died young (such as 'Week's En In Zummer In The Wold Vo'ks Time' and 'The Vaices That Be Gone').

In this, as in his philological desires to take the language back to a purer form, Barnes was harking back to a traditional past and traditional values. Barnes' idealisation of the smallholder and of rustic communities, where there was a place for everyone and all knew their place, reflects an outlook more common to the eighteenth century than to the nineteenth. His daughter wrote in her biography of her father:

The vale of Blackmore, in which all these houses of his forebears were situated, is a kind of Tempé – a happy valley – so shut in by its sheltering hills, that up to quite modern times the outer world had sent few echoes to disturb its serene and rustic quiet. Life in Blackmore was practically the life of the seventeenth and eighteenth centuries, until the nineteenth was actually far advanced. [8]

Barnes took a dim view of the more intensive farming methods which impinged on the old rural ways. He had first hand experience of the value of common rights, for his father made use of Bagber Common (which was to be the subject of an Act to enclose 95 acres in 1836). The use of common land had been a valuable means by which poor families could supplement their income by keeping geese or an animal on it. Barnes' early poetry expresses the plight of the rural poor in such poems as 'The Common A-Took In' and 'Father Come Hwome'.

Barnes' critical comments sprang from the same roots as William Cobbett's. Cobbett, who started off as a Conservative, a notable anti-Jacobin pamphleteer, similarly was very critical of the new ways in agriculture which undermined the old cottage economy. [9] However, Barnes' views did not become as advanced as Cobbett's. Thus, in commenting on the loss of the commons, Barnes' remedy was far from radical. In both poetry and newspaper articles he advocated the provision of allotments – and it is notable that in the eclogue 'The 'Lotments' the reform is seen as coming from above, from 'the squire .... a worthy man'. This might be a shrewd way to encourage such provision, given the well-to-do readership of *The Dorset County Chronicle*, but it also coincides with the idealised role he had in mind for the local landed interest. Barnes was very critical of the idle rich, but he could exclude the local squirearchy from this, both in poetry which recalled 'The good wold squire' who 'did know the poor so well' and in such writings as *Views of Labour and Gold*. In the latter he warned of the idle rich:

So, the more may be the unworking men, who yield no service or hand or mind to the community, the worse is the task of the burdened workers; and therefore in a community of many rich idlers, care should be taken of the honest working classes, or else they will become degraded and dangerous. (p. 162)

The squire and his lady are a great social good when they live among the poor, and keep before their eyes the graceful pattern of Christian life, and raise their tone of feeling by kindness and sober bearing. Nay it is good to expose to the eyes of the poor toilers, for the bare animal man, the clean gravel path, the shrub adorned lawn, the bright windows, and the amenities of a good house. But on the other hand to increase of a truly idle class, a class who may do nothing for the bodily man, and cannot work any good to the intellectual one, is a social evil. (p. 173)

Barnes looked back with considerable nostalgia to pre-industrial values. He admired the independent craftsmen as well as the independent small holder. He deplored the division of labour being taken too far, as it could make the workman 'a man of only one skill and so narrowing the sphere within which he may win his livelihood'.

In contrast he observed, 'If a man in a less refined community made needles for his household, the grinding of them would happen so seldom, and hold on through so short a time, that it would never break up his health; whereas with our division of labour, a man takes the grinding of needles as his only work, and breathes steel dust all day, and from day to day, and thus inhales disease and hasty death'.

Barnes saw manual labour, alongside intellectual activity, as an important ingredient of a well balanced life. 'Hard labour', he observed, 'is the lot of man, his main if not only true wealth, and the upholder of his life'. [10] He regretted that industrialisation, by providing goods cheaply, had undermined self-reliance. In such views he was not far removed from John Ruskin's complaint in his *The Stones of Venice* (1853):

We have much studied and much perfected, of late, the great civilised invention of the division of labour; only we have given it a false name. It is not, truly speaking, the labour that is divided; but the men: divided into mere segments of men, broken into small fragments and crumbs of life, so that all the little pieces of intelligence that is left in a man is not enough to make a pin or a nail but exhausts itself in making the point of a pin and the head of a nail.

In the late 1820s and 1830s the virtues of self reliance were something very much in evidence in Barnes' writings. It was a popular theme. Books such as Alfred Buckland's *Letters on the Importance, Duty and Advantages of Early Rising* (1819) sold extremely well – as did Samuel Smiles' famous *Self Help* (1859) later. [11] Barnes argued that self-help could give the working man his independence and self respect (and, incidentally, thereby avoid him being a burden on the parish). As he grew older, and as his own worthiness did not automatically reap its due rewards (notably with the decline of his school), he became less brash in his claims for the efficacy of self help. But throughout his life he emphasised the need for society to encourage self-reliance and independence among the working class.

Barnes saw the possibility of social mobility as an essential element in the regeneration of rural society. In his eclogue, 'Two Farms in Woone' he deplored the removal of the possibility for families to advance themselves by hard work on a small holding. Later, in 1867, in written evidence to the Royal Commission on Employment of Children, Young Persons and Women in Agriculture (published 1869), he urged,

What is wanted for the land labourer is a 'rung' in the ladder of rural life, by which he may hope to raise himself by his industry towards a higher position. He cannot now hope ever to step from day labour to farming. The smallest of our new great farms is beyond his wildest hope, and so he toils without the hope that has led on the poor lad in commercial work to the honourable estate of the high risen merchant.

One pre-condition for self improvement was more leisure time. Barnes urged that working people, whether on the land, in industry or in shops, should have a half day holiday each week. This would improve family life as well as give more time for reflection and learning. Thus self-help was not just a matter of self advancement but also a matter of self improvement. Barnes always had a notion of the balanced life – and tried to live it himself. He abhorred the worship of money. He warned in his *Views of Labour and Gold* (p. 18) that men obsessed with money 'may rise from a bolted meal, cast their child from their knee, slight the soothing hour of prattle with their wife, and the meditation in the field or bench at eventide, give up the sight of the blue vault of heaven, the cheering sunlight and the air of the sweet summer field ... may slight the seeking of higher forms of knowledge, and purer forms of pleasure, things better than money, and die a wreck in health and happiness'. In his emphasis on a balanced life, Barnes' views were close to Ruskin's observations in *Unto this Last* (1860) that:

THERE IS NO WEALTH BUT LIFE. Life, including all its powers of love, of joy, and of admiration. That country is the richest which nourishes the greatest number of noble and happy human beings; that man is the richest who, having perfected the functions of his own life to the utmost, has also the widest helpful influence, both personal, and by means of his possessions, over the lives of others.

Of Ruskin, it is worth remembering that, whilst he was to be a major influence on the first Labour M.P.s, he himself began his autobiography, *Praeterita* (1885–9), with the sentence: 'I am, and my father was before me, a violent Tory of the old school; Walter Scott's school, that is to say, and Homer's'. Barnes' values were also based on traditional conservatism. Barnes' outlook put emphasis on the social hierarchy and the duties of property and also included a heightened view of the role of the clergy in society. In pointing to the duties of property and even the economic inbalance in society Barnes' comments could come near to Christian socialism. In fact paternalistic Conservatism and

Christian socialism could come close, both emphasising a duty to the community and both abhorring the making of money as an end in itself.

Barnes' values were well away from those of the dominant *laissez-faire* Liberalism of Cobden and Bright, and even from the main stream Conservatism of the latter part of the nineteenth century. He deplored

the money-making mind which looks on the work of God or the pursuits of man mainly, if not only, as sources of wealth, and on the promotion of trade as an end that is well gained over every other good. Such a mind may look on time only as a form of space for the doing of business; on education only as a qualification for gainful employment; on a handsome tree only as a loss or gain upon a balance of the commercial value of its yearly growth and the yield of the ground it takes up; on a waterfall only as a power for an overshot wheel; on the discovery of a new land only as that of new resources of trade; on a newly reached people only as buyers of our wares; and on a war on a people who have never lifted a hand against us, other than as meddlers with their own laws and towns, as a fine opening up of trade. [12]

Perhaps Barnes' poetry also offered the same reassuring hierarchic values that Wordsworth's poetry offered. As one historian has recently written, 'Wordsworth's deep sense of the rightness of nature and God's ways, of the value of simple personal truths and simple and personal acts of goodness, assured many readers that all was not Benthamite calculus, political economy, and Whig complacency'. [13]

*　*　*

Barnes' reputation today rests on his poetry not his prose. Since his death in 1886, William Barnes has always held his place as a significant, if not major, poet.

There is a certain degree of agreement, over the century since then, on his place in English Literature. George Saintsbury, who wrote *A Short History of English Literature* (1898), a textbook of remarkable longevity, placed Barnes in a chapter headed 'The Minor Poets of 1800–1830' in which he observed, 'He wrote wholly in Dorset dialect, and chiefly on gentle, domestic and pastoral themes, two features which attract many, revolt some, and perhaps count little one way or other with the critic'. Later guides make much the same point, but George Saintsbury's remarks point to one nagging doubt about Barnes' reputation: whether it rests on Dorset quaintness or on major poetical merit. Saintsbury was, as the first section of this collection shows, wrong in believing that Barnes wrote 'wholly in dialect'; though very few would disagree with the view that his best poetry is in dialect. That Barnes' poetry has remained in print owes much to his status as 'the Dorset poet' and as an important influence on Thomas Hardy; yet his poetry would not have continued to attract interest for a hundred years after his death simply on grounds of 'local interest' and the Hardy connection. [14]

The essence of much of Barnes' verse is a deceptive simplicity: the subject matter is straightforward and intelligible to all, but the means by which it is put over is often very subtle. Such gifted writers as Thomas Hardy, John Drinkwater and Geoffrey Grigson have all admired the skill in his versification. John Drinkwater observed 'Barnes had a lyric heart, but he was a grave gentleman, a scholar, and in the most agreeable sense a precisian, and he delighted to exercise his singing gift in the terms of a very agile and conscious art'. [15] Earlier Thomas Hardy put the point colourfully:

Primarily spontaneous, he was academic closely after; and we find him warbling his native wood-notes with a watchful eye on the predetermined score, a far remove from the popular impression of him as the naif and rude bard who sings only because he must, and who submits the uncouth lines of his page to us without knowing how they came there. Goethe never knew better of his; nor Milton; nor in their rhymes, Poe; nor in their whimsical alliterations here and there, Langland and the versifiers of the fourteenth and fifteenth centuries. [16]

Barnes' craftmanship in poetry was intimately linked with his remarkable linguistic learning. He was deeply interested in the Welsh language and Welsh verse forms – an interest aroused by visits to Wales, as early as 1831 when visiting Julia's parents, and fostered by help from Welsh neighbours in Dorset. Barnes took up various techniques of Welsh verse and used them pure or adapted them. The best known is his use of the cynghanned, where there is repetition of the sounds of consonants in two parts of a line, divided by a pause (the caesura). It is employed, for example, in such a well known poem as 'My Orcha'd In Linden Lea'; thus

'Do lean down low in Linden Lea'.

Bardic poetry appealed to Barnes as it had been a way that various peoples had remembered their lores without books. He experimented not only in Welsh but also in Irish, Anglo-Saxon, Hebrew and Persian verse forms. In the poem 'Went Hwome'

Barnes uses 'cymmeriad', which he defined as 'the keeping of the same word through sundry verses, for the sake of oneness of time, or subject or thought'; so each stanza ends with the name of where home was – 'Meldonley'.

In other poems he borrowed a technique called 'union' from Irish poetry, which he described as 'a kind of under-rhyme' where there is 'under-rhyming or rhyming of the last word or breath-sound in one line, with one in the middle of the following one'. So in 'Times O' Year', for example, there is:

> Soon shall grass, a-vrosted *bright*,
> Glisten *white* instead o' green,
> An' the wind shall smite the *cows*,
> Where the *boughs* be now their screen.

He adapted the use of alliteration from Anglo-Saxon verse. In 'The Elm in Home Ground' one finds three alliterative words used in couplets; two in words emphasised in the first line and the third as the first emphasised word or syllable in the second line. Thus:

> O then, how *s*oothing will it *s*eem
> To *s*ee they meadow and its stream,
> While *n*ear thy shadow *n*o bird cleaves
> The *n*ightly air that shakes thy leaves:
> And, *b*rining *b*ack the mellow light
> Of *b*ygone days in darksome night,
> In wordless thought to *d*raw the *d*ead
> Where *d*aylight's living do not tread.

He also used Persian poetical forms, such as, in 'Woak Hill', the 'pearl', where rhymes run through the verses of the poem; in 'Woak Hill' with the '-en' and 'Woak Hill' endings to lines and 'guide', 'bride' etc. rhyme early in the final line of each stanza. He took various forms from Hebrew. One of the more attractive is used in 'White and Blue', where there is a repetition of ideas in the first two lines of each stanza – the idea being expressed in two different ways.

> She came by the down with tripping walk,
> By daisies and shining banks of chalk.

The poem is also remarkable for its use of contrasts of colour; thus this stanza ends:

> And brooks with the crowfoot flow'rs to strew,
> The sky-tinted water, white on blue [17]

Whilst Barnes drew on his wide ranging learning, he also made use of, and adapted, the inflections of ordinary speech. This is notable in his eclogues. Several of his poems were based on a vivid incident or phrase. This is not to say that he did not improve on the incident or the words expressed. As Bernard Jones has perceptively suggested in his 'Forewords' to his collected edition of Barnes' poems, Barnes did this not only to meet the needs of his poetry but also to adjust the dialect closer to what he perceived to be its Anglo-Saxon roots.[18] Barnes had a very deep love of the Dorset dialect. A year before he died, when looking at the first copy of his 'Glossary of the Dorset Language', he said 'I have done some little to preserve the speech of our fore-fathers, but I fear a time will come when it will be scarcely remembered, and none will be found who can speak it with the purity I have heard it spoken in my youth'.[19]

His dialect verse was not a learned obscurity. Much of it was verse to be read out and enjoyed. The Reverend Francis Kilvert, who visited Barnes in 1874, recorded in his diary how Barnes reading out 'John Bloom in Lon'on' had his visitors 'in roars of laughter'. Barnes poetry readings were great successes. Thus of one meeting in Langport in 1868 the local newspaper recorded:

both stairs were crowded long before the time announced for opening the doors, and such was the crush on the market house stairs that the committee found it impossible to open the door and sell tickets on the landing as usual. As many as the room would comfortably hold were admitted on the other side and afterwards the number that remained was augmented by a rush from the market house. The bannisters were broken and the policeman was pressed so closely upon the dilapidated railings that he and a number of other persons had a narrow escape from being precipitated on the stones in the passage beneath ....[20]

Today, at many 'socials' in the East Midlands, especially in or near Derbyshire, a few dialect poems are very popular in intervals between periods of dancing.

In nineteenth century Dorset, long before radio and television, verse such as Barnes' was genuinely a popular oral entertainment. Barnes recognised this and appears to have been happy to leaven his educational lectures with poetry. Thus, in writing to accept an invitation to lecture to Bridport Working Men's Association, he offered:

How would they like one on 'Work and Welfare' with some of the substance of my *Views of Labour and Gold*. It would treat of Labour as bearing on capital, health, and social well being etc.

I could read a few Dorset Poems ....[21]

Tennyson admired Barnes' dialect verse and wrote 'The Northern Farmer' poems in dialect. In 1863, on one of the two occasions when they met, Tennyson and Barnes enjoyed talking of 'Ancient Britons, barrows and roads', and Tennyson probably endeared himself further to Barnes by declaring, 'Modern fame is nothing: I'd rather have an acre of land'.[22] However Barnes had reservations about Tennyson's dialect verse. Kilvert on his visit to Barnes recorded:

He spoke of Tennyson's *Northern Farmer*. 'Tennyson', he said, 'even if he did not mean to ridicule the Northern Farmer, at least had no love for him and no sympathy with him'. Which is probably true and a just criticism. The Poet went on to say that in all which he himself had written there was not a line which was not inspired by love for and kindly sympathy with the things and people described.

Barnes' rustic verse does contain sadness, concerning time passing, premature deaths or girls committing suicide because of pregnancies; but, overall, it shows the happier side of rural life. The Bishop of Salisbury remembered Barnes as having said to him words to the effect 'That many persons thought that he had painted our folk in too bright colours, but that everything which he had written was true of some one in the classes described in the poems; that he was painting in fact, from life, though the level might be somewhat above the average'.[23] His love of country life is in accord with his later vocation as Anglican clergyman; he writes of the beauties of God's works and of the transient joys of human life. His is not the worship of Nature of the Romantic poets but the poetry of an agricultural society.

Barnes kept faith with those who had gone before, the earlier generations, and with the language and way of life of the Dorset of his youth. His daughter recalled that he often used to go to the deserted village of Farringdon, which lay within his parish: 'It was one of the poet's favourite musing places, to sit in the shadow of that old ruin and think of the parishioners whose very homes had disappeared, leaving only uneven spots in the waving grass to show where they had been.' He wrote of it in his poem 'The Depopulated Village'. It epitomises an aspect of his verse, the communion with the past.

William Barnes is 'The Dorset Poet', but he is also a poet of national stature. W. H. Auden once wrote, when trying to define 'minor' and 'major' poets, that it was not simply 'a matter of the pleasure the poet gives an individual reader: I cannot enjoy one poem by Shelley and am delighted by every line of William Barnes, but I know perfectly well that Shelley is a major poet and Barnes a minor one'. Others have been less keen about every line of Barnes – but few have claimed him to be a poet of the first order. [24] However, many have agreed with Auden in expressing the pleasure they have gained from reading the best of his verse.

For me Barnes' rural poetry is unforgettable. It brings back the flavour of nineteenth century rural society, and yet, in many of its features, it has a universality not restricted to place or time. The more I read Barnes' poetry, the more I admire his skill in writing verse.

Barnes deserves a wider audience. I hope this selection brings the enjoyment of reading his poetry to many more people.

References to Introduction

1 – Lucy Baxter ('Leader Scott'), *The Life of William Barnes: Poet and Philologist* (1887), p. 105. Lucy Baxter (1837–1902) was the third of Barnes' four daughters.

2 – Barnes often re-used parts of his newspaper pieces in his books. Much of 'Auctions' appears in his *Views of Labour and Gold* (1859), p. 146.

3 – Julia Miles to William Barnes, 16 April 1823; printed in Giles Dugdale, *William Barnes of Dorset* (1953), pp. 52–3.

4 – He used material in 'Gardening' again in his *Views of Labour and Gold*, pp. 124–6.

5 – Trevor Hearl in his *William Barnes: The Schoolmaster* (1966), p. 256, which is the essential work on this aspect of his life.

6 – June Wilson, *Green Shadows: The Life of John Clare* (1951), pp. 89–90.

7 – In his Preface to the former he wrote, 'If I have cast any new light on the subjects under hand, it has been by a careful use of my little knowledge of the British language, which I believe Antiquaries have too often neglected'.

8 – Lucy Baxter, *op. cit.*, pp. 5–6.

9 – For a discussion of Cobbett's criticism of 'the new developments in the terms and accents of an older England' see Raymond Williams, *Culture and Society 1780–1950* (1958), pp. 23–39. For a more detailed discussion of Barnes' views on social matters see my 'William Barnes and the Social Problem', Dorset Natural History and Archaeological Society, *Proceedings for 1977*, pp. 19–27.

10 – *Views of Labour and Gold*, p. 76, p. 3, and p. 94.

11 – Tim Chilcott, *A Publisher And His Circle* (1972), p. 67. For samples of Barnes' writings on this theme, see 'Gardening' and 'Association' in Section 3 of this volume.

12 – *Views of Labour and Gold*, p. 57. Of later leading Conservatives, Lord Robert Cecil (1864–1958), a devoted Anglican, probably comes nearest to sharing some of Barnes' views.

13 – David Roberts, *Paternalism in Early Victorian England* (1979), p. 68.

14 – Barnes' verse appears in many of the anthologies of Victorian verse. This is true both of Sir Arthur Quiller Couch's *The Oxford Book of Victorian Verse* (first published in 1912 and repeatedly reprinted subsequently) and more recent anthologies as the selections by George MacBeth, *The Penguin Book of Victorian Verse* (1969), N. P. Messenger and J. R. Watson, *Victorian Poetry* (1974) and B. Richards, *English Verse 1830–1890* (1980).

15 – In his Introduction to *Twenty Poems in Common English by William Barnes* (1925), p. 10.

16 – In his Preface to his *Select Poems of William Barnes* (1908), p. ix. For Grigson's assessment see his Introduction to his *Selected Poems of William Barnes* (1950), especially pp. 14–18.

17 – For discussions of his metrical experiments see, among others, Lucy Baxter, *op. cit.*, pp. 97–8 and 247–51; Grigson, *op. cit.*, pp. 17–21; and R. A. Forsyth, 'The Conserving Myth of William Barnes' in Ian Fletcher (ed.), *Romantic Mythologies* (1967), pp. 137–67, especially pp. 147–50.

18 – *The Poems of William Barnes* (1962), pp. 17–18.

19 – Laura Barnes' diary, 21 November 1885; quoted in Dugdale, *op. cit.*, p. 226.

20 – Quoted by Patrick Keane in his 'Prophet In The Wilderness: Rev. William Barnes As An Adult Educator', *Dorset Natural History and Archaeological Society Proceedings for* 1978, Vol. 100, p. 20. The Kilvert extract comes from his diary, 30 April 1874, Wiliam Plomer (ed.), *Kilvert's Diary*, Vol. 2 (1960 ed.), p. 441.

21 – Letter to Thomas Colfox, 5 September 1864; Barnes Papers, Dorset County Museum.

22 – William Allingham's diary, 4 October 1863; quoted by Hallam Tennyson, *Alfred, Lord Tennyson: A Memoir* (1 vol. ed., 1899), Appendix, p. 878.

23 – The Bishop was recalling visiting Barnes in January 1886; Lucy Baxter, *op. cit.*, pp. 321–2.

24 – For Auden, see his introduction to his anthology, *Nineteenth Century Minor Poets* (1967), p. 17. For one advocate of Barnes as a great poet, see Arthur Bryant, 'Our Notebook', *The Illustrated London News*, 17 September 1949.

PART I
POEMS IN NATIONAL
ENGLISH

WHITE AND BLUE

My love is of comely height and straight,
And comely in all her ways and gait,
She shows in her face the rose's hue,
And her lids on her eyes are white on blue.

When Elemley club-men walk'd in May,
And folk came in clusters every way,
As soon as the sun dried up the dew,
And clouds in the sky were white on blue,

She came by the down with tripping walk,
By daisies and shining banks of chalk,
And brooks with the crowfoot flow'rs to strew
The sky-tinted water, white on blue;

She nodded her head as play'd the band,
She tapp'd with her foot as she did stand,
She danc'd in a reel, and wore all new
A skirt with a jacket, white with blue.

I singled her out from thin and stout,
From slender and stout I chose her out,
And what in the evening could I do
But give her my breast-knot, white and blue?

MELHILL FEAST

Aye up at the feast, by Melhill's brow,
So softly below the clouds in flight,
There swept on the wood the shade and light,
Tree after tree, and bough by bough.

And there, as among the crowd I took
My wandering way, both to and fro,
Full comely were shapes that day could show,
Face upon face, and look by look.

And there, among girls on left and right,
On one with a winsome smile I set
My looks; and the more, the more we met,
Glance upon glance, and sight by sight.

The road she had come by then was soon
The one of my paths that best I knew,
By glittering gossamer and dew,
Evening by evening, moon by moon.

First by the doors of maidens fair,
As fair as the best till she is nigh,
Though now I can heedless pass them by,
One after one, or pair by pair.

Then by the orchards dim and cool,
And then along Woodcombe's elmy side,
And then by the meads, where waters glide,
Shallow by shallow, pool by pool.

And then to the house, that stands alone,
With roses around the porch and wall,
Where up by the bridge the waters fall,
Rock under rock, and stone by stone.

Sweet were the hopes I found to cheer
My heart as I thought on time to come,
With one that would bless my happy home,
Moon upon moon, and year by year.

RUSTIC CHILDHOOD

No city primness train'd my feet
To strut in childhood through the street,
But freedom let them loose to tread
The yellow cowslip's downcast head;
Or climb, above the twining hop
And ivy, to the elm-tree's top;
Where southern airs of blue-sky'd day
Breath'd o'er the daisy and the may.
   I knew you young, and love you now,
   O shining grass, and shady bough.

Far off from town, where splendour tries
To draw the looks of gather'd eyes,
And clocks, unheeded, fail to warn
The loud-tongued party of the morn,
I spent in woodland shades my day
In cheerful work or happy play,

And slept at night where rustling leaves
Threw moonlight shadows o'er my eaves.
  I knew you young, and love you now,
  O shining grass, and shady bough.

Or in the grassy drove by ranks
Of white-stemm'd ashes, or by banks
Of narrow lanes, in-winding round
The hedgy sides of shelving ground;
Where low-shot light struck in to end
Again at some cool-shaded bend,
Where I might see through darkleav'd boughs
The evening light on green hill-brows.
  I knew you young, and love you now,
  O shining grass, and shady bough.

Or on the hillock where I lay
At rest on some bright holyday;
When short noon-shadows lay below
The thorn in blossom white as snow;
And warm air bent the glist'ning tops
Of bushes in the lowland copse,
Before the blue hills swelling high
And far against the southern sky.
  I knew you young, and love you now,
  O shining grass, and shady bough.

THE WOODLAND HOME

My woodland home, where hillocks swell
With flow'ry sides, above the dell,
And sedge's hanging ribbons gleam
By meadow withies in the stream;
And elms, with ground-beglooming shades,
Stand high upon the sloping glades;
When toilsome day at evening fades,
    And sorrow heaves within my breast,
      By fancy brought,
      I come in thought
    To thee my home, my spirit's rest.

I left thy woody fields that lay
So fair below my boyhood's play,
To toil in busy life that fills
The world with strife of wayward wills;
Where mortals in their little day
Of pride disown their brother clay.
But when my soul can steal away
   From such turmoil, with greater zest,
     By fancy brought,
     I come in thought
   To thee my home, my spirit's rest.

For I behold thee fresh and fair
In summer light, and summer air,
As when I rambled, pulling low
The hazel bough that, when let go,
Flew back, with high-toss'd head, upright,
To rock again in airy light,
Where brown-stemm'd elms and ashes white
   Rose tall upon the flow'ry breast
     Of some green mound,
     With timber crown'd,
   My woodland home, my spirit's rest.

And there my fancy will not find
The loveless heart or selfish mind,
Nor scowling hatred mutt'ring aught
To break my heart-intrancing thought;
But manly souls above deceit,
And lively girls with smiles to greet
The bright'ning eyes they love to meet.
   The fairest in their looks, and best
     In heart, I found
     On thy lov'd ground,
   My woodland home, my spirit's rest.

THE LANE

I love the narrow lane's dark bows,
When summer glows or winter blows;
Or when the hedge-born primrose hides
Its head upon the dry banksides,

26

By ribby-rinded maple shoots,
Or round the dark-stemm'd hazel's roots;
Where weather-beaten ivy winds
Unwith'ring o'er the elms' brown rinds,
And where the ashes white bough whips
The whistling air with coal-black tips;
And where the grassy ground, beside
The gravel-washing brook, lies wide,
And leaping lambs, with shrill-toned throats,
Bleat loudly in their first white coats,
And rooks through clear air cleave, in black,
And cloud-high flocks, their unmark'd track,
And merry larks are whistling loud,
Aloft, unshaded by a cloud.

I like the narrow lane's dark bows,
When winter blows or summer glows;
Where under summer suns, between
The sappy boughs of lively green,
The playful shadows mutely mock
The moving trees that breezes rock,
And robinhoods bloom red below
The rough-stemm'd bramble's flow'ry bow,
And stitchwort's bending stalks upbear
Their starlike cups to sultry air,
Where I may hear the wind-brought words
Of workfolk, with the songs of birds,
And rubb'd scythes reared upon their sneades,
And ringing in the roadside meads.

I love the narrow lane's dark bows,
When summer glows or winter blows;
Or in the fall, when leaves all fade,
Yet flutt'ring in the airy shade,
And in the shelter'd shaw the blast
Has shaken down the green-cupp'd mast,
And time is black'ning blue-skinn'd sloes,
And blackberries on bramble bows,
And ripening haws are growing red
Around the grey-rin'd hawthorn's head
And hazel branches, brokentipp'd
And brown, of all their nuts are stripp'd,

And in the leazes, whiffling white,
The whirling thistle seeds alight
In sunshine, struck from bents' brown stalks
By strolling girls in Sunday walks.

I love the narrow lane's dark bows,
When summer glows or winter blows;
And wildly driven wet is cast
Through windy gates upon the blast,
And trickling down the trees, around
Their trunks, the rain drops fall to ground,
And wither'd leaves, too wet to ride
The winds, line ev'ry ditches side,
Nor songs of birds, nor merry sounds
Of souls at work, are in the grounds:
O then the lane affords its lee
Of limber bough, and sturdy tree,
And so I love its winding bows
When summer glows or winter blows.

AUTUMN

The waning days now waft us on
From world-enlight'ning summer gone,
And shrill cold winds, above the shrouds
Of shaken trees, drive darksome clouds
O'er gloomy grass within the glades,
Where glowing lights and quiv'ring shades
Were lately lying, in the heat
Of longer days, beneath our feet.

The bending stream that bubbled by
Its bank among the stones half dry,
When in the heat of high-sunn'd noon
Our hay was rustling grey in June,
With yellow waves is rolling wide
And wild along the wet rock's side;
And bending trees now bow and twist
All beaten by the wind-borne mist,

And on below them lightly leap
Their leaves adown the leeward steep;
Where lately in a ring, around
The ridge, their boughs begloomed the ground,
And they in fading fell as light
As feathers from their airy height,
In bleak air softly blowing through
The black-thorn with its sloes of blue.

O blue-sky'd summer, now the bloom
Of blowing flowers, and the gloom
Of leaves but lately green, where grows
The grove of elms in goodly rows,
With thy soft air, and long days' light,
Are lost for winter's storms and night.
For never-tiring time but gives
To take away, and so man lives
With less to love till he, at last,
Is lost with all he held so fast.

MOSS

O rain-bred moss that now dost hide
The timber's bark and wet rock's side,
Upshining to the sun, between
The darksome storms, in lively green,
And wash'd by pearly rain drops clean,
   Steal o'er my lonely path, and climb
   My wall, dear child of silent time.
      O winter moss, creep on, creep on,
      And warn me of the time that's gone.

Green child of winter, born to take
Whate'er the hands of man forsake,
That makest dull, in rainy air,
His labour-brighten'd works; so fair
While newly left in summer's glare;
   And stealest o'er the stone that keeps
   His name in mem'ry where he sleeps.
      O winter moss, creep on, creep on,
      And warn us of the time that's gone.

Come lowly plant that lov'st, like me,
The shadow of the woodland tree,
And waterfall where echo mocks
The milkmaid's song by dripping rocks,
And sunny turf for roving flocks,
   And ribby elms extending wide
   Their roots within the hillock's side.
      Come winter moss, creep on, creep on,
      And warn me of the time that's gone.

Come, meet me wandering, and call
My mind to some green mould'ring hall
That once stood high, the fair-wall'd pride
Of hearts that lov'd, and hoped, and died,
Ere thou hadst climb'd around its side:
   Where blooming faces once were gay
   For eyes no more to know the day.
      Come winter moss, creep on, creep on,
      And warn me of the time that's gone.

While there in youth, – the sweetest part
Of life, – with joy-believing heart,
They liv'd their own dear days, all fraught
With incidents for after-thought
In later life, when fancy brought
   The outline of some faded face
   Again to its forsaken place.
      Come winter moss, creep on, creep on,
      And warn me of the time that's gone.

Come where thou climbedst, fresh and free,
The grass-beglooming apple-tree,
That, hardly shaken with my small
Boy's strength, with quiv'ring head, let fall
The apples we lik'd most of all,
   Or elm I climb'd, with clasping legs,
   To reach the crow's high-nested eggs.
      Come winter moss, creep on, creep on,
      And warn me of the time that's gone.

Or where I found thy yellow bed
Below the hill-borne fir-tree's head,
And heard the whistling east wind blow
Above, while wood-screen'd down below

I rambled in the spring-day's glow,
   And watch'd the low-ear'd hares upspring
   From cover, and the birds take wing.
      Come winter moss, creep on, creep on,
      And warn me of the time that's gone.

Or where the bluebells bent their tops
In windless shadows of the copse;
Or where the misty west wind blew
O'er primroses that peer'd out through
Thy bankside bed, and scatter'd dew
   O'er grey spring grass I watch'd alone
   Where thou hadst grown o'er some old stone.
      Come winter moss, creep on, creep on,
      And warn me of the time that's gone.

TO A GARDEN – ON LEAVING IT

Sweet garden! peaceful spot! no more in thee
   Shall I e'er while away the sunny hour.
Farewell each blooming shrub, and lofty tree;
   Farewell the mossy path and nodding flow'r:
   I shall not hear again from yonder bow'r
The song of birds, or humming of the bee,
Nor listen to the waterfall, nor see
   The clouds float on behind the lofty tow'r.

No more, at cool-air'd eve, or dewy morn,
   My gliding scythe shall shear thy mossy green:
My busy hands shall never more adorn,

   My eyes no more may see, this peaceful scene.
But still, sweet spot, wherever I may be,
My love-led soul will wander back to thee.

THE BIRD-BOY'S DINNER TOKEN

      Ah, then, a boy, I rov'd below
      The sun that seem'd to go so slow,
      While keeping birds beside the hill,
      With little wind-blown voice so shrill,

And flapping clacker, seldom still;
   And longed to see the snow-white patch
   Upon the hedge beside our hatch;
     Poor mother's dinner token.

For I, a child, was then too small
To see from home, and out of call;
And my best clock, the shifting shade
Of some high elm-tree on the glade,
Below a cloud would often fade;
   And so, at dinner time, beside
   The hatch my mother open'd wide
     A sheet, her dinner token.

And while the dew-drops dried away
Below the heat of blue-sky'd day,
With thoughts of home, alone and dumb,
I whiled the time a-cutting some
New plaything out for days to come:
   Till when, at dinner time, hound-light,
   I ran down homeward, catching sight
     Of mother's snow-white token.

But when another year came on
My mother, poor dear soul, was gone;
And left behind no hands to spread
Her sheet for me when she was dead.
And so I ate my lonesome bread
   Afield, more selfmourn'd now than then;
   And never ran down home again,
     At mother's dinner token.

And when the Sunday church-peals, toss'd
With swelling winds, were heard and lost;
And when I saw go slowly through
The fields from church, the folk I knew,
Gay maids in white, and lads in blue;
   How sadd'ning seem'd the sounds I caught
   From o'er her grave, the while I thought
     On mother's dinner token.

LEAVES

Leaves of the summer, lovely summer's pride,
  Sweet is the shade below your lofty tree,
Whether in waving copses, where ye hide
  My roamings, or in fields that let me see
  The open sky; and whether ye may be
Around the low-stemm'd oak, outspreading wide;
Or taper ash upon the mountain side;
  Or lowland elm; your shade is sweet to me.

Whether ye wave above the early flow'rs
  In lively green; or whether, rustling sere,
    Ye fly on playful winds, around my feet,

In dying autumn; lovely are your bow'rs,
  Ye early-dying children of the year;
    Holy the silence of your calm retreat.

RURAL SECLUSION

As o'er the hill with waving timber crown'd,
  In yonder drove, beneath an ash I lay;
    Where bloom'd the hawthorn with its snow-white may,
And gilt-cups brightly deck'd the grassy ground;
While merry hinds within the fields around,
  A-singing, ended some enliv'ning lay;
    I heard a waterfall, so far away
That stillness only brought its sullen sound;

  And thought in silence, O thou peaceful place;
I would that summer weather could but last;
  And, in this northern land, the lovely face

Of nature could withstand the winter's blast;
  And I, from all my worldly cares set free,
  Could have, awhile, a happy home in thee.

THE HOME-GROUND

How welcome came before my sight
That old face seen by this day's light,
Although his cheeks no longer glow
With burning redness; and although

His hair, once black's the glossy crow,
  Is white; for when he spoke my name,
  I found his voice was still the same
    As I had heard in home-ground;

When ruddy suns withdrew the day
From games that we had met to play,
And quoits rose up, in high-bow'd flight,
From strong arms clad in snowy white,
And outstretched hands, and eager sight,
  Were bent to stop the flying balls,
  With eager strides, and slips, and falls,
    On summer grass in home-ground.

There, touching light, with flying feet,
The grassy ground, we ran, wind-fleet;
Or sprang, hound-light, with lofty springs
O'er gate and stream in lively strings;
The while our sisters, in their swings,
  Were laughing loud in merry mood,
  At play, in blushing maidenhood,
    Below the trees in home-ground.

With backs of white and legs of red,
There cackling geese, in summer, fed;
While rustling barley, load by load,
With loose-straw'd sides that hardly show'd
The rolling wheels, so slowly rode
  Behind the horses, nodding low
  Their halter'd heads, and coming slow
    To barton up through home-ground.

When o'er the fields the night lay brown
Ere father yet was come from town,
There stood our mother, list'ning round
With holden breath, to hear the sound
Of horses' footsteps on the ground,
  And went in griev'd to find she heard
  Naught else but whisp'ring winds that stirr'd
    The ashes' leaves in home-ground.

There, north of us, a knoll swell'd high
Before the ever sunless sky,
And trees that bore the rook's high nest
Sprang tall before the stormy west

And keen-air'd east; and left the best
  Of winds, the south ones, free to blow
  O'er open meadows, in the glow
    Of sunshine, up through home-ground.

And so I love the well-known names
We once heard there in youthful games;
Before our mother, hollow-eyed,
Had wept for father that had died;
Or we lost her, all scatter'd wide,
  Each struggling in the world alone,
  No more to share our mirth now flown
    For ever from the home-ground.

THE ELM IN HOME-GROUND

Green elm, whose shade, in open light,
Steals o'er the mead from morn till night,
As I have known it reach at rest
O'er rimy grass-blades to the west,
Or under low-gone suns to lie
Outlength'ning to the eastern sky;
O let thy shelt'ring shroud, dear tree,
Yet shed its airy gloom on me,
As once it fell around the feet
Of forms I never more shall meet,
In quick-limb'd youth, all laughing loud,
Below thy hillock-screening shroud;
While o'er the water's weedy bed
The willow bent its grey-leav'd head,
And dragonflies were darting through
The drooping rushes, dazzling blue.

For while the summer ground is green
With grass below thy midday screen,
How fain am I to come and find
The few that time has left behind,
Of those whose well-known tongues can tell
Their tales of all that once befell
The laughing lad, and giggling lass,
That lean'd below thee on the grass.

But when the moonlight marks anew
Thy murky shadow on the dew,
So slowly o'er the sleeping flow'rs
Onsliding through the nightly hours,
While smokeless on the houses height
The higher chimney gleams in light,
Above yon reedy roof where now,
With rosy cheeks, and lily brow,
No watchful mother's ward, within
The window, sleeps for me to win:

O then, how soothing will it seem
To see thy meadow and its stream,
While near thy shadow no bird cleaves
The nightly air that shakes thy leaves:
And, bringing back the mellow light
Of bygone days in darksome night,
In wordless thought to draw the dead
Where daylight's living do not tread.
For those who look with heavy heart
On happy times that soon depart,
In fancy's fairy dreams may leave
The faithless world in which they grieve,
And live o'er days the mourning mind
Likes most to look to back behind;
And I will seek some youthful scene
Of summer on thy hillock green.

MOONLIGHT

O when, with weary limbs, we lose
The light, with day-time's thousand hues,
And when, from shady shapes of night,
We shut in sleep our weary sight,
All heedless how the stars may light
The hoary fogs of airy night;
To light the road for later eyes
The lofty moon then climbs the skies,
And southern sides of boughs grow bright
Above the darksome shades of night,
Where cheeks in glimm'ring gloom may hide

Their glowing by a sweetheart's side;
As when in younger years we took
Home you up hill beyond the brook,
With lightsome limbs all skipping through
The leazes wet with sparkling dew,
Below the shining moon that show'd
The sharp-edg'd hollows night our road,
With wan light on the water's face
To warn us off the darksome place,
Where more than one had miss'd their ground
On moonless evenings, and been drown'd.
There lengthen'd shadows, lying dim
Below the gravelpit's sharp brim,
Marked out its form, lest folk should go
And fall o'er headlong down below;
And show'd us plainly where the planks
Were placed athwart the gullies' banks,
And hard things stood to hit the eyes
Of heads abroad with lightless skies.

So, when the dusk of day is gone,
The duller moon comes slowly on,
Up-rising round her star-bound bow
For roving mortals here below.
But still, of light that she has lent
To lead me on the ways I went,
The welcomest to me was while
I watch'd my Fanny's parting smile,
As she bestow'd outstanding nigh
The stone at door her sweet 'Good bye,'
With moon-bright forehead, marble fair
Among her locks of sloe-black hair,
That wav'd in summer winds before
The wall-side jessamine at door,
In seemly loops between my sight
And some pale star of early night.

THE EEGRASS

With stricken heart, and melting mood,
I rov'd along the mead to brood
In freedom, at the eventide,
On souls that time has scatter'd wide;

As by the boughy hedge's side
　　The shadows darken'd into night,
　　And cooling airs, with wanton flight,
　　　Were blowing o'er the eegrass.

There fancy roam'd from place to place,
From year to year, to find some face
That I no more shall look upon,
Or see in sadness, sorrow-wan,
Or time-worn with its brightness gone;
　　And my own Lucy, fair to see,
　　Seem'd there to come again to me,
　　　Up o'er the shining eegrass.

As when upon a summer's day,
While we were there at hawling hay,
With downcast look she lightly drew
Her rake-head to her shapely shoe,
With hands well skill'd to bring it through
　　The tangled crowfoot-stems, that broke
　　The rakes for us poor clumsy folk,
　　　And still are in the eegrass.

And there the storms that spring clouds shed
Fell lately on her hooded head,
The while she sat, at eventide,
A-milking by her dun cow's side;
And there, when summer, sunny-skied
　　And boughy-wooded, brought its heat,
　　She trod the flow'rs with light-shod feet,
　　　But comes not o'er the eegrass.

O summer all thy crops are down,
And copse and leaze are turning brown,
And cuckoos leave the boughs to fade
Through waning fall, within the glade;
And we have lost our blooming maid.
　　So all thou broughtest fresh and fair
　　Begins to wither ev'ry where,
　　　But this bright-bladed eegrass.

My business brought me in my way
To Burnley back the other day;
And, sitting there in some old hall
Beside the gloomy-window'd wall,
I saw a wither'd woman throwing
Her wrinkled arm up backward, sewing,
Downlooking low, with glass-help'd sight,
To lead her slow-drawn stitches right;
Though never turning ear or eye
To us that happen'd to be nigh:
But when she heard my name, she held
Her hand upon the seam she fell'd,
And, taking off her eyes, made free
To ask who might my mother be?
I told her; and my tongue upstirr'd
Her torpid heart's blood by the word:
And in her lap she lightly laid
Her long-boned arm, from labor stay'd,
And open'd all the hidden store
Of olden joys her mem'ry bore,
And told me of her heart-lov'd home,
And holidays that let her roam,
With my lost mother wand'ring wild
A winning child, with her a child;
Or moving forth, more staid in mood
And mien, in high-soul'd womanhood:
Of wakes, and days that broke to bring
The brisk youths to the maypole ring,
Where folks, now all grown old, were then
But air-light girls, and spry young men:
Of joys the shyfaced maiden shares
With shifting crowds in deaf'ning fairs,
Where, conscious of the growth and grace
That greet her on her glasses face,
She goes, with seemly softness, by,
Look-seeking still, but ever shy:
Of feats that folks did once, but few
Are fit in later times to do:
Of lonesome widows left in woe,
That lost their husbands years ago;

When strong-wav'd streams o'erflow'd their banks,
Or storms o'erthrew the elms' high ranks;
And others that were lost, for lack
Of light the ling'ring moon kept back,
When over darksome eastern skies
No evening star was seen to rise,
And no slow team, in shining train,
Was travelling with Charles's wain;
And tales of bridegrooms, hale and bold,
With burning hearts by death made cold,
Or youth bewilder'd, weeping near
His wax-cold maid upon her bier,
For God she told us takes the best
Betimes to everlasting rest.
And as she follow'd, line by line,
My long-lost mother's face in mine,
She told us what a trusty part
Was taken by her good young heart,
When first her father died, and all
His family but she were small:
And how she met, a thoughtful maid,
Her mother's weary hands with aid,
And did the most she ever might
To make her heavy loss seem light.
And thus the old soul led us on
Through all her heart-dear seasons gone,
With tales of mourning minds of old,
That my poor mother left untold.
For ere we leave the light that show'd
The looks that blest our short abode,
Our burden'd heart is fain to find
That faithful mortals, left behind,
Will hold, with hearts of kindred clay,
The hist'ry of our little day;
And thus the hoary headstone prays
For heedful thought in after days,
And fellow-mortals still hold fast
Their fleeting earth-loves to the last,
And lay upon the last they see
Their love's injunction, 'Think of me.'
But God knows all the ills forlorn
And overgrieving hearts have borne,

And ne'er o'erlooking, though they lie
In lowly dust, the griefs that try
Them now, will weigh with equal weight
Their woe, and make the crooked straight.

LEARNING

Heavenly source of guiltless joy!
    Holy friend through good and ill;
When all idle pleasures cloy,
    Thou canst hold my spirit still.

Give the idle their delights,
    Wealth unblest, and splendor vain;
Empty days and sleepless nights,
    Seeming bliss in real pain.

Give the sensual their joys;
    Wild excitement, heartless glee,
Madd'ning wine and giddy noise;
    I will spend my hours with thee.

Take me to some still abode,
    Underneath some woody hill;
By some timber-skirted road,
    By some willow-shaded rill.

Where along the rocky brook,
    Flying echoes sweetly sound,
And the hoarsely-croaking rook
    Builds upon the trees around.

Take me to some lofty room
    Lighted from the western sky,
Where no glare dispels the gloom
    Till the golden eve is nigh.

Where the works of searching thought,
    Chosen books, may still impart
What the wise of old have taught,
    What has tried the meek of heart.

Books in long-dead tongues, that stirr'd
  Living hearts in other climes;
Telling to my eyes, unheard,
  Glorious deeds of olden times.

Books that purify the thought,
  Spirits of the learned dead,
Teachers of the little taught,
  Comforters when friends are fled.

Learning! source of guiltless joy!
  Holy friend through good and ill;
When all idle pleasures cloy,
  Thou canst hold my spirit still.

ATHELHAMTON HOUSE

O once dear home of those that told
Their days in unknown years of old,
Here thoughtful let me wander round
Thy long-worn floors, and hallow'd ground;
Where still thy gloomy arches spread
O'er unseen footsteps of the dead; –
Where once thy lodge's op'ning gate
Swung slowly back, with creaking weight,
When, vassal-girt, thy lord drew near
With clinking mail, and long-beam'd spear, –
And round thy mossy walls with stains
Of twice two hundred winters' rains, –
And hall where merry-worded tongue
And sweetly-singing voice once rung; –
And ladies' bow'r, where beauty blest,
With smiles, the young heart now at rest;
And still, from painted windows, brood
The glowing sunlights, rainbow-hued.
When first the wind-bent timber grew
Around thy walls all fair and new,
And bow-neck'd steeds bore out the train
Of merry hunters to the plain,
No gun's light thunder, rolling wide,
Struck wave-wash'd rock, or green hill-side;
But from the hand uplifted high,

The hawk soar'd upwards to the sky,
And on his quarry, from afar,
Shot downward like a falling star.
Among the flow'rs thy garden knew
Of sweetest smell, or gayest hue,
To set off beauty's living bloom,
Or spend their odour in her room,
No cactus blush'd, no dahlia tall
Yet bow'd to suns of dewy fall;
No tall magnolia rose to spread
Her high-borne blossoms over head;
No Fuchsia's scarlet tassels fell;
And, overlook'd in woody dell,
The hearts-ease had not come to spread
Her colours on thy garden bed,
Where marigolds came forth below
The lily, white as driven snow.
And some would tell us now, with praise
Reserved alone for latter days,
That, since for those whose love has clung
To thee, grey pile, when thou wast young,
No coach yet bore its living load
Its hundred fast-told miles of road,
Nor smoke-trail'd steam-car, engine-sped,
Outstripp'd the wild-bird overhead,
Nor senseless wheels could yet fulfil
The hand's hard tasks of strength and skill;
So their cold hearts were far below
The happiness that ours may know!
O had they then no air that shook
The green-leav'd bough above the brook?
No flow'ry meads? no high-bough'd copse?
No airy shades of elm-tree tops?
No summer days, with health to ride
O'er downs and dingles far and wide?
No winter-mirth within their walls?
No crackling fires within their halls?
Had love no smile, and joy no tongue?
Had no sweet voices ever sung?
And had no mother yet a child
To clasp in fondness when he smiled?
O you whom that light oriel

Held smiling once, come back and tell,
That we may set our richer store
Of happiness by yours of yore.
You left that oriel behind,
Man's love-built gift to woman's mind,
That she, although the fairest share
Of gayest sights, might see them there.
O woman, heart-enthralling queen
Of fairest beings eyes have seen,
In thee a loving God bestows
The best of blessings man e'er knows;
When, walking in thy maiden grace
With purest thought, and fairest face,
And leading him to rise above
Unworthy deeds to win thy love,
Or blessing, through a toilsome life,
His trying days, a faithful wife;
Or moulding, with thy soft controul,
To goodness, childhood's love-train'd soul.
Where amber sunlight, in the glade,
Breaks, streaming, through the green bough's shade,
While softly-wheeling eddies gleam
Below the rock upon the stream,
All still is dead, though winning fair,
Till fancy sets thine image there,
The brightest gem, and fairer found
Thus set in all that's bright around.
Have not thy portals opened wide,
Grey pile, before the coming bride?
And has no daughter left with tears
Thy roof, the home of maiden years?
How fondly yearns my heart to know
Thy many tales of joy and woe;
And though they all are lost, grey pile,
May man still spare thee to beguile
Some other soul, when mine is fled,
With touching fancies of thy dead.

FRIENDLY LIGHT

And when the evening star arose,
   And blink'd to me with glitt'ring ray,
   Along the eastward-reaching way
I took as day began to close,
As there it hung on high, and flung
   Its light abroad, it seem'd to say
'I'm up above the house you love,
   Come on before I pass away.'

And when again the moon was full,
   And clear, and true-rimm'd all around,
   And shone on softly-lighted ground,
From shining clouds as soft as wool,
To me before the porched door;
   In all my joy she seem'd to say
'I light your track both here and back,
   And give you yet a while to stay.'

And when again along the west
   She roll'd above the hills her rim,
   And in the shaded wall left dim
The window where my love should rest:
'Now take your way,' she seem'd to say,
   'From this old court, though dear it be;
I fall, I sink, ere my last blink
   Pick out your road the while you see.'

PLORATA VERIS LACHRYMIS

O now, my true and dearest bride,
Since thou hast left my lonely side,
My life has lost its hope and zest.
The sun rolls on from east to west,
But brings no more that evening rest,
Thy loving-kindness made so sweet,
And time is slow that once was fleet,
   As day by day was waning.

The last sad day that show'd thee lain
Before me, smiling in thy pain,
The sun soar'd high along his way
To mark the longest summer day,
And show to me the latest play
Of thy sweet smile, and thence, as all
The days' lengths shrunk from small to small,
    My joy began its waning.

And now 'tis keenest pain to see
Whate'er I saw in bliss with thee.
The softest airs that ever blow,
The fairest days that ever glow,
Unfelt by thee, but bring me woe.
And sorrowful I kneel in pray'r,
Which thou no longer, now, canst share,
    As day by day is waning.

How can I live my lonesome days?
How can I tread my lonesome ways?
How can I take my lonesome meal?
Or how outlive the grief I feel?
Or how again look on to weal?
Or sit, at rest, before the heat
Of winter fires, to miss thy feet,
    When evening light is waning?

Thy voice is still I lov'd to hear,
Thy voice is lost I held so dear.
Since death unlocks thy hand from mine,
No love awaits me such as thine.
Oh! boon the hardest to resign!
But if we meet again at last
In heav'n, I little care how fast
    My life may now be waning.

MY DEAREST JULIA

Oh! can or can I not live on,
Forgetting thee, my love forgone?
'Tis true, where joyful faces crowd
And merry tongues are ringing loud,

Or where some needful work unwrought
May call for all my care and thought,
Or where some landscape, bath'd in light,
May spread to fascinate my sight,
Thy form may melt awhile, as fade
Our shades within some welkin shade,
    And I awhile may then live on,
    Forgetting thee, my love forgone.

But then the thrilling thought comes on,
    Of all thy love that's now forgone;
Thy daily toil to earn me wealth,
Thy grief to see me out of health,
Thy yearning readiness to share
The burden of my toil and care,
And all the blessings thou hast wrought
In my behalf by deed and thought.
And then I seem to hear thee calling,
Gloomy fac'd with tear drops falling,
    'Canst thou then so soon live on,
    Forgetful of my love forgone?'

THE WIND AT THE DOOR

As daylight darken'd on the dewless grass,
There still, with no one come by me,
To stay awhile at home by me,
Within the house, now dumb by me,
I sitting let the voiceless evening pass.

And there a windblast shook the rattling door,
And sounded in a moan without,
As if my love, alone without,
And standing on the stone without,
Had there come back with happiness once more.

I went to door, and out from trees above
My head, upon the blast by me,
Sweet blossoms there were cast by me,
As if my love had pass'd by me,
And flung them down, a token of her love.

Sweet blossoms of the tree where now I mourn,
I thought, if you could blow for her,
For apples that should grow for her,
And fall red-ripe below for her,
O then how happy I should see you kern.

But no. Too soon my fond illusion broke.
No comely soul in white like her –
No fair one tripping light like her –
No wife of comely height like her –
Went by; but all my grief again awoke.

SEE OR HEAR

'Tis pleasing to see the waters fall,
    Albeit their sound may not be heard;
Or hear from the wood the blackbird's call,
    Although we may not behold the bird;
To find what is sweet in sound, or fair
To meet, with our sight, in daylight air.

The head of the tree may catch the light,
    While underwood hides its stem in gloom;
The house may uphold its roof in sight,
    With door hidden back by apple bloom,
As often we find things fair conceal'd
Behind what is fair over hill and field.

At Meldon the tow'r, with bells all still,
    May show on the knap its comely height,
Or send out his peals below the hill,
    Though hidden itself in darksome night.
O could I but be by Meldon's brow,
To see and to hear its people now!

THE BANK STEPS

Where the hollow lane lies, deepen'd
Down below two banks, high steepen'd,
    And o'ergrown with flow'rs and wood,
Rose our elm tree, big and lofty,

By the high ground, rough and tofty,
　　Where of old a house had stood –
Stood before the tree was seen
Green-bough'd up above the green.

There the bank had crumbled, showing
Some of his long roots, outgrowing,
　　As in rongs for us to tread,
Which, with little legs outstriding,
We upclimbed, not seldom sliding
　　To the bottom, heels o'erhead –
Head, aye, with a head all bare
To its locks of shining hair.

Near our house-wall, lichen-dappled,
Rose the orchard, bloom'd or appled,
　　In the spring, or in the fall,
And the rook'ry, newly nested,
Or with rooklings glossy-breasted,
　　Loud with many a croaking call –
Calls well match'd by many a sound
Of our shrill voices on the ground.

BEECHLEY

Oh! the beech lawns at Beechley, how charming they wound
By the long eastern landridge of highwooded ground;
And its low-lying dingle, with wandering rill,
And low-leaning beech-lawns, that reached to the hill;
　　　May its dairies do well,
　　　　And may God speed its plough,
　　　For those I knew dwell there,
　　　　But where are they now?

And there stood the houses, some high and some small,
With their flow'r-warding pales and their rose-behung wall,
And westward and northward outsprang a long streech
Of grass-land, bestudded with elm and with beech.
　　　And late in the day,
　　　　Some maid by her cow
　　　Was singing full gay there,
　　　　But where is she now?

And there, in the dusk, in fine weather, we played
At our game 'Hide and seek' in the nook and the shade,
With 'I spy,' or 'Run yonder,' or 'Am I not near,
Jane Hunt or John Hine?' or 'Ha! ha! you are here;'
   Or cunning Ned Knoles,
    By stall or by mow,
   Finds out such queer holes there,
    And where is he now?

Or at cricket, while one, in a quick-handed fight
With the ball, saw in glory his wicket upright,
The ball fleetly roll'd and it sprang, and it flew,
It was out in the field, and at home at the shoe;
   Or it hit a man out,
    Oh! he could not tell how;
   While others would shout there
    'Well where are you now?'

'Tis long since my footsteps have trodden the ground
Where few, I should fear, of my friends would be found.
But tell me, I pray you, all ever you can
Of the life and the loss of the maid and the man,
   The Hinds, and the Harleys,
    Oh! How are they? How?
   And the Burnleys and Deans; there
    Oh! where are they now?

SEASON TOKENS

The shades may show the time of day,
And flowers how summer wanes away.

Where thyme on turfy banks may grow,
Or mallows by the laneside ledge,
About the blue-barr'd gate, may show
Their grey-blue heads beside the hedge,
Or where the poppy's scarlet crown
May nod by clover, dusky red,
Or where the field is ruddy brown,
By brooks with shallow-water'd bed,

The shades may show the time of day,
And flowers how summer wanes away.

Or, where the light of dying day
May softly shine against the wall,
Below the sloping thatch, brown-grey,
Or over pale-green grass, may fall,
Or where, in fields that heat burns dry,
May show the thistle's purple studs,
Or beds of dandelions ply
Their stems with yellow fringed buds,

There shades may show the time of day,
And flowers how summer wanes away.

THE CHURCH TOWER

To see the high tower, so stately and tall,
Above all the houses, looking so small,
  How fell back our head with uplooking sight
To reach up its height of smooth-sided wall,
As there we beheld his pinnacles stand
As sound as they first were put out of hand.

With battlements back'd by clear-shining sky,
And windows a higher over a high,
  In winds that flung out the bells' chiming sound,
The daws flew around with high-screaming cry,
Up over the yew that cast down a gloom
On weak-bladed grass beside the grey tomb.

In summer, when day with sweltering glare
Had melted away in dim-blowing air,
  And men, when at last the night-bell had pealed,
Had come from the field in weather yet fair,
How peaceful within my window beside
The lawn was my hour of still eventide.

And then, if the moon might scatter her light
On monument stones unheeded at night,
  No stone idly show'd while people all slept
A name I had wept by chisel to write;
But lives given me were still coming on,
All hopeful and gay, with none of them gone.

While clock-strokes may ring from fewer to more,
As climbs up the sun above the warm door,
    And then give again new hours after one
Till evening's low sun shines low as a floor,
Oh! sweet be the day and peaceful the hour
Of evening to souls below the tall tow'r.

THE NEWS OF THE DAY

As fell the red leaves o'er the full-running stream
That whiten'd in foam at its fall;
Where rose the tall trees in two rows by the side
Of the walk on the ledge by the wall;
Up there we all gather'd as evening was grey
To talk of the news of the day.

There day-sunder'd friends at the dewfall came out,
To be mates at the day's shady end,
With night-fearing girls feeling naught of their dread
On the arm of a brother or friend,
To meet with their neighbours who came every way
To talk of the news of the day.

No numbness then slacken'd their nimble-tipp'd tongues,
And quick rose their laughter and shout
At funny men's words, or at fine people's ways,
Or queer things the day had brought out,
In mirth at their work, or at pranks in their play,
And news they had heard in the day.

If a loud-whistling lad took the lead in a tune,
It was soon taken up all around;
If he jogg'd on his way with a jig on his lips
The girls beat, on tiptoe, the ground;
And so, as they met, they were merry in play,
If they heard not the news of the day.

To one within housewalls had waned the soft day,
To one open sunshine had glow'd,
By wide-arched bridge, or by wood-shelter'd tower,
Another had come a long road,
And each as he thither had taken his way
Had brought out some news of the day.

But moon-meted years both of man and of maid
Have emptied the ridge-reaching walk,
And the air brings no more to the ear on their path
The words of their gay-sounding talk;
And little you know as you saunter that way
The news – all the news of their day.

BROWN BENNETS

With the acorns yet green on the wide-spreading oak,
    While the grass was yet green in his shade,
That had holden it cool from the sun's burning stroke
    As it brown'd all the hill and the glade;
There the wind of the fall, in a blast
Flitted fast, o'er the dry-headed bennets.

With folk that, on Sunday, then tripp'd o'er the ground
    To the grey-tower'd church on the height,
There the sound of the bells' mellow chiming was drown'd
    By the bough-sweeping wind in its flight,
As it made the white thistle-down fly
Low and high, by the brown-headed bennets.

And from hence, on a workday, by gateways and stiles,
    And by brook-brim and elm-shaded bank,
We all merrily wended o'er quick-trodden miles
    On the pathways, that climb'd or that sank,
To the fair under Hambledon's side,
Sinking wide, with the brown-headed bennets.

There the close-thronging people, the great with the small,
    Were all streaming about on the ground,
Like the pool-filling water that, under its fall,
    Will keep giddily wallowing round,
Where to-day all the down is left bare
To the air-blast that shakes the brown bennets.

And dear are the paths of their quick-tripping feet
    Out by Manston and Sturminster tow'rs,
And the high-shooting maypole in Shillingston street
    For the may-dance, with spring-quickened flow'rs;
Or Hammoon, or by Ockford, with wide-reaching ground,
Green, or brown'd with the dry-headed bennets.

BENIGHTED

Invited by your sire's good-will
   To me, I took the road
By Downley, over heath and hill,
   To go to your abode;
And o'er my mare, as white as snow,
   Full fain I sprightly threw
My leg, and in my stirrup's bow
   I set my shining shoe,
And merry-hearted,
Briskly started
   Out by our old yew.

But when, at last, the sun had set
   Upon my road, too soon,
I found myself where three ways met
   Below the western moon.
There stood a shining holly tree,
   With firs of five-fold height,
But yet no guide-post held for me
   An arm to send me right,
As I benighted,
Moon-belighted,
   Turn'd my wheeling sight.

And one road down a ground-slope sank,
   A darken'd, hollow way;
And one beside a heathy bank
   Ran on as light as day;
And nigh it wound a shining brook,
   Adown a shallow bed,
And thitherward my mare would look
   With ever-steadfast head,
As if well knowing,
Without showing,
   Whitherward I sped.

And shortly, from the eastern sky,
   I found five bell-sounds sweep;
Your peal of bells – one shrill, one high,
   One loud, one low, one deep –

And with my moonshade on before
  My mare's two ears' white tips,
I soon had reached your gate, your door,
  Your fire of blazing chips,
Where I, at meeting,
Found a greeting,
  Out of many lips.

I never after that mistook
  The right road of the three,
And well I knew the shallow brook,
  And firs, and holly tree;
I ne'er mistook the road when day
  Show'd houses from afar,
Nor when the moon was o'er my way,
  Nor by the evening star,
As I rode spanking
On by banking,
  Gapp'd for gate or bar.

THE DEPOPULATED VILLAGE

As oft I see by sight, or oft
  In mind, the ridges on the ground,
The mark of many a little croft
  And house where now no wall is found,
I call the folk to life again
  And build their houses up anew;
  I ween I shape them wrong, but who
Can now outmark their shapes to men?

I call them back to path or door
  In warm-cheek'd life below the sun,
And see them tread their foot-worn floor
  That now is all by grass o'errun.
To me the most of them may seem
  Of fairer looks than were their own,
  Yet some of all their lives were shown
As fair's the fairest of my dream.

I seem to see the church's wall
   And some grey tomb below a yew,
And hear the churchyard wicket fall
   Behind the people passing through.
I seem to hear, above my head,
   The bell that in the tow'r was hung;
   But whither went its iron tongue
That here bemoaned the long lost dead?

GOODY TIRED

Home, thank God, but like to fall
   O'er the threshold of the door;
I can hardly walk at all,
   And could not a half-mile more.
Oh! how weary are my feet!
And I'm spent with dust and heat.
Bit of meat? No; give me first
Just some tea to quench my thirst.
No; not wine – e'er so fine.
No; not gold – heap'd untold;
   But a cup or two of tea.

With what heavy steps I put
   On the ground my last two miles,
Lifting each lead–heavy foot
   O'er the road and over stiles.
At the best I fain would stop,
But at hills was like to drop;
Leaving pretty sights behind
That no more could take my mind.
No; not hills. No; not mills.
Not a thing, but a spring,
   Whence I drank, but wish'd for tea.

I was glad to leave so well
   All within my sister's door;
But I'm sure I cannot tell
   How to reach her any more;
For to me, if I must beat
Longsome ways in burning heat,

Why 'tis worth the very grounds
Just to toil athwart their bounds.
No; not now, land or cow.
No; not here, park or deer,
    By my little pot of tea.

HOME-FIELD

But ah! the long gone happy hours
    Of sunny days, in summer-tide,
In home-field bright with shining flow'rs,
    Or sweet with new-mown grass, half-dried;
Where voices laugh'd at merry words,
Below the songs of many birds,
    As slid the time away,
In tree shades wheeling round so slow
That they to me seem'd not to go,
    But linger at a stay.

But now, as I by night come through
    The lonely field with thoughts of day,
The cows lie sleeping in the lew,
    Where then our friends were young and gay;
And cooler winds now scatter down
The elm leaves, faded into brown,
    As slides the hour away,
Where moon cast tree shades wheel so slow,
That they to me seem not to go,
    But linger at a stay.

There seems but little change to me
    In field or path where'er I roam;
The change is where I miss to see
    The life that lived in this old home.
At yonder house, no sun or fire
Shines now on its old dame or sire,
    Whose time is pass'd away;
And yet to us who linger on,
It seems as if it had not gone,
    But this were still their day.

A SABBATH LAY

'Why hast Thou forsaken me?'
                    Mark, Chap. 15, v. 34

The joy that shone in early days
    Is dark, and peace is fled,
And I, cut off from human ways,
    Am number'd with the dead.
And while my soul in fear and pain
    Is peaceless as the sea,
I call on Thee but call in vain.
            LAMA SABACHTHANI?

Is it to purge me of my pride,
    Of ev'ry vain desire,
That I am in affliction tried
    As silver in the fire?
If thus of mercy and of love
    The visitation be,
Oh! send me comfort from above.
            LAMA SABACHTHANI?

Before Thy frowning face, O God!
    I fly as driven chaff;
But while I groan beneath Thy rod
    Support me with Thy staff.
And after heaviness and pain
    In mercy let me see
The brightness of Thy face again.
            LAMA SABACHTHANI?

PART II
POEMS IN DORSET
DIALECT

THE SPRING

When wintry weather's all a–done,
An' brooks do sparkle in the zun,
An' naïsy-builden rooks do vlee
Wi' sticks toward their elem tree;
When birds do zing, an' we can zee
   Upon the boughs the buds o' spring, –
   Then I'm as happy as a king,
     A-vield wi' health an' zunsheen.

Vor then the cowslip's hangen flow'r
A-wetted in the zunny show'r,
Do grow wi' vi'lets, sweet o' smell,
Bezide the wood-screen'd grægle's bell;
Where drushes' aggs, wi' sky-blue shell,
   Do lie in mossy nest among
   The thorns, while they do zing their zong
     At evenen in the zunsheen.

An' God do meäke his win' to blow
An' raïn to vall vor high an' low,
An' bid his mornen zun to rise
Vor all alike, an' groun' an' skies
Ha' colors vor the poor man's eyes:
   An' in our trials He is near,
   To hear our mwoan an' zee our tear,
     An' turn our clouds to zunsheen.

An' many times when I do vind
Things all goo wrong, an' vo'k unkind,
To zee the happy veeden herds,
An' hear the zingen o' the birds,
Do soothe my sorrow mwore than words;
   Vor I do zee that 'tis our sin
   Do meäke woone's soul so dark 'ithin,
     When God would gi'e woone zunsheen.

EASTER ZUNDAY

Last Easter Jim put on his blue
Frock cwoat, the vu'st time – vier new;
Wi' yollow buttons all o' brass,
That glitter'd in the zun lik' glass;

An' pok'd 'ithin the button-hole
A tutty he'd a–begg'd or stole.
A span–new wes'co't, too, he wore,
Wi' yollow stripes all down avore;
An' tied his breeches' lags below
The knee, wi' ribbon in a bow;
An' drow'd his kitty-boots azide,
An' put his laggens on, an' tied
His shoes wi' strings two vingers wide,
    Because 'twer Easter Zunday.

An' after mornen church wer out
He come back hwome, an' stroll'd about
All down the vields, an' drough the leäne,
Wi' sister Kit an' cousin Jeäne,
A–turnen proudly to their view
His yollow breast an' back o' blue.
The lambs did plaÿ, the grounds wer green,
The trees did bud, the zun did sheen;
The lark did zing below the sky,
An' roads wer all a–blown so dry,
As if the zummer wer begun;
An' he had sich a bit o' fun!
He meäde the maïdens squeäl an' run,
    Because 'twer Easter Zunday.

EASTER MONDAY

An' zoo o' Monday we got drough
Our work betimes, an ax'd a vew
Young vo'k vrom Stowe an' Coom, an' zome
Vrom uncle's down at Grange, to come.
An' they so spry, wi' merry smiles,
Did beät the path an' leäp the stiles,
Wi' two or dree young chaps bezide,
To meet an' keep up Easter tide:
Vor we'd a–zaid avore, we'd git
Zome friends to come, an' have a bit
O' fun wi' me, an' Jeäne, an' Kit,
    Because 'twer Easter Monday.

An' there we plaÿ'd away at quaïts,
An' weigh'd ourzelves wi' sceäles an' waïghts;
An' jump'd to zee who jump'd the spryest,
An' sprung the vurdest an' the highest;
An' rung the bells vor vull an hour,
An' plaÿ'd at vives ageän the tower.
An' then we went an' had a taît,
An' cousin Sammy, wi' his waïght,
Broke off the bar, he wer so fat!
An' toppled off, an' vell down flat
Upon his head, an' squot his hat,
  Because 'twer Easter Monday.

DOCK-LEAVES

The dock-leaves that do spread so wide
Up yonder zunny bank's green zide,
Do bring to mind what we did do
At plaÿ wi' dock-leaves years agoo:
How we, – when nettles had a-stung
Our little hands, when we wer young, –
Did rub 'em wi' a dock, an' zing
'Out nettl', in dock. In dock, out sting.'
An' when your feäce, in zummer's het,
Did sheen wi' tricklen draps o' zweat,
How you, a–zot bezide the bank,
Didst toss your little head, an' pank,
An' teäke a dock-leaf in your' han',
An' whisk en lik' a leädy's fan;
While I did hunt, 'ithin your zight,
Vor streaky cockle-shells to fight.

In all our plaÿ-geämes we did bruise
The dock-leaves wi' our nimble shoes;
Bwoth where we merry chaps did fling
You maïdens in the orcha'd swing,
An' by the zaw-pit's dousty bank,
Where we did taït upon a plank.
– (D'ye mind how woonce, you cou'den zit
The bwoard, an' vell off into pit?)

An' when we hunted you about
The grassy barken, in an' out
Among the ricks, your vlee-en frocks
An' nimble veet did strik' the docks.
An' zoo they docks, a-spread so wide
Up yonder zunny bank's green zide,
Do bring to mind what we did do
Among the dock-leaves years agoo.

WOODCOM' FEAST

Come, Fanny, come! put on thy white,
'Tis Woodcom' feäst, good now! to-night.
Come! think noo mwore, you silly maïd,
O' chicken drown'd or ducks a-straÿ'd;
Nor mwope to vind thy new frock's taïl
A-tore by hitchen in a naïl;
Nor grieve an' hang thy head azide,
A-thinken o' thy lam' that died.
The flag's a-vlee-en wide an' high,
An' ringen bells do sheäke the sky;
The fifes do plaÿ, the horns do roar,
An' boughs be up at ev'ry door:
They'll be a-dancen soon, – the drum
'S a-rumblen now. Come, Fanny, come!
Why father's gone, an' mother too.
They went up leäne an hour agoo;
An' at the green the young an' wold
Do stan' so thick as sheep in vwold:
The men do laugh, the bwoys do shout, –
Come out you mwopen wench, come out,
An' go wi' me, an' show at leäst
Bright eyes an' smiles at Woodcom' feäst.

Come, let's goo out, an' fling our heels
About in jigs an' vow'r-han' reels;
While all the stiff-lagg'd wolder vo'k,
A-zitten roun', do talk an' joke
An' smile to zee their own wold rigs,
A-show'd by our wild geämes an' jigs.
Vor ever since the wold church speer

64

Vu'st prick'd the clouds, vrom year to year,
When grass in meäd did reach woone's knees,
An' blooth did kern in apple-trees,
Zome merry day 'v' a-broke to sheen
Above the dance at Woodcom' green,
An' all o' they that now do lie
So low all roun' the speer so high,
Woonce, vrom the biggest to the leäst,
Had merry hearts at Woodcom' feäst.

Zoo keep it up, an' gi'e it on
To other vo'k when we be gone.
Come out; vor when the zetten zun
Do leäve in sheäde our harmless fun,
The moon a-risèn in the east
Do gi'e us light at Woodcom' feäst.
Come, Fanny, come! put on thy white,
'Tis merry Woodcom' feäst to-night:
There's nothen vor to mwope about, –
Come-out, you leäzy jeäde, come out!
An' thou wult be, to woone at leäst,
The prettiest maïd at Woodcom' feäst.

THE GIRT WOAK TREE THAT'S IN THE DELL

The girt woak tree that's in the dell!
There's noo tree I do love so well;
Vor times an' times when I wer young,
I there've a-climb'd, an' there've a-zwung,
An' pick'd the eäcorns green, a-shed
In wrestlen storms vrom his broad head.
An' down below's the cloty brook
Where I did vish with line an' hook,
An' beät, in plaÿsome dips and zwims,
The foamy stream, wi' white-skinn'd lim's.
An' there my mother nimbly shot
Her knitten-needles, as she zot
At evenen down below the wide
Woak's head, wi' father at her zide.
An' I've a-plaÿed wi' many a bwoy,
That's now a man an' gone awoy;
    Zoo I do like noo tree so well
    'S the girt woak tree that's in the dell.

An' there, in leäter years, I roved
Wi' thik poor maïd I fondly lov'd, –
The maïd too feäir to die so soon, –
When evenen twilight, or the moon,
Cast light enough 'ithin the pleäce
To show the smiles upon her feäce,
Wi' eyes so clear's the glassy pool,
An' lips an cheäks so soft as wool.
There han' in han', wi' bosoms warm,
Wi' love that burn'd but thought noo harm,
Below the wide-bough'd tree we past
The happy hours that went too vast;
An' though she'll never be my wife,
She's still my leädèn star o' life.
She's gone: an' she've a-left to me
Her mem'ry in the girt woak tree;
   Zoo I do love noo tree so well
    'S the girt woak tree that's in the dell.

An' oh! mid never axe nor hook
Be brought to spweil his steätely look;
Nor ever roun' his ribby zides
Mid cattle rub their heäiry hides;
Nor pigs rout up his turf, but keep
His lwonesome sheäde vor harmless sheep;
An' let en grow, an' let en spread,
An' let en live when I be dead.
But oh! if men should come an' vell
The girt woak tree that's in the dell,
An' build his planks 'ithin the zide
O' zome girt ship to plough the tide,
Then, life or death! I'd goo to sea,
A-saïlen wi' the girt woak tree:
An' I upon his planks would stand,
An' die a-fighten vor the land, –
The land so dear, – the land so free, –
The land that bore the girt woak tree;
   Vor I do love noo tree so well
    'S the girt woak tree that's in the dell.

VELLEN O' THE TREE

Aye, the girt elem tree out in little hwome-groun'
Wer a-stannen this mornen, an' now's a-cut down.
Aye, the girt elem tree, so big roun' an' so high,
Where the mowers did goo to their drink, an' did lie
In the sheäde ov his head, when the zun at his heighth
Had a-drove em vrom mowen, wi' het an' wi' drith,
Where the haÿ-meäkers put all their picks an' their reäkes,
An' did squot down to snabble their cheese an' their ceäkes,
An' did vill vrom their flaggons their cups wi' their eäle,
An' did meäke theirzelves merry wi' joke an wi' teäle.

Ees, we took up a rwope an' we tied en all round
At the top o'n, wi' woone end a-hangen to ground,
An' we cut, near the ground, his girt stem a'most drough,
An' we bent the wold head o'n wi' woone tug or two;
An' he swaÿ'd all his limbs, an' he nodded his head,
Till he vell away down like a pillar o' lead:
An' as we did run vrom en, there, clwose at our backs,
Oh! his boughs come to groun' wi' sich whizzes an' cracks;
An' his top wer so lofty that, now he is down,
The stem o'n do reach a'most over the groun'.
Zoo the girt elem tree out in little hwome-groun',
Wer a-stannen this mornen, an' now's a-cut down.

EVENEN TWILIGHT

Ah! they vew zummers brought us round
The happiest days that we've a-vound,
When in the orcha'd, that did stratch
To westward out avore the patch
Ov high-bough'd wood, an' shelve to catch
   The western zun-light, we did meet
    Wi' merry tongues an' skippen veet
     At evenen in the twilight.

The evenen aïr did fan, in turn,
The cheäks the midday zun did burn,
An' zet the russlen leaves at plaÿ,
An' meäke the red stemm'd brembles swaÿ

In bows below the snow-white maÿ;
　　An' whirlen roun' the trees, did sheäke
Jeäne's raven curls about her neck,
　　They evenens in the twilight.

An' there the yollow light did rest
Upon the bank toward the west,
An' twitt'ren birds did hop in drough
The hedge, an' many a skippen shoe
Did beät the flowers, wet wi' dew,
　　As underneäth the tree's wide limb
　　Our merry sheäpes did jumpy, dim,
　　They evenens in the twilight.

How sweet's the evenen dusk to rove
Along wi' woone that we do love!
When light enough is in the sky
To sheäde the smile an' light the eye
'Tis all but heaven to be by;
　　An' bid, in whispers soft an' light
　　'S the russlen ov a leaf, 'Good night,'
　　At evenen in the twilight.

An' happy be the young an' strong,
That can but work the whole day long
So merry as the birds in spring;
An' have noo ho vor any thing
Another day mid teäke or bring;
　　But meet, when all their work's a–done,
　　In orcha'd vor their bit o' fun
　　At evenen in the twilight.

EVENEN IN THE VILLAGE

Now the light o' the west is a-turn'd to gloom,
　　An' the men be at hwome vrom ground;
An' the bells be a-zenden all down the Coombe
　　From tower, their mwoansome sound.
　　　　An' the wind is still,
　　　　An' the house-dogs do bark,
An' the rooks be a-vled to the elems high an' dark,
　　An' the water do roar at mill.

68

An' the flickeren light drough the window-peäne
Vrom the candle's dull fleäme do shoot,
An' young Jemmy the smith is a-gone down leäne,
A-playen his shrill-vaïced flute.
      An' the miller's man
      Do zit down at his ease
On the seat that is under the cluster o' trees,
  Wi' his pipe an' his cider can.

MAY

Come out o' door, 'tis Spring! 'tis Maÿ!
The trees be green, the vields be gaÿ;
The weather's warm, the winter blast,
Wi' all his traïn o' clouds, is past;
The zun do rise while vo'k do sleep,
To teäke a higher daily zweep,
Wi' cloudless feäce a-flingen down
His sparklen light upon the groun'.

The aïr's a-streamen soft, – come drow
The windor open; let it blow
In drough the house, where vire, an' door
A-shut, kept out the cwold avore.
Come, let the vew dull embers die,
An' come below the open sky;
An' wear your best, vor fear the groun'
In colours gaÿ mid sheäme your gown:
An' goo an' rig wi' me a mile
Or two up over geäte an' stile,
Drough zunny parrocks that do leäd,
Wi' crooked hedges, to the meäd,
Where elems high, in steätely ranks,
Do rise vrom yollow cowslip-banks,
An' birds do twitter vrom the spraÿ
O' bushes deck'd wi' snow-white maÿ;
An' gil'cups, wi' the deäisy bed,
Be under ev'ry step you tread.

We'll wind up roun' the hill, an' look
All down the thickly-timber'd nook,
Out where the squier's house do show
His grey-wall'd peaks up drough the row

O' sheädy elems, where the rook
Do build her nest; an' where the brook
Do creep along the meäds, an' lie
To catch the brightness o' the sky;
An' cows, in water to their knees,
Do stan' a-whisken off the vlees.

Mother o' blossoms, and ov all
That's feäir a-vield vrom Spring till Fall,
The gookoo over white-weäv'd seas
Do come to zing in thy green trees,
An' buttervlees, in giddy flight,
Do gleäm the mwost by thy gaÿ light.
Oh! when, at last, my fleshly eyes
Shall shut upon the vields an' skies,
Mid zummer's zunny days be gone,
An' winter's clouds be comen on:
Nor mid I draw upon the e'th,
O' thy sweet aïr my leätest breath;
Alassen I mid want to staÿ
Behine for thee, O flow'ry Maÿ!

BOB THE FIDDLER

Oh! Bob the fiddler is the pride
O' chaps an' maïdens vur an' wide;
They can't keep up a merry tide,
   But Bob is in the middle.
If merry Bob do come avore ye,
He'll zing a zong, or tell a story;
But if you'd zee en in his glory,
   Jist let en have a fiddle.

Aye, let en tuck a crowd below
His chin, an' gi'e his vist a bow,
He'll dreve his elbow to an' fro',
   An' plaÿ what you do please.
At Maÿpolen, or feäst, or feäir,
His eärm wull zet off twenty peäir,
An' meäke em dance the groun' dirt-beäre,
   An' hop about lik' vlees.

Long life to Bob! the very soul
O' me'th at merry feäst an' pole;
Vor when the crowd do leäve his jowl,
    They'll all be in the dumps.
Zoo at the dance another year,
At Shillinston or Hazelbur',
Mid Bob be there to meäke em stir,
    In merry jigs, their stumps!

THE WHITE ROAD UP ATHIRT THE HILL

When hot-beam'd zuns do strik right down,
An' burn our zweaty feäzen brown;
An' zunny slopes, a-lyen nigh,
Be back'd by hills so blue's the sky;
Then, while the bells do sweetly cheem
Upon the champen high-neck'd team,
How lively, wi' a friend, do seem
    The white road up athirt the hill.

The zwellen downs, wi' chalky tracks
A-climmen up their zunny backs,
Do hide green meäds an' zedgy brooks,
An' clumps o' trees wi' glossy rooks,
An' hearty vo'k to laugh an' zing,
An' parish-churches in a string,
Wi' tow'rs o' merry bells to ring,
    An' white roads up athirt the hills.

At feäst, when uncle's vo'k do come
To spend the day wi' us at hwome,
An' we do lay upon the bwoard
The very best we can avvword,
The wolder woones do talk an' smoke,
An' younger woones do plaÿ an' joke,
An' in the evenen all our vo'k
    Do bring em gwaïn athirt the hill.

An' while the green do zwarm wi' wold
An' young, so thick as sheep in vwold,
The bellows in the blacksmith's shop,
An' miller's moss-green wheel do stop,

An' lwonesome in the wheelwright's shed
'S a-left the wheeless waggon-bed;
While zwarms o' comen friends do tread
   The white road down athirt the hill.

An' when the winden road so white,
A-climmen up the hills in zight,
Do leäd to pleäzen, east or west,
The vu'st a-known, an' lov'd the best,
How touchen in the zunsheen's glow,
Or in the sheädes that clouds do drow
Upon the zunburnt downs below,
   'S the white road up athirt the hill.

What peacevul hollows here the long
White roads do windy round among!
Wi' deäiry cows in woody nooks,
An' haÿmeäkers among their pooks,
An' housen that the trees do screen
From zun an' zight by boughs o' green!
Young blushen beauty's hwomes between
   The white roads up athirt the hills.

THE WOODY HOLLOW

If mem'ry, when our hope's a-gone,
Could bring us dreams to cheat us on,
Ov happiness our hearts voun' true
In years we come too quickly drough;
What days should come to me, but you,
   That burn'd my youthvul cheäks wi' zuns
   O' zummer, in my plaÿsome runs
    About the woody hollow.

When evenen's risèn moon did peep
Down drough the hollow dark an' deep,
Where gigglen sweethearts meäde their vows
In whispers under waggen boughs;
When whisslen bwoys, an' rott'len ploughs
   Wer still, an' mothers, wi' their thin
   Shrill vaïces, call'd their daughters in,
    From walken in the hollow;

What souls should come avore my zight,
But they that had your zummer light?
The litsome younger woones that smil'd
Wi' comely feäzen now a-spweil'd;
Or wolder vo'k, so wise an' mild,
    That I do miss when I do goo
        To zee the pleäce, an' walk down drough
            The lwonesome woody hollow?

When wrongs an' overbearen words
Do prick my bleeden heart lik' swords,
Then I do try, vor Christes seäke,
To think o' you, sweet days! an' meäke
My soul as 'twer when you did weäke
    My childhood's eyes, an' when, if spite
        Or grief did come, did die at night
            In sleep 'ithin the hollow.

JENNY'S RIBBONS

Jeän ax'd what ribbon she should wear
'Ithin her bonnet to the feäir?
She had woone white, a-gi'ed her when
She stood at Meäry's chrissenen;
She had woone brown, she had woone red,
A keepseäke vrom her brother dead,
That she did like to wear, to goo
To zee his greäve below the yew.

She had woone green among her stock,
That I'd a-bought to match her frock;
She had woone blue to match her eyes,
The colour o' the zummer skies,
An' thik, though I do like the rest,
Is he that I do like the best,
Because she had en in her heäir
When vu'st I walk'd wi' her at feäir.

The brown, I zaid, would do to deck
Thy heäir; the white would match thy neck;
The red would meäke thy red cheäk wan
A-thinken o' the gi'er gone;
The green would show thee to be true;

73

But still I'd sooner zee the blue,
Because 'twer he that deck'd thy heäir
When vu'st I walked wi' thee at feäir.

Zoo, when she had en on, I took
Her han' 'ithin my elbow's crook,
An' off we went athirt the weir
An' up the meäd toward the feäir;
The while her mother, at the geäte,
Call'd out an' bid her not staÿ leäte,
An' she, a-smilen wi' her bow
O' blue, look'd roun' an' nodded, *No*.

ECLOGUE: THE 'LOTMENTS
JOHN AND RICHARD

JOHN

Zoo you be in your groun' then, I do zee,
A-worken and a-zingen lik' a bee.
How do it answer? what d'ye think about it?
D'ye think 'tis better wi' it than without it?
A-reck'nen rent, an' time, an' zeed to stock it,
D'ye think that you be any thing in pocket?

RICHARD

O, 'tis a goodish help to woone, I'm sure o't.
If I had not a-got it, my poor bwones
Would now ha' eäch'd a-cracken stwones
Upon the road; I wish I had zome mwore o't.

JOHN

I wish the girt woones had a-got the greäce
To let out land lik' this in ouer pleäce;
But I do fear there'll never be nwone vor us,
An' I can't tell whatever we shall do:
We be a'most a-starven, an' we'd goo
To 'merica, if we'd enough to car us.

RICHARD

Why 'twer the squire, good now! a worthy man,
That vu'st brought into ouer pleäce the plan;
He zaid he'd let a vew odd eäcres

O' land to us poor leäb'ren men;
An', faïth, he had enough o' teäkers
Vor that, an' twice so much ageän.
Zoo I took zome here, near my hovel,
To exercise my speäde an' shovel;
An' what wi' dungen, diggen up, an' zeeden,
A-thinnen, cleänen, howen up an' weeden,
I, an' the biggest o' the childern too,
Do always vind some useful jobs to do.

JOHN

Aye, wi' a bit o' ground, if woone got any,
Woone's bwoys can soon get out an' eärn a penny;
An' then, by worken, they do learn the vaster
The way to do things when they have a meäster;
Vor woone must know a deäl about the land
Bevore woone's fit to lend a useful hand,
In geärden or a-vield upon a farm.

RICHARD

An' then the work do keep em out o' harm;
Vor vo'ks that don't do nothen wull be vound
Soon doen woorse than nothen, I'll be bound.
But as vor me, d'ye zee, wi' theäse here bit
O' land, why I have ev'ry thing a'mwost:
Vor I can fatten vowels vor the spit,
Or zell a good fat goose or two to rwoast;
An' have my beäns or cabbage, greens or grass,
Or bit o' wheat, or, sich my happy feäte is,
That I can keep a little cow, or ass,
An' a vew pigs to eat the little teäties.

JOHN

An' when your pig's a-fatted pretty well
Wi' teäties, or wi' barley an' some bran,
Why you've a-got zome vlitches vor to zell,
Or hang in chimney-corner, if you can.

RICHARD

Aye, that's the thing; an' when the pig do die,
We got a lot ov offal vor to fry,
An' netlens vor to bwoil; or put the blood in,
An' meäke a meal or two o' good black-pudden.

75

JOHN

I'd keep myzelf from parish, I'd be bound,
If I could get a little patch o' ground.

ECLOGUE: A BIT O' SLY COORTEN
JOHN AND FANNY

JOHN

Now, Fanny, 'tis too bad, you teazen maïd!
How leäte you be a–come! Where have ye staÿ'd?
How long you have a–meäde me waït about!
I thought you werden gwaïn to come ageän.
I had a mind to goo back hwome ageän.
This idden when you promis'd to come out.

FANNY

Now tidden any good to meäke a row,
Upon my word, I cooden come till now.
Vor I've a–been kept in all day by mother,
At work about woone little job an' tother.
If you do want to goo, though, don't ye staÿ
Vor me a minute longer, I do praÿ.

JOHN

I thought you mid be out wi' Jemmy Bleäke.

FANNY

An' why be out wi' him, vor goodness' seäke?

JOHN

You walk'd o' Zunday evenen wi'n, d'ye know,
You went vrom church a–hitch'd up in his eärm.

FANNY

Well, if I did, that werden any harm.
Lauk! that *is* zome'at to teäke notice o'.

JOHN

He took ye roun' the middle at the stile,
An' kiss'd ye twice 'ithin the ha'f a mile.

FANNY

Ees, at the stile, because I shoulden vall,
He took me hold to help me down, that's all;

76

An' I can't zee what very mighty harm
He could ha' done a-lenden me his eärm.
An' as vor kissen o' me, if he did,
I didden ax en to, nor zay he mid:
An' if he kiss'd me dree times, or a dozen,
What harm wer it? Why idden he my cousin?
An' I can't zee, then, what there is amiss
In cousin Jem's jist gi'en me a kiss.

JOHN

Well, he shan't kiss ye, then; you shan't be kiss'd
By his girt ugly chops, a lanky houn'!
If I do zee'n, I'll jist wring up my vist
An' knock en down.
I'll squot his girt pug-nose, if I don't miss en;
I'll warn I'll spweil his pretty lips vor kissen!

FANNY

Well, John, I'm sure I little thought to vind
That you had ever sich a jealous mind.
What then! I s'pose that I must be a dummy,
An' mussen goo about nor wag my tongue
To any soul, if he's a man, an' young;
Or else you'll work yourzelf up mad wi' passion,
An' talk away o' gi'en vo'k a drashen,
An' breaken bwones, an' beätèn heads to pummy!
If you've a–got sich jealous ways about ye,
I'm sure I should be better off 'ithout ye.

JOHN

Well, if girt Jemmy have a-won your heart,
We'd better break the coortship off, an' peärt.

FANNY

He won my heart! There, John, don't talk sich stuff;
Don't talk noo mwore, vor you've a-zaid enough.
If I'd a–lik'd another mwore than you,
I'm sure I shoulden come to meet ye zoo;
Vor I've a–twold to father many a storry,
An' took o' mother many a scwolden vor ye.
              (weeping)
But 'twull be over now, vor you shan't zee me
Out wi' ye noo mwore, to pick a quarrel wi' me.

JOHN

Well, Fanny, I woon't zay noo mwore, my dear.
Let's meäke it up. Come, wipe off thik there tear.
Let's goo an' zit o' top o' theäse here stile,
An' rest, an' look about a little while.

FANNY

Now goo away, you crabbed jealous chap!
You shan't kiss me, – you shan't! I'll gi' ye a slap.

JOHN

Then you look smilen; don't you pout an' toss
Your head so much, an' look so very cross.

FANNY

Now, John! don't squeeze me roun' the middle zoo.
I woon't stop here noo longer, if you do.
Why, John! be quiet, wull ye? Fie upon it!
Now zee how you've a–wrumpl'd up my bonnet!
Mother 'ill zee it after I'm at hwome,
An' gi'e a guess directly how it come.

JOHN

Then don't you zay that I be jealous, Fanny.

FANNY

I wull: vor you *be* jealous, Mister Jahnny.
There's zomebody a–comen down the groun'
Towards the stile. Who is it? Come, get down.
I must run hwome, upon my word then, now;
If I do staÿ, they'll kick up sich a row.
Good night. I can't staÿ now.

JOHN

         Then good night, Fanny!
Come out a bit to–morrow evenen, can ye?

WHITSUNTIDE AN' CLUB WALKEN

Ees, last Whit-Monday, I an' Meäry
Got up betimes to mind the deäiry;
An' gi'ed the milken païls a scrub,
An' dress'd, an' went to zee the club.

Vor up at public-house, by ten
O'clock the pleäce wer vull o' men,
A-dress'd to goo to church, an' dine,
An' walk about the pleäce in line.
Zoo off they started, two an' two,
Wi' païnted poles an' knots o' blue,
An' girt silk flags, – I wish my box
'D a-got em all in ceäpes an' frocks, –
A-weäven wide an' flappen loud
In plaÿsome winds above the crowd;
While fifes did squeak an' drums did rumble,
An' deep beäzzoons did grunt an' grumble,
An' all the vo'k in gath'ren crowds
Kick'd up the doust in smeechy clouds,
That slowly rose an' spread abrode
In streamen aïr above the road.
An' then at church there wer sich lots
O' hats a-hangen up wi' knots,
An' poles a-stood so thick as iver
The rushes stood bezide a river.
An' Mr. Goodman gi'ed em warnen
To spend their evenen lik' their mornen;
An' not to praÿ wi' mornen tongues,
An' then to zwear wi' evenen lungs;
Nor vu'st sheäke hands, to let the wrist
Lift up at last a bruisen vist:
Vor clubs were all a-meän'd vor friends,
He twold em, an' vor better ends
Than twiten vo'k an' picken quarrels,
An' tipplen cups an' empten barrels, –
Vor meäken woone man do another
In need the kindness ov a brother.

An' after church they went to dine
'Ithin the long-wall'd room behine
The public-house, where you remember,
We had our dance back last December.
An' there they meäde sich stunnen clatters
Wi' knives an' forks, an' pleätes an' platters;
An' waïters ran, an' beer did pass
Vrom tap to jug, vrom jug to glass:
An' when they took away the dishes,

They drink'd good healths, an' wish'd good wishes,
To all the girt vo'k o' the land,
An' all good things vo'k took in hand;
An' woone cried *hip, hip, hip!* an' hollow'd,
An' tothers all struck in, an' vollow'd;
An' grabb'd their drink wi' eager clutches,
An' swigg'd it wi' sich hearty glutches,
As vo'k, stark mad wi' pweison stuff,
That thought theirzelves not mad enough.

An' after that they went all out
In rank ageän, an' walk'd about,
An' gi'ed zome parish vo'k a call;
An' then went down to Narley Hall
An' had zome beer, an' danc'd between
The elem trees upon the green.
An' down along the road they done
All sorts o' mad-cap things vor fun;
An' danc'd, a-poken out their poles,
An' pushen bwoys down into holes:
An' Sammy Stubbs come out o' rank,
An' kiss'd me up ageän the bank,
A saucy chap; I ha'nt vorgi'ed en
Not yet, – in short, I han't a-zeed en.
Zoo in the dusk ov evenen, zome
Went back to drink, an' zome went hwome.

WOODLEY

Sweet Woodley! oh! how fresh an' gaÿ
Thy leänes an' vields be now in Maÿ,
The while the broad-leav'd clotes do zwim
In brooks wi' gil'cups at the brim;
An' yellow cowslip-beds do grow
By thorns in blooth so white as snow;
An' win' do come vrom copse wi' smells
O' grægles wi' their hangen bells!

Though time do dreve me on, my mind
Do turn in love to thee behind,
The seäme's a bulrush that's a-shook
By wind a-blowen up the brook:

The curlen stream would dreve en down,
But plaÿsome aïr do turn en roun',
An' meäke en seem to bend wi' love
To zunny hollows up above.

Thy tower still do overlook
The woody knaps an' winden brook,
An' leänes wi' here an' there a hatch,
An' house wi' elem sheäded thatch,
An' vields where chaps do vur outdo
The Zunday sky, wi' cwoats o' blue;
An' maïdens' frocks do vur surpass
The whitest deäises in the grass.

What peals to–day from thy wold tow'r
Do strike upon the zummer flow'r,
As all the club, wi' dousty lags,
Do walk wi' poles an' flappen flags,
An' wind, to music, roun' between
A zwarm o' vo'k upon the green!
Though time do dreve me on, my mind
Do turn wi' love to thee behind.

THE BROOK THAT RAN BY GRAMFER'S

When snow-white clouds wer thin an' vew
Avore the zummer sky o' blue,
An' I'd noo ho but how to vind
Zome plaÿ to entertaïn my mind;
Along the water, as did wind
  Wi' zedgy shoal an' hollow crook,
  How I did ramble by the brook
  That ran all down vrom gramfer's.

A-holden out my line beyond
The clote-leaves, wi' my withy wand,
How I did watch, wi' eager look,
My zwimmen cork, a-zunk or shook
By minnows nibblen at my hook,
  A-thinken I should catch a breäce
  O' perch, or at the leäst some deäce,
  A-zwimmen down vrom gramfer's.

Then ten good deäiries wer a-ved
Along that water's winden bed,
An' in the lewth o' hills an' wood
A half a score farm-housen stood:
But now, – count all o'm how you would,
    So many less do hold the land, –
    You'd vind but vive that still do stand,
    A-comen down vrom gramfer's.

There, in the midst ov all his land,
The squier's ten-tunn'd house did stand,
Where he did meäke the water clim'
A bank, an' sparkle under dim
Bridge arches, villen to the brim
    His pon', an' leäpen, white as snow,
    Vrom rocks a-glitt'ren in a bow,
    An' runnen down to gramfer's.

An' now woone wing is all you'd vind
O' thik girt house a-left behind;
An' only woone wold stwonen tun
'S a-stannen to the raïn an' zun, –
An' all's undone that he'd a-done;
    The brook ha' now noo call to staÿ
    To vill his pon' or clim' his baÿ,
    A-runnen down to gramfer's.

When woonce, in heavy raïn, the road
At Grenley bridge wer overflow'd,
Poor Sophy White, the pleäce's pride,
A-gwaïn vrom market, went to ride
Her pony droo to tother side;
    But vound the streäm so deep an' strong,
    That took her off the road along
    The hollow down to gramfer's.

'Twer dark, an' she went on too vast
To catch hold any thing she pass'd;
Noo bough hung over to her hand,
An' she could reach noo stwone nor land,
Where woonce her little voot could stand;
    Noo ears were out to hear her cries,
    Nor wer she woonce a-zeen by eyes,
    Till took up dead at gramfer's.

SWEET MUSIC IN THE WIND

When evenen is a–drawen in,
I'll steal vrom others' naïsy din;
An' where the whirlen brook do roll
Below the walnut-tree, I'll stroll
An' think o' thee wi' all my soul,
Dear Jenny; while the sound o' bells
Do vlee along wi' mwoansome zwells,
    Sweet music in the wind!

I'll think how in the rushy leäze
O' zunny evenens jis' lik' theäse,
In happy times I us'd to zee
Thy comely sheäpe about the tree,
Wi' païl a–held avore thy knee;
An' lissen'd to thy merry zong
That at a distance come along,
    Sweet music in the wind!

An' when wi' me you walk'd about
O' Zundays, after church wer out,
Wi' hangen eärm an' modest look;
Or zitten in zome woody nook
We lissen'd to the leaves that shook
Upon the poplars straïght an' tall,
Or rottle o' the watervall,
    Sweet music in the wind!

An' when the playvul aïr do vlee,
O' moonlight nights, vrom tree to tree,
Or whirl upon the sheäkèn grass,
Or rottle at my window glass:
Do seem, – as I do hear it pass, –
As if thy vaïce did come to tell
Me where thy happy soul do dwell,
    Sweet music in the wind!

UNCLE AN' AUNT

How happy uncle us'd to be
O' zummer time, when aunt an' he
O' Zunday evenens, eärm in eärm,
Did walk about their tiny farm,

While birds did zing an' gnats did zwarm,
Drough grass a'most above their knees,
An' roun' by hedges an' by trees
    Wi' leafy boughs a-swayen.

His hat wer broad, his cwoat wer brown,
Wi' two long flaps a-hangen down;
An' vrom his knee went down a blue
Knit stocken to his buckled shoe;
An' aunt did pull her gown-tail drough
Her pocket-hole, to keep en neat,
As she mid walk, or teäke a seat
    By leafy boughs a-swayen.

An' vu'st they'd goo to zee their lots
O' pot-eärbs in the geärden plots;
An' he, i'-may-be, by the hatch,
Would zee aunt's vowls upon a patch
O' zeeds, an' vow if he could catch
Em wi' his gun, they shoudden vlee
Noo mwore into their roosten tree,
    Wi' leafy boughs a-swayen.

An' then vrom geärden they did pass
Drough orcha'd out to zee the grass,
An' if the apple-blooth, so white,
Mid be at all a-touch'd wi' blight;
An' uncle, happy at the zight,
Did guess what cider there mid be
In all the orcha'd, tree wi' tree,
    Wi' tutties all a-swayen.

An' then they stump'd along vrom there
A-vield, to zee the cows an' meäre;
An' she, when uncle come in zight,
Look'd up, an' prick'd her ears upright,
An' whicker'd out wi' all her might;
An' he, a-chucklen, went to zee
The cows below the sheädy tree,
    Wi' leafy boughs a-swayen.

An' last ov all, they went to know
How vast the grass in meäd did grow;
An' then aunt zaid 'twer time to goo
In hwome, – a-holden up her shoe,

To show how wet he were wi' dew.
An' zoo they toddled hwome to rest,
Lik' doves a-vlee-en to their nest,
    In leafy boughs a-swaÿen.

HAVEN WOONE'S FORTUNE A-TWOLD

In leäne the gipsies, as we went
A-milken, had a-pitch'd their tent,
Between the gravel-pit an' clump
O' trees, upon the little hump:
An' while upon the grassy groun'
    Their smoken vire did crack an' bleäze,
    Their shaggy-cwoated hoss did greäze
Among the bushes vurder down.

An' zoo, when we brought back our païls,
The woman met us at the raïls,
An' zaid she'd tell us, if we'd show
Our han's, what we should like to know.
Zoo Poll zaid she'd a mind to try
    Her skill a bit, if I would vu'st;
    Though, to be sure, she didden trust
To gipsies any mwore than I.

Well; I agreed, an' off all dree
O's went behind an elem tree;
An' after she'd a-zeed 'ithin
My han' the wrinkles o' the skin,
She twold me – an' she must a-know'd
    That Dicky met me in the leäne, –
    That I'd a-walk'd, an' should ageän,
Wi' zomebody along thik road.

An' then she twold me to bewar
O' what the letter M stood vor.
An' as I walk'd, o' Monday night,
Drough Meäd wi' Dicky overright
The Mill, the Miller, at the stile,
    Did stan' an' watch us teäke our stroll,
    An' then, a blabben dousty-poll!
Twold Mother o't. Well wo'th his while!

An' Poll too wer a-bid bewar
O' what the letter F stood vor;
An' then, because she took, at Feäir,
A bosom-pin o' Jimmy Heäre,
Young Franky beät en black an' blue.
    'Tis F vor Feäir; an' 'twer about
    A Feäiren Frank an' Jimmy foüght,
Zoo I do think she twold us true.

In short, she twold us all about
What had a-vell, or would vall out;
An' whether we should spend our lives
As maïdens, or as wedded wives;
But when we went to bundle on,
    The gipsies' dog wer at the raïls
    A-lappen milk vrom ouer païls, –
A pretty deäl o' Poll's wer gone.

MEAKEN UP A MIFF

Vorgi'e me, Jenny, do! an rise
Thy hangen head an' teary eyes,
An' speak, vor I've a-took in lies,
    An' I've a–done thee wrong;
But I wer twold, – an' thought 'twer true, –
That Sammy down at Coome an' you
Wer at the feäir, a-walken drough
    The pleäce the whole day long.

An' tender thoughts did melt my heart,
An' zwells o' viry pride did dart
Lik' lightnen drough my blood; a peärt
    Ov your love I should scorn,
An' zoo I vow'd, however sweet
Your looks mid be when we did meet,
I'd trample ye down under veet,
    Or let ye goo forlorn.

But still thy neäme would always be
The sweetest, an' my eyes would zee
Among all maïdens nwone lik' thee
    Vor ever any mwore;

Zoo by the walks that we've a-took
By flow'ry hedge an' zedgy brook,
Dear Jenny, dry your eyes, an' look
   As you've a-look'd avore.

Look up, an' let the evenen light
But sparkle in thy eyes so bright,
As they be open to the light
   O' zunzet in the west;
An' let's stroll here vor half an hour,
Where hangen boughs do meäke a bow'r
Above theäse bank, wi' eltrot flow'r
   An' robinhoods a-drest.

HAY-MEAKEN

'Tis merry ov a zummer's day,
Where vo'k be out a-meäken haÿ;
Where men an' women, in a string,
Do ted or turn the grass, an' zing,
Wi' cheemen vaïces, merry zongs,
A-tossen o' their sheenen prongs
Wi' eärms a-zwangen left an' right,
In colour'd gowns an' shirtsleeves white;
Or, wider spread, a-reäken round
The rwosy hedges o' the ground,
Where Sam do zee the speckled sneäke,
An' try to kill en wi' his reäke;
An' Poll do jump about an' squall,
To zee the twisten slooworm crawl.

'Tis merry where a gaÿ-tongued lot
Ov haÿ-meäkers be all a-squot,
On lightly-russlen haÿ, a-spread
Below an elem's lofty head,
To rest their weary limbs an' munch
Their bit o' dinner, or their nunch;
Where teethy reäkes do lie all round
By picks a-stuck up into ground.
An' wi' their vittles in their laps,
An' in their hornen cups their draps
O' cider sweet, or frothy eäle,
Their tongues do run wi' joke an' teäle.

An' when the zun, so low an' red,
Do sheen above the leafy head
O' zome broad tree, a-rizèn high
Avore the vi'ry western sky,
'Tis merry where all han's do goo
Athirt the groun', by two an' two,
A-reäken, over humps an' hollors,
The russlen grass up into rollers.
An' woone do row it into line,
An' woone do clwose it up behine;
An' after them the little bwoys
Do stride an' fling their eärms all woys,
Wi' busy picks, an' proud young looks
A-meäken up their tiny pooks.
An' zoo 'tis merry out among
The vo'k in haÿ-vield all day long.

HAY-CARREN

'Tis merry ov a zummer's day,
When vo'k be out a-haulen haÿ,
Where boughs, a-spread upon the ground,
Do meäke the staddle big an' round;
An' grass do stand in pook, or lie
In long-back'd weäles or parsels, dry.
There I do vind it stir my heart
To hear the frothen hosses snort,
A-haulen on, wi' sleek-heäir'd hides,
The red-wheel'd waggon's deep-blue zides.
Aye; let me have woone cup o' drink,
An' hear the linky harness clink,
An' then my blood do run so warm,
An' put sich strangth 'ithin my eärm,
That I do long to toss a pick,
A-pitchen or a-meäken rick.

The bwoy is at the hosse's head,
An' up upon the waggon bed
The lwoaders, strong o' eärm do stan',
At head, an' back at taïl, a man,
Wi' skill to build the lwoad upright

An' bind the vwolded corners tight;
An' at each zide o'm, sprack an' strong,
A pitcher wi' his long-stemm'd prong,
Avore the best two women now
A-call'd to reäky after plough.

When I do pitchy, 'tis my pride
Vor Jenny Hine to reäke my zide,
An' zee her fling her reäke, an' reach
So vur, an' teäke in sich a streech;
An' I don't shatter haÿ, an' meäke
Mwore work than needs vor Jenny's reäke.
I'd sooner zee the weäles' high rows
Lik' hedges up above my nose,
Than have light work myzelf, an' vind
Poor Jeäne a-beät an' left behind;
Vor she would sooner drop down dead,
Than let the pitchers get a-head.

'Tis merry at the rick to zee
How picks do wag, an' haÿ do vlee.
While woone's unlwoaden, woone do teäke
The pitches in; an' zome do meäke
The lofty rick upright an' roun',
An' tread en hard, an' reäke en down,
An' tip en, when the zun do zet,
To shoot a sudden vall o' wet.
An' zoo 'tis merry any day
Where vo'k be out a-carren haÿ.

ECLOGUE: THE BEST MAN
IN THE VIELD
SAM AND BOB

SAM

That's slowish work, Bob. What'st a-been about?
Thy pooken don't goo on not over sprack.
Why I've a-pook'd my weäle, lo'k zee, clear out,
An' here I be ageän a-turnen back.

89

BOB

I'll work wi' thee then, Sammy, any day,
At any work dost like to teäke me at,
Vor any money thou dost like to lay.
Now, Mister Sammy, what dost think o' that?
My weäle is nearly twice so big as thine,
Or else, I warnt, I shoudden be behin'.

SAM

Ah! hang thee, Bob! don't tell sich whoppen lies.
My weäle's the biggest, if do come to size.
'Tis jist the seäme whatever bist about;
Why, when dost goo a–tedden grass, you sloth,
Another hand's a–fwo'c'd to teäke thy zwath,
An' ted a half way back to help thee out;
An' then a–reäken rollers, bist so slack,
Dost keep the very bwoys an' women back.
An' if dost think that thou canst challenge I
At any thing, – then, Bob, we'll teäke a pick a–piece,
An' woonce theäse zummer, goo an' try
To meäke a rick a–piece.
A rick o' thine wull look a little funny,
When thou'st a–done en, I'll bet any money.

BOB

You noggerhead! last year thou meäd'st a rick,
An' then we had to trig en wi' a stick.
An' what did John that tipp'd en zay? Why zaid
He stood a–top o'en all the while in dread,
A–thinken that avore he should a–done en,
He'd tumble over slap wi' him upon en.

SAM

You yoppen dog! I warnt I meäde my rick
So well's thou meädst thy lwoad o' haÿ last week.
They hadden got a hunderd yards to haul en,
An' then they vound 'twer best to have en boun',
Vor if they hadden, 'twould a–tumbl'd down;
An' after that I zeed en all but vallèn,
An' trigg'd en up wi' woone o'm's pitchen pick,
To zee if I could meäke en ride to rick;
An' when they had the dumpy heap unboun',
He vell to pieces flat upon the groun'.

BOB

Do shut thy lyen chops! What dosten mind
Thy pitchen to me out in Gully-plot,
A meäken o' me waït (wast zoo behind)
A half an hour vor ev'ry pitch I got?
An' how didst groun' thy pick? an' how didst quirk
To get en up on end? Why hadst hard work
To rise a pitch that wer about so big
'S a goodish crow's nest, or a wold man's wig!
Why bist so weak, dost know, as any roller:
Zome o' the women vo'k will beät thee hollor.

SAM

You snub-nos'd flopperchops! I pitch'd so quick,
That thou dost know thou hadst a hardish job
To teäke in all the pitches off my pick;
An' dissen zee me groun' en, nother, Bob.
An' thou bist stronger, thou dost think, than I?
Girt bandy-lags! I jist should like to try.
We'll goo, if thou dost like, an' jist zee which
Can heave the mwost, or car the biggest nitch.

BOB

There, Sam, do meäke me zick to hear thy braggen!
Why bissen strong enough to car a flagon.

SAM

You grinnen fool! why I'd zet thee a-blowen,
If thou wast wi' me vor a day a-mowen.
I'd wear my cwoat, an' thou midst pull thy rags off,
An' then in half a zwath I'd mow thy lags off.

BOB

Thee mow wi' me! Why coossen keep up wi' me:
Why bissen fit to goo a-vield to skimmy,
Or mow down docks an' thistles! Why I'll bet
A shillen, Samel, that thou cassen whet.

SAM

Now don't thee zay much mwore than what'st a-zaid,
Or else I'll knock thee down, heels over head.

Thou knock me down, indeed! Why cassen gi'e
A blow half hard enough to kill a bee.

Well, thou shalt veel upon thy chops and snout.

Come on then, Samel; jist let's have woone bout.

WHERE WE DID KEEP OUR FLAGON

When we in mornen had a–drow'd
The grass or russlen' haÿ abrode,
The lit'some maïdens an' the chaps,
Wi' bits o' nunchens in their laps,
Did all zit down upon the knaps
   Up there, in under hedge, below
   The highest elem o' the row,
     Where we did keep our flagon.

There we could zee green vields at hand,
Avore a hunderd on beyand,
An' rows o' trees in hedges roun'
Green meäds, an' zummerleäzes brown,
An' thorns upon the zunny down,
   While aïr, vrom the rocken zedge
   In brook, did come along the hedge,
     Where we did keep our flagon.

There laughen chaps did try in plaÿ
To bury maïdens up in haÿ,
As gigglen maïdens tried to roll
The chaps down into zome deep hole,
Or sting wi' nettles woone o'm's poll;
   While John did hele out each his drap
   O' eäle or cider, in his lap
     Where he did keep the flagon.

Woone day there spun a whirlwind by
Where Jenny's clothes wer out to dry;
An' off vled frocks, a'most a–catch'd
By smock–frocks wi' their sleeves outstratch'd,

An' caps a-frill'd an' eäperns patch'd;
  An' she a-steären in a fright,
    Wer glad enough to zee em light
      Where we did keep our flagon.

An' when white clover wer a-sprung
Among the eegrass, green an' young,
An' elder-flowers wer a-spread
Among the rwosen white an' red,
An' honeyzucks wi hangen head, –
  O' Zunday evenens we did zit
    To look all roun' the grounds a bit,
      Where we'd a-kept our flagon.

WEEK'S END IN ZUMMER IN THE WOLD VO'K'S TIME

His aunt an' uncle, – ah! the kind
Wold souls be often in my mind:
A better couple never stood
In shoes, an' vew be vound so good.
She cheer'd the work-vo'k in their tweils
Wi' timely bits an' draps, an' smiles;
An' *he* païd all o'm at week's end,
Their money down to goo an' spend.

In zummer, when week's end come roun',
The haÿ-meäkers did come vrom groun',
An' all zit down, wi' weary bwones,
Within the yard a-peäved wi' stwones,
Along avore the peäles, between
The yard a-steän'd an' open green.
There women zot wi' beäre-neck'd chaps,
An' maïdens wi' their sleeves an' flaps
To screen vrom het their eärms an' polls,
An' men wi' beards so black as coals:
Girt stocky Jim, an' lanky John,
An' poor wold Betty dead an' gone;
An' cleän-grown Tom so spry an' strong,
An' Liz the best to pitch a zong,

That now ha' nearly half a score
O' childern zwarmen at her door;
An' whindlen Ann, that cried wi' fear
To hear the thunder when 'twer near, –
A zickly maïd, so peäle's the moon,
That voun' her zun goo down at noon;
An' blushen Jeäne so shy an' meek,
That seldom let us hear her speak,
That wer a–coorted an' undone
By Farmer Woodley's woldest son;
An' after she'd a–been vorzook,
Wer voun' a–drown'd in Longmeäd brook.

An' zoo, when *he*'d a–been all roun',
An' païd em all their wages down,
She us'd to bring vor all, by teäle,
A cup o' cider or ov eäle,
An' then a tutty meäde o' lots
O' blossoms vrom her flower-nots,
To wear in bands an' button–holes
At church, an' in their evenen strolls.
The pea that rangled to the oves,
An' columbines an' pinks an' cloves,
Sweet rwosen vrom the prickly tree,
An' jilliflow'rs, an' jessamy;
An' short–liv'd pinies, that do shed
Their leaves upon a eärly bed.
She didden put in honeyzuck:
She'd nwone, she zaïd, that she could pluck
Avore wild honeyzucks, a–vound
In ev'ry hedge ov ev'ry ground.

Zoo maïd an' woman, bwoy an' man,
Went off, while zunzet aïr did fan
Their merry zunburnt feäzen; zome
Down leäne, an' zome drough parrocks hwome.

Ah! who can tell, that ha'n't a–vound,
The sweets o' week's–end comen round!
When Zadurday do bring woone's mind
Sweet thoughts o' Zunday clwose behind;
The day that's all our own to spend
Wi' God an' wi' an e'thly friend.

The worold's girt vo'k, wi' the best
O' worldly goods mid be a-blest;
But Zunday is the poor man's peärt,
To seäve his soul an' cheer his heart.

THE EVENEN STAR O' ZUMMER

When vu'st along theäse road vrom mill,
I zeed ye hwome all up the hill,
The poplar tree, so straïght an' tall,
Did rustle by the watervall;
An' in the leäze the cows wer all
    A-lyen down to teäke their rest,
    An' slowly zunk toward the west
        The evenen star o' zummer.

In parrock there the haÿ did lie
In weäle below the elems, dry;
An' up in hwome-groun' Jim, that know'd
We all should come along thik road,
'D a-tied the grass in knots that drow'd
    Poor Poll, a-watchen in the West
    Woone brighter star than all the rest, –
        The evenen star o' zummer.

The stars that still do zet an' rise,
Did sheen in our forefather's eyes;
They glitter'd to the vu'st men's zight,
The last will have em in their night;
But who can vind em half so bright
    As I thought thik peäle star above
    My smilen Jeäne, my zweet vu'st love,
        The evenen star o' zummer.

How sweet's the mornen fresh an' new,
Wi' sparklen brooks an' glitt'ren dew;
How sweet's the noon wi' sheädes a-drow'd
Upon the groun' but leätely mow'd,
An' bloomen flowers all abrode;
    But sweeter still, as I do clim'
    Theäse woody hill in evenen dim,
        'S the evenen star o' zummer.

I GOT TWO VIELDS

I got two vields, an' I don't ceäre
What squire mid have a bigger sheäre.
My little zummer-leäze do stratch
All down the hangen, to a patch
O' meäd between a hedge an' rank
Ov elems, an' a river bank.
Where yollow clotes, in spreaden beds
O' floaten leaves, do lift their heads
By benden bulrushes an' zedge
A-swayen at the water's edge,
Below the withy that do spread
Athirt the brook his grey-leav'd head.
An' eltrot flowers, milky white,
Do catch the slanten evenen light;
An' in the meäple boughs, along
The hedge, do ring the blackbird's zong;
Or in the day, a-vlee-en drough
The leafy trees, the whoa'se gookoo
Do zing to mowers that do zet
Their zives on end, an' stan' to whet.
From my wold house among the trees
A leäne do goo along the leäze
O' yollow gravel, down between
Two mossy banks vor ever green.
An' trees, a-hangen overhead,
Do hide a trinklen gully-bed,
A-cover'd by a bridge vor hoss
Or man a-voot to come across.
Zoo wi' my hwomestead, I don't ceäre
What squire mid have a bigger sheäre!

BE'MI'STER

Sweet Be'mi'ster, that bist a-bound
By green an' woody hills all round,
Wi' hedges reachen up between
A thousan' vields o' zummer green,

Where elems' lofty heads do drow
Their sheädes vor haÿ-meäkers below,
An' wild hedge-flow'rs do charm the souls
O' maïdens in their evenen strolls.

When I o' Zunday nights wi' Jeäne
Do saunter drough a vield or leäne,
Where elder-blossoms be a-spread
Above the eltrot's milk-white head,
An' flow'rs o' blackberries do blow
Upon the brembles, white as snow,
To be outdone avore my zight
By Jeäne's gaÿ frock o' dazzlen white;

Oh! then there's nothen that's 'ithout
Thy hills that I do ho about, –
Noo bigger pleäce, noo gaÿer town,
Beyond thy sweet bells' dyen soun',
As they do ring, or strike the hour,
At evenen vrom thy wold red tow'r.
No: shelter still my head, an' keep
My bwones when I do vall asleep.

ECLOGUE: THE VEAIRIES
SIMON AN' SAMEL

SIMON

There's what the vo'k do call a veäiry ring
Out there, lo'k zee. Why, 'tis an oddish thing.

SAMEL

Ah! zoo do seem. I wonder how do come!
What is it that do meäke it, I do wonder?

SIMON

Be hang'd if I can tell, I'm sure! But zome
Do zay do come by lightnen when do thunder;
An' zome do zay sich rings as thik ring there is,
Do grow in dancen-tracks o' little veäiries,
That in the nights o' zummer or o' spring
Do come by moonlight, when noo other veet
Do tread the dewy grass, but their's, an' meet
An' dance away together in a ring.

SAMEL

An' who d'ye think do work the fiddlestick?
A little veäiry too, or else wold Nick!

SIMON

Why, they do zay, that at the veäiries' ball,
There's nar a fiddle that's a-heär'd at all;
But they do plaÿ upon a little pipe
A-meäde o' kexes or o' straws, dead ripe,
A-stuck in row (zome short an' longer zome)
Wi' slime o' snaïls, or bits o' plum-tree gum,
An' meäke sich music that to hear it sound,
You'd stick so still's a pollard to the ground.

SAMEL

What do em dance? 'Tis plaïn by theäse green wheels,
They don't frisk in an' out in dree-hand reels;
Vor else, instead o' theäse here girt round O,
They'd cut us out a figure aïght, d'ye know.

SIMON

Oh! they ha' jigs to fit their little veet.
They woulden dance, you know, at their fine ball,
The dree an' vow'r han' reels that we do sprawl
An' kick about in, when we men do meet.

SAMEL

An' zoo have zome vo'k, in their midnight rambles,
A-catch'd the veäiries, then, in theäsem gambols?

SIMON

Why, yes; but they be off lik' any shot,
So soon's a man's a-comen near the spot.

SAMEL

But in the day-time where do veäiries hide?
Where be their hwomes, then? where do veäiries bide?

SIMON

Oh! they do get awaÿ down under ground,
In hollow pleäzen where they can't be vound.
But still my gramfer, many years agoo,
(He liv'd at Grenley-farm, an' milk'd a deäiry),
If what the wolder vo'k do tell is true,
Woone mornen eärly vound a veäiry.

An' did he stop, then, wi' the good wold bwoy?
Or did he soon contrive to slip awoy?

SIMON

Why, when the vo'k were all asleep, a-bed,
The veäiries us'd to come, as 'tis a-zaid,
Avore the vire wer cwold, an' dance an hour
Or two at dead o' night upon the vloor;
Var they, by only utteren a word
Or charm, can come down chimney lik' a bird;
Or draw their bodies out so long an' narrow,
That they can vlee drough keyholes lik' an arrow.
An' zoo woone midnight, when the moon did drow
His light drough window, roun' the vloor below,
An' crickets roun' the bricken he'th did zing,
They come an' danced about the hall in ring;
An' tapp'd, drough little holes noo eyes could spy,
A kag o' poor aunt's meäd a-stannen by.
An' woone o'm drink'd so much, he coulden mind
The word he wer to zay to meäke en small;
He got a-dather'd zoo, that after all
Out tothers went an' left en back behind.
An' after he'd a-beät about his head,
Ageän the keyhole till he wer half dead,
He laid down all along upon the vloor
Till gramfer, comen down, unlocked the door:
An' then he zeed en ('twer enough to frighten en)
Bolt out o' door, an' down the road lik' lightenen.

A-HAULEN O' THE CORN

Ah! yesterday, you know, we carr'd
    The piece o' corn in Zidelen Plot,
An' work'd about it pretty hard,
    An' vound the weather pretty hot.
'Twer all a-tied an' zet upright
In tidy hile o' Monday night;
Zoo yesterday in afternoon
We zet, in eärnest, ev'ry woone
    A-haulen o' the corn.

The hosses, wi' the het an' lwoad,
   Did froth, an' zwang vrom zide to zide,
A-gwaïn along the dousty road,
   An' seem'd as if they would a-died.
An' wi' my collar all undone,
An' neck a-burnen wi' the zun,
I got, wi' work, an' doust, an' het,
So dry at last, I coulden spet,
   A-haulen o' the corn.

At uncle's orcha'd, gwaïn along,
   I begged some apples, vor to quench
My drith, o' Poll that wer among
   The trees: but she, a saucy wench,
Toss'd over hedge some crabs vor fun.
I squaïl'd her, though, an' meäde her run;
An' zoo she gi'ed me, vor a treat,
A lot o' stubberds vor to eat,
   A-haulen o' the corn.

An' up at rick, Jeäne took the flagon,
   An' gi'ed us out zome eäle; an' then
I carr'd her out upon the waggon,
   Wi' bread an' cheese to gi'e the men.
An' there, vor fun, we dress'd her head
Wi' nodden poppies bright an' red,
As we wer catchen vrom our laps,
Below a woak, our bits an' draps,
   A-haulen o' the corn.

HARVEST HWOME
The vu'st Peärt. The Supper

Since we were striplens naïghbour John,
The good wold merry times be gone:
But we do like to think upon
   What we've a-zeed an' done.
When I wer up a hardish lad,
At harvest hwome the work-vo'k had
Sich suppers, they wer jumpen mad
   Wi' feästen an' wi' fun.

At uncle's, I do mind, woone year,
I zeed a vill o' hearty cheer;
Fat beef an' pudden, eäle an' beer,
    Vor ev'ry workman's crop.
An' after they'd a-gi'ed God thanks,
They all zot down, in two long ranks,
Along a teäble-bwoard o' planks,
    Wi' uncle at the top.

An' there, in platters, big and brown,
Wer red fat beäcon, an' a roun'
O' beef wi' gravy that would drown
    A little rwoasten pig;
Wi' beäns an' teäties vull a zack,
An' cabbage that would meäke a stack,
An' puddens brown, a-speckled black
    Wi' figs, so big's my wig.

An' uncle, wi' his elbows out,
Did carve, an' meäke the gravy spout;
An' aunt did gi'e the mugs about
    A-frothen to the brim.
Pleätes werden then ov e'then ware,
They ate off pewter, that would bear
A knock; or wooden trenchers, square,
    Wi' zalt-holes at the rim.

An' zoo they munch'd their hearty cheer,
An' dipp'd their beards in frothy-beer,
An' laughed, an' jok'd – they coudden hear
    What woone another zaid.
An' all o'm drink'd, wi' woone accword,
The wold vo'k's health: an' beät the bwoard,
An' swung their eärms about, an' roar'd,
    Enough to crack woone's head.

HARVEST HWOME
Second Peärt. *What they did after Supper*

Zoo after supper wer a-done,
They clear'd the teäbles, an' begun
To have a little bit o' fun,
    As long as they mid stop.

The wold woones took their pipes to smoke,
An' tell their teäles, an' laugh an' joke,
A-looken at the younger vo'k,
   That got up vor a hop.

Woone screäp'd away, wi' merry grin,
A fiddle stuck below his chin;
An' woone o'm took the rollen pin,
   An' beät the fryen pan.
An' tothers, dancen to the soun',
Went in an' out, an droo an' roun',
An' kick'd, an' beät the tuen down,
   A-laughen, maïd an' man.

An' then a maïd, all up tip-tooe,
Vell down; an' woone o'm wi' his shoe
Slit down her pocket-hole in two,
   Vrom top a'most to bottom.
An' when they had a-danc'd enough,
They got a-playen blindman's buff,
An' sard the maïdens pretty rough,
   When woonce they had a-got em.

An' zome did drink, an' laugh, an' roar,
An' lots o' teäles they had in store,
O' things that happen'd years avore
   To them, or vo'k they know'd.
An' zome did joke, an' zome did zing,
An' meäke the girt wold kitchen ring;
Till uncle's cock, wi' flappen wing,
   Stratch'd out his neck an' crow'd.

A ZONG OV HARVEST HWOME

The ground is clear. There's nar a ear
   O' stannen corn a-left out now,
Vor win' to blow or raïn to drow;
   'Tis all up seäfe in barn or mow.
   Here's health to them that plough'd an' zow'd;
   Here's health to them that reap'd an' mow'd,
   An' them that had to pitch an' lwoad,
   Or tip the rick at Harvest Hwome.
The happy zight, – the merry night,
The men's delight, – the Harvest Hwome.

An' mid noo harm o' vire or storm
  Beval the farmer or his corn;
An' ev'ry zack o' zeed gi'e back
  A hunderd-vwold so much in barn.
  An' mid his Meäker bless his store,
  His wife an' all that she've a-bore,
  An' keep all evil out o' door,
    Vrom Harvest Hwome to Harvest Hwome.
The happy zight, – the merry night,
The men's delight, – the Harvest Hwome.

Mid nothen ill betide the mill,
  As day by day the miller's wheel
Do dreve his clacks, an' heist his zacks,
  An' vill his bins wi' show'ren meal:
  Mid's water never overflow
  His dousty mill, nor zink too low,
  Vrom now till wheat ageän do grow,
    An' we've another Harvest Hwome.
The happy zight, – the merry night,
The men's delight, – the Harvest Hwome.

Drough cisterns wet an' malt-kil's het,
  Mid barley paÿ the malter's païns;
An' mid noo hurt beval the wort,
  A-bweilen vrom the brewer's graïns.
  Mid all his beer keep out o' harm
  Vrom bu'sted hoop or thunder storm,
  That we mid have a mug to warm
    Our merry hearts nex' Harvest Hwome.
The happy zight, – the merry night,
The men's delight, – the Harvest Hwome.

Mid luck an' jaÿ the beäker paÿ,
  As he do hear his vier roar,
Or nimbly catch his hot white batch,
  A-reeken vrom the oven door.
  An mid it never be too high
  Vor our vew zixpences to buy,
  When we do hear our childern cry
  Vor bread, avore nex' Harvest Hwome.
The happy zight, – the merry night,
The men's delight, – the Harvest Hwome.

Wi' jaÿ o' heart mid shooters start
   The whirren pa'tridges in vlocks;
While shots do vlee drough bush an' tree,
   An' dogs do stan' so still as stocks.
An' let em ramble round the farms
   Wi' guns 'ithin their bended eärms,
In goolden zunsheen free o' storms,
   Rejaïcen vor the Harvest Hwome.
The happy zight, – the merry night,
The men's delight, – the Harvest Hwome.

GRENLEY WATER

The sheädeless darkness o' the night
Can never blind my mem'ry's zight;
An' in the storm my fancy's eyes
Can look upon their own blue skies.
The laggen moon mid faïl to rise,
   But when the daylight's blue an' green
   Be gone, my fancy's zun do sheen
     At hwome at Grenley Water.

As when the work-vo'k us'd to ride
In waggon, by the hedge's zide,
Drough evenen sheädes that trees cast down
Vrom lofty stems athirt the groun';
An' in at house the mug went roun',
   While ev'ry merry man praïs'd up
   The pretty maïd that vill'd his cup,
     The maïd o' Grenley Water.

There I do seem ageän to ride
The hosses to the water-zide,
An' zee the visher fling his hook
Below the withies by the brook;
Or Fanny, wi' her blushen look,
   Car on her païl, or come to dip
   Wi' ceäreful step, her pitcher's lip
     Down into Grenley Water.

If I'd a farm wi' vower ploughs,
An' vor my deäiry fifty cows;
If Grenley Water winded down
Drough two good miles o' my own groun';

If half ov Ashknowle Hill 'wer brown
  Wi' my own corn, – noo growen pride
  Should ever meäke me cast azide
  The maïd o' Grenley Water.

OUT A-NUTTEN

Last week, when we'd a-haul'd the crops,
We went a-nutten out in copse,
Wi' nutten-bags to bring hwome vull,
An' beaky nutten-crooks to pull
The bushes down; an' all o's wore
Wold clothes that wer in rags avore,
An' look'd, as we did skip an' zing,
Lik' merry gipsies in a string,
  A-gwaïn a-nutten.

Zoo drough the stubble, over rudge
An' vurrow, we begun to trudge;
An' Sal an' Nan agreed to pick
Along wi' me, an' Poll wi' Dick;
An' they went where the wold wood, high
An' thick, did meet an' hide the sky;
But we thought we mid vind zome good
Ripe nuts among the shorter wood,
  The best vor nutten.

We voun' zome bushes that did feäce
The downcast zunlight's highest pleäce,
Where clusters hung so ripe an' brown,
That some slipp'd shell an' vell to groun'.
But Sal wi' me zoo hitch'd her lag
In brembles, that she coulden wag;
While Poll kept clwose to Dick, an' stole
The nuts vrom's hinder pocket-hole,
  While he did nutty.

An' Nanny thought she zaw a sneäke,
An' jumped off into zome girt breäke,
An' tore the bag where she'd a-put
Her sheäre, an' shatter'd ev'ry nut.

An' out in vield we all zot roun'
A white-stemm'd woak upon the groun',
Where yollor evenen light did strik'
Drough yollow leaves, that still wer thick
  In time o' nutten,

An' twold ov all the luck we had
Among the bushes, good an' bad!
Till all the maïdens left the bwoys,
An' skipped about the leäze all woys
Vor musherooms, to car back zome,
A treat vor father in at hwome.
Zoo off we trudg'd wi' clothes in slents
An' libbets, jis' lik' Jack-o'-lents,
  Vrom copse a-nutten.

SHRODON FEAIR
The vu'st Peärt

An' zoo's the day wer warm an' bright,
An' nar a cloud wer up in zight,
We wheedled father vor the meäre
An' cart, to goo to Shrodon feäir.
An' Poll an' Nan run off up stairs,
To shift their things, as wild as heäres;
An' pull'd out, each o'm vrom her box,
Their snow-white leäce an' newest frocks,
An' put their bonnets on, a-lined
Wi' blue, an' sashes tied behind;
An' turn'd avore the glass their feäce
An' back, to zee their things in pleäce;
While Dick an' I did brush our hats
An' cwoats, an' cleän ourzelves lik' cats.
At woone or two o'clock, we vound
Ourzelves at Shrodon seäfe and sound,
A-strutten in among the rows
O' tilted stannens an' o' shows,
An' girt long booths wi' little bars
Chock-vull o' barrels, mugs, an' jars,
An' meat a-cooken out avore
The vier at the upper door;

Where zellers bwold to buyers shy
Did hollow round us, 'What d'ye buy?'
An' scores o' merry tongues did speak
At woonce, an' childern's pipes did squeak,
An' horns did blow, an' drums did rumble,
An' bawlen merrymen did tumble;
An' woone did all but want an edge
To peärt the crowd wi', lik' a wedge.

We zaw the dancers in a show
Dance up an' down, an' to and fro,
Upon a rwope, wi' chalky zoles,
So light as magpies up on poles;
An' tumblers, wi' their streaks an' spots,
That all but tied theirzelves in knots.
An' then a conjurer burn'd off
Poll's han'kerchief so black's a snoff,
An' het en, wi' a single blow,
Right back ageän so white as snow.
An' after that, he fried a fat
Girt ceäke inzide o' my new hat;
An' yet, vor all he did en brown,
He didden even zweal the crown.

SHRODON FEAIR

The rest o't

An' after that we met wi' zome
O' Mans'on vo'k, but jist a–come,
An' had a raffle vor a treat
All roun', o' gingerbread to eat;
An' Tom meäde leäst, wi' all his sheäkes,
An' païd the money vor the ceäkes,
But wer so lwoth to put it down
As if a penny wer a poun'.
Then up come zidelen Sammy Heäre,
That's fond o' Poll, an' she can't bear,
A–holden out his girt scram vist,
An' ax'd her, wi' a grin an' twist,
To have zome nuts; an' she, to hide
Her laughen, turn'd her head azide,

An' answer'd that she'd rather not,
But Nancy mid. An' Nan, so hot
As vier, zaid 'twer quite enough
Vor Poll to answer vor herzuf:
She had a tongue, she zaid, an' wit
Enough to use en, when 'twer fit.
An' in the dusk, a-riden round
Drough Okford, who d'ye think we vound
But Sam ageän, a-gwaïn vrom feäir
Astride his broken-winded meäre.
An' zoo, a-hetten her, he tried
To keep up clwose by ouer zide:
But when we come to Haÿward-brudge,
Our Poll gi'ed Dick a meänen nudge,
An' wi' a little twitch our meäre
Flung out her lags so light's a heäre,
An' left poor Sammy's skin an' bwones
Behind, a-kicken o' the stwones.

MARTIN'S TIDE

Come, bring a log o' cleft wood, Jack,
An' fling en on ageän the back,
An' zee the outside door is vast, –
The win' do blow a cwoldish blast.
Come, so's! come, pull your chairs in roun'
Avore the sparklen zun is down:
An' keep up Martin's-tide, vor I
Shall keep it up till I do die.
'Twer Martinmas, and ouer feäir,
When Jeäne an' I, a happy peäir,
Vu'st walk'd, a-keepen up the tide,
Among the stannens, zide by zide;
An' thik day twel'month, never faïlen,
She gi'ed me at the chancel raïlen
A heart – though I do sound her praïse –
As true as ever beät in staÿs.
How vast the time do goo! Do seem
But yesterday, – 'tis lik' a dream!

Ah, so's! 'tis now zome years agoo
You vu'st knew me, an' I knew you;
An' we've a-had zome bits o' fun,
By winter vire an' zummer zun.
Aye; we've a-prowl'd an' rigg'd about
Like cats, in harm's way mwore than out,
An' busy wi' the tricks we plaÿ'd
In fun, to outwit chap or maïd.
An' out avore the bleäzen he'th,
Our naïsy tongues, in winter me'th,
'V a-shook the warmen-pan, a-hung
Bezide us, till his cover rung.
There, 'twer but tother day thik chap,
Our Robert, wer a child in lap;
An' Poll's two little lags hung down
Vrom thik wold chair a span vrom groun',
An' now the saucy wench do stride
About wi' steps o' dree veet wide.
How time do goo! A life do seem
As 'twer a year; 'tis lik' a dream!

GUY FAUX'S NIGHT

Guy Faux's night, dost know, we chaps,
A-putten on our woldest traps,
Went up the highest o' the knaps,
    An' meäde up such a vier!
An' thou an' Tom wer all we miss'd,
Vor if a sarpent had a-hiss'd
Among the rest in thy sprack vist,
    Our fun'd a-been the higher.

We chaps at hwome, an' Will our cousin,
Took up a half a lwoad o' vuzzen;
An' burn'd a barrel wi' a dozen
    O' faggots, till above en
The fleämes, a-risèn up so high
'S the tun, did snap, an' roar, an' ply,
An' drow a gleäre ageän the sky
    Lik' vier in an oven.

An' zome wi' hissen squibs did run,
To paÿ off zome what they'd a-done,
An' let em off so loud's a gun
    Ageän their smoken polls;
An' zome did stir their nimble pags
Wi' crackers in between their lags,
While zome did burn their cwoats to rags,
    Or wes'cots out in holes.

An' zome o'm's heads lost half their locks,
An' zome o'm got their white smock-frocks
Jist fit to vill the tinder-box,
    Wi' half the backs o'm off;
An' Dick, that all o'm vell upon,
Vound woone flap ov his cwoat-taïl gone,
An' tother jist a-hangen on,
    A-zweal'd so black's a snoff.

ECLOGUE: THE COMMON A-TOOK IN
THOMAS AN' JOHN

THOMAS

Good morn t'ye, John. How b'ye? how b'ye?
Zoo you be gwaïn to market, I do zee.
Why, you be quite a-lwoaded wi' your geese.

JOHN

Ees, Thomas, ees.
Why, I'm a-getten rid ov ev'ry goose
An' goslen I've a-got: an' what is woose,
I fear that I must zell my little cow.

THOMAS

How zoo, then, John? Why, what's the matter now?
What, can't ye get along? B'ye run a-ground?
An' can't paÿ twenty shillens vor a pound?
What, can't ye put a lwoaf on shelf?

JOHN

Ees, now;
But I do fear I shan't 'ithout my cow.
No; they do meän to teäke the moor in, I do hear,
An' 'twill be soon begun upon;
Zoo I must zell my bit o' stock to-year,
Because they woon't have any groun' to run upon.

THOMAS

Why, what d'ye tell o'? I be very zorry
To hear what they be gwaïn about;
But yet I s'pose there'll be a 'lotment vor ye,
When they do come to mark it out.

JOHN

No; not vor me, I fear. An' if there should,
Why 'twoulden be so handy as 'tis now;
Vor 'tis the common that do do me good,
The run vor my vew geese, or vor my cow.

THOMAS

Ees, that's the job; why 'tis a handy thing
To have a bit o' common, I do know,
To put a little cow upon in Spring,
The while woone's bit ov orcha'd grass do grow.

JOHN

Aye, that's the thing, you zee. Now I do mow
My bit o' grass, an' meäke a little rick;
An' in the zummer, while do grow,
My cow do run in common vor to pick
A bleäde or two o' grass, if she can vind em,
Vor tother cattle don't leäve much behind em.
Zoo in the evenen, we do put a lock
O' nice fresh grass avore the wicket;
An' she do come at vive or zix o'clock,
As constant as the zun, to pick it.
An' then, bezides the cow, why we do let
Our geese run out among the emmet hills;
An' then when we do pluck em, we do get
Vor zeäle zome veathers an' zome quills;

An' in the winter we do fat em well,
An' car em to the market vor to zell
To gentlevo'ks, vor we don't oft avvword
To put a goose a-top ov ouer bwoard;
But we do get our feäst, – vor we be eäble
To clap the giblets up a-top o' teäble.

THOMAS

An' I don't know o' many better things,
Than geese's heads and gizzards, lags an' wings.

JOHN

An' then, when I ha' nothen else to do,
Why I can teäke my hook an' gloves, an' goo
To cut a lot o' vuzz and briars
Vor heten ovens, or vor lighten viers.
An' when the childern be too young to eärn
A penny, they can g'out in zunny weather,
An' run about, an' get together
A bag o' cow-dung vor to burn.

THOMAS

'Tis handy to live near a common;
But I've a-zeed, an' I've a-zaid,
That if a poor man got a bit o' bread,
They'll try to teäke it vrom en.
But I wer twold back tother day,
That they be got into a way
O' letten bits o' groun' out to the poor.

JOHN

Well, I do hope 'tis true, I'm sure;
An' I do hope that they will do it here,
Or I must goo to workhouse, I do fear.

ECLOGUE: TWO FARMS IN WOONE
ROBERT AN' THOMAS

ROBERT

You'll lose your meäster soon, then, I do vind;
He's gwaïn to leäve his farm, as I do larn,
At Miëlmas; an' I be sorry vor'n.
What, is he then a little bit behind?

O no! at Miëlmas his time is up,
An' thik there sly wold fellow, Farmer Tup,
A-fearen that he'd get a bit o' bread,
'V a-been an' took his farm here over's head.

ROBERT

How come the Squire to treat your meäster zoo?

THOMAS

Why, he an' meäster had a word or two.

ROBERT

Is Farmer Tup a-gwaïn to leäve his farm?
He han't a-got noo young woones vor to zwarm.
Poor over-reachen man! why to be sure
He don't want all the farms in parish, do er?

THOMAS

Why ees, all ever he can come across.
Last year, you know, he got away the eäcre
Or two o' ground a-rented by the beäker,
An' what the butcher had to keep his hoss;
An' vo'k do beänhan' now, that meäster's lot
Will be a-drow'd along wi' what he got.

ROBERT

That's it. In theäse here pleäce there used to be
Eight farms avore they were a-drow'd together,
An' eight farm-housen. Now how many be there?
Why after this, you know, there'll be but dree.

THOMAS

An' now they don't imploy so many men
Upon the land as work'd upon it then,
Vor all they midden crop it worse, nor stock it.
The lan'lord, to be sure, is into pocket;
Vor half the housen be-en down, 'tis clear,
Don't cost so much to keep em up, a-near.
But then the jobs o' work in wood an' morter
Do come I 'spose, you know, a little shorter;

An' many that wer little farmers then,
Be now a-come all down to leäb'ren men;
An' many leäb'ren men, wi' empty hands,
Do live lik' drones upon the workers' lands.

ROBERT

Aye, if a young chap, woonce, had any wit
To try an' screäpe together zome vew pound,
To buy some cows an' teäke a bit o' ground,
He mid become a farmer, bit by bit.
But, hang it! now the farms be all so big,
An' bits o' groun' so skeä'ce, woone got no scope;
If woone could seäve a poun', woone coudden hope
To keep noo live stock but a little pig.

THOMAS

Why here wer vourteen men, zome years agoo,
A-kept a-drashen half the winter drough;
An' now, woone's drashels be'n't a bit o' good.
They got machines to drashy wi', plague teäke em!
An' he that vu'st vound out the way to meäke em,
I'd drash his busy zides vor'n if I could!
Avore they took away our work, they ought
To meäke us up the bread our leäbour bought.

ROBERT

They hadden need meäke poor men's leäbour less,
Vor work a'ready is uncommon skeä'ce.

THOMAS

Ah! Robert! times be badish vor the poor;
An' worse will come, I be afeärd, if Moore
In theäse year's almanick do tell us right.

ROBERT

Why then we sartainly must starve. Good night!

ECLOGUE:
RUSTICUS RES POLITICAS ANIMADVERTENS
THE NEW POOR LAWS
JOHN AND THOMAS

JOHN

Well, what d'ye think o' thiese new laes they got
A miade about the parishes an' poor?

THOMAS

Why I da hardly know, I'm sure,
Whether tha'l do the naytion good or not.
But I da hope, drough GOD, the workhouse laes
Wull miake but little odds to I.
I hope to kip myzelf till I da die,
An' miake my own han's always veed my jaes.
I aleways scarn'd as I da hope to scarn
To ax var money that I diden yarn.

JOHN

True, Thomas, true: that's right; that's very right.
But still thiese laes da seem a little tight.
They woon't allow a vard'n out o' door,
An' tis but scanty prog tha'l gi'e within
The house; 't'll kip em plaguy thin,
T'oon't be so well as 'twer afore;
An' ther's to be oone poorhouse in the town,
Zix miles awoy, var al the pliazes roun',
Zoo if a man should come to want relief,
An' goo an' ax the auverzeer var't,
Tha'l tiake an' put en up into a cart,
An' car en out o' parish like a thief,
An' shove en in to bed an' tiable
Amang a house vull o' fresh fiazes,
Wi' scores o' volk vrom fifty pliazes
Like hosses in a common stiable.

THOMAS

That's very right; a honest man would vind
Al that a little gallen to his mind.
But then, ya know, hardworken men

115

Wull kip therzelves awoy, nine out o' ten.
An' ther wer zome'hat wrong in the wold plan.
Var if a chap wer liazy, an' a sot,
The parish kept his house, an' zoo 'e got
As good a liven as a steady man.
An' noggerheaded buoys that wer too young
To yarn ther zalt and tiaties, got a miate:
An' then wi' two ar dree poor children flung
Therzelves upon the parish riate.

JOHN

Aye, they be guain, ya know, to kip asunder
The menvolk in the poorhouse, vrom their wives.
How wull the women like thick plan I wonder?
How wull the menvolk like to liead such lives?
They mid as well, I think, each wi' his bride
Goo back to Church an' have ther knot untied.
Thiese lae, upon my word, is rather hard.
But I suppuose tha'l let em, var a trieat,
Goo oonce or twice a week into the yard
An' look at oone another drough a giate.

THOMAS

Ees, that's an oddish job; but mid be good,
Var they da want to bring volk, if they can,
To have muore forezight; an' to miake a man
Trust only to his zelf var food.
They woon't kip liazy volk noo muore, nar gi'e
The drone the honey o' the worken bee.
I have a liabour'd pirty hard,
An' reared zix childern in my time,
An' tried to teach 'em var to fear the LARD
An' yarn ther bread, an' shun a crime.
I have a vound good friends, thank GOD, and many,
But never ax'd the parish var a penny;
Zoo I can now look buoldly in the fiace
O' th' girtest man that is in al the pliace,
An' veel that I be free, an' tell my name
To al the wordle without fear or shiame.
But if I wer a liazy man, an' willen
To zell my freedom for a parish shillen,
I must a skulked about a looken down

Wi' shiame an' mieanness, like a slinken houn'.
My trust a bin in GOD, an' not in man,
Var HE've a promised us to gi'e
Whate'er is good for us; an' HE can zee;
Var all the wordle da belong to HE.

JOHN

Aye, that's al right, 'tis no use var to trust
In wicked an' weak men, that be but dust.
But then if volk da want to miake the poor
Good men they ought to fiavour goodness muore.
Volk do esteem a rogue in a high pliace
Muore than a poorer man that's rich in griace.
An' honesty, when 'tis avoun' disguised
Under a plain smockfrock, is now despised.
A fop o' hossback is ashiamed to meet
A poorer neighbour down upon his veet;
An' thick siame fop would be uncommon proud
To ta'ke wi' a fine rascal in a crowd.
Thiese laes mid do some good; but volk mast show
Esteem var goodness if they'd zee it grow.
A farmer woulden git much vrom his zeeds
If they wer left to struggle wi' the weeds.

THOMAS

That's very true. The wordle don't ax what
A body is, but only what 'e got.

GRAMMER'S SHOES

I do seem to zee Grammer as she did use
Vor to show us, at Chris'mas, her wedden shoes,
An' her flat spreaden bonnet so big an' roun'
As a girt pewter dish a-turn'd upside down;
    When we all did draw near
    In a cluster to hear
O' the merry wold soul how she did use
To walk an' to dance wi' her high-heel shoes.

She'd a gown wi' girt flowers lik' hollyhocks,
An' zome stockens o' gramfer's a-knit wi' clocks,
An' a token she kept under lock an' key, –
A small lock ov his heäir off avore 't wer grey.

An' her eyes wer red,
    An' she shook her head,
When we'd all a-look'd at it, an' she did use
To lock it away wi' her wedden shoes.

She could tell us such teäles about heavy snows,
An' o' raïns an' o' floods when the waters rose
All up into the housen, an' carr'd awoy
All the bridge wi' a man an' his little bwoy;
    An' o' vog an' vrost,
    An' o' vo'k a-lost,
An' o' peärties at Chris'mas, when she did use
Vor to walk hwome wi' gramfer in high-heel shoes.

Ev'ry Chris'mas she lik'd vor the bells to ring,
An' to have in the zingers to heär em zing
The wold carols she heärd many years a-gone,
While she warm'd em zome cider avore the bron';
    An' she'd look an' smile
    At our dancen, while
She did tell how her friends now a-gone did use
To reely wi' her in their high-heel shoes.

Ah! an' how she did like vor to deck wi' red
Holly-berries the window an' wold clock's head,
An' the clavy wi' boughs o' some bright green leaves,
An' to meäke twoast an' eäle upon Chris'mas eves;
    But she's now, drough greäce,
    In a better pleäce,
Though we'll never vorget her, poor soul, nor lose
Gramfer's token ov heäir, nor her wedden shoes.

ZUNSHEEN IN THE WINTER

The winter clouds, that long did hide
The zun, be all a-blown azide,
An' in the light, noo longer dim,
Do sheen the ivy that do clim'
The tower's zide an' elem's stim;
    An' holmen bushes, in between
    The leafless thorns, be bright an' green
        To zunsheen o' the winter.

The trees, that yesterday did twist
In winds a–drevèn raïn an' mist,
Do now drow sheädes out, long an' still;
But roaren watervalls do vill
Their whirlen pools below the hill,
  Where, wi' her païl upon the stile,
  A–gwaïn a–milken Jeäne do smile
    To zunsheen o' the winter.

The birds do sheäke, wi' plaÿsome skips,
The raïn–drops off the bushes' tips,
A–chirripen wi' merry sound;
While over all the grassy ground
The wind's a–whirlen round an' round
  So softly, that the day do seem
  Mwore lik' a zummer in a dream,
    Than zunsheen in the winter.

The wold vo'k now do meet abrode,
An' tell o' winters they've a–know'd;
When snow wer long above the groun',
Or floods broke all the bridges down,
Or wind unheal'd a half the town, –
  The teäles o' wold times long a–gone,
  But ever dear to think upon,
    The zunsheen o' their winter.

Vor now to them noo brook can run,
Noo hill can feäce the winter zun,
Noo leaves can vall, noo flow'rs can feäde,
Noo snow can hide the grasses bleäde,
Noo vrost can whiten in the sheäde,
  Noo day can come, but what do bring
  To mind ageän their early spring,
    That's now a–turn'd to winter.

THE SETTLE AN' THE GIRT WOOD VIRE

Ah! naïghbour John, since I an' you
Wer youngsters, ev'ry thing is new.
My father's vires wer all o' logs
O' cleft–wood, down upon the dogs

119

Below our clavy, high, an' brode
Enough to teäke a cart an' lwoad,
Where big an' little all zot down
At bwoth zides, an' bevore, all roun'.
An' when I zot among em, I
Could zee all up ageän the sky
Drough chimney, where our vo'k did hitch
The zalt-box an' the beäcon vlitch,
An' watch the smoke on out o' vier,
All up an' out o' tun, an' higher.
An' there wer beäcon up on rack,
An' pleätes an' dishes on the tack;
An' roun' the walls wer heärbs a-stowed
In peäpern bags, an' blathers blowed.
An' just above the clavy-bwoard
Wer father's spurs, an' gun, an' sword;
An' there wer then, our girtest pride,
The settle by the vier-zide.
   Ah! gi'e me, if I wer a squier,
   The settle an' the girt wood vier.

But they've a-wall'd up now wi' bricks
The vier pleäce vor dogs an' sticks,
An' only left a little hole
To teäke a little greäte o' coal,
So small that only twos or drees
Can jist push in an' warm their knees.
An' then the carpets they do use,
Ben't fit to tread wi' ouer shoes;
An' chairs an' couches be so neat,
You mussen teäke em vor a seat:
They be so fine, that vo'k mus' pleäce
All over em an' outer ceäse,
An' then the cover, when 'tis on,
Is still too fine to loll upon.
   Ah! gi'e me, if I wer a squier,
   The settle an' the girt wood vier.

Carpets indeed! You coulden hurt
The stwone-vloor wi' a little dirt;
Vor what wer brought in doors by men,
The women soon mopp'd out ageän.
Zoo we did come vrom muck an' mire,

120

An' walk in straïght avore the vier;
But now, a man's a-kept at door
At work a pirty while, avore
He's screäp'd an' rubb'd, an' cleän and fit
To goo in where his wife do zit.
An' then if he should have a whiff
In there, 'twould only breed a miff:
He can't smoke there, vor smoke woon't goo
'Ithin the footy little flue.
　　Ah! gi'e me, if I wer a squier,
　　The settle an' the girt wood vier.

KEEPEN UP O' CHRIS'MAS

An' zoo you didden come athirt,
To have zome fun last night: how wer't?
Vor we'd a-work'd wi' all our might
To scour the iron things up bright,
An' brush'd an' scrubb'd the house all drough;
An' brought in vor a brand, a plock
O' wood so big's an uppen-stock,
An' hung a bough o' misseltoo,
An' ax'd a merry friend or two,
　　To keepen up o' Chris'mas.

An' there wer wold an' young; an' Bill,
Soon after dark, stalk'd up vrom mill.
An' when he wer a-comen near,
He whissled loud vor me to hear;
Then roun' my head my frock I roll'd,
An' stood in orcha'd like a post,
To meäke en think I wer a ghost.
But he wer up to't, an' did scwold
To vind me stannen in the cwold,
　　A-keepen up o' Chris'mas.

We plaÿ'd at forfeits, an' we spun
The trencher roun', an' meäde such fun!
An' had a geäme o' dree-ceärd loo,
An' then begun to hunt the shoe.
An' all the wold vo'k zitten near,
A-chatten roun' the vier pleäce,

Did smile in woone another's feäce,
An' sheäke right hands wi' hearty cheer,
An' let their left hands spill their beer,
    A-keepen up o' Chris'mas.

ZITTEN OUT THE WOLD YEAR

Why, raïn or sheen, or blow or snow,
    I zaid, if I could stand so's,
I'd come, vor all a friend or foe,
    To sheäke ye by the hand, so's;
An' spend, wi' kinsvo'k near an' dear,
A happy evenen, woonce a year,
        A-zot wi' me'th
        Avore the he'th
    To zee the new year in, so's.

There's Jim an' Tom, a-grown the size
    O' men, girt lusty chaps, so's,
An' Fanny wi' her sloo–black eyes,
    Her mother's very daps, so's;
An' little Bill, so brown's a nut,
An' Poll, a gigglen little slut,
        I hope will shoot
        Another voot
    The year that's comen in, so's.

An' there, upon his mother's knee,
    So peärt do look about, so's,
The little woone ov all, to zee
    His vu'st wold year goo out, so's.
An' zoo mid God bless all o's still,
Gwaïn up or down along the hill,
        To meet in glee
        Ageän to zee
    A happy new year in, so's.

The wold clock's han' do softly steal
    Up roun' the year's last hour, so's;
Zoo let the han'–bells ring a peal,
    Lik' them a–hung in tow'r, so's.
Here, here be two vor Tom, an' two

Vor Fanny, an' a peäir vor you;
   We'll meäke em swing,
   An' meäke em ring,
The merry new year in, so's.

Tom, mind your time there; you be wrong.
   Come let your bells all sound, so's:
A little clwoser, Poll; ding, dong!
   There, now 'tis right all round, so's.
The clock's a-striken twelve, d'ye hear?
Ting, ting, ding, dong! Farewell, wold year!
   'Tis gone, 'tis gone! –
   Goo on, goo on,
An' ring the new woone in, so's!

ECLOGUE: FATHER COME HWOME
JOHN, WIFE, AN' CHILD

CHILD

O mother, mother! be the teäties done?
Here's father now a-comen down the track.
He's got his nitch o' wood upon his back,
An' such a speäker in en! I'll be bound,
He's long enough to reach vrom ground
Up to the top ov ouer tun;
'Tis jist the very thing vor Jack an' I
To goo a–colepecksen wi', by an' by.

WIFE

The teäties must be ready pretty nigh;
Do teäke woone up upon the fork an' try.
The ceäke upon the vier, too, 's a-burnen,
I be afeärd: do run an' zee, an' turn en.

JOHN

Well, mother! here I be woonce mwore, at hwome.

WIFE

Ah! I be very glad you be a-come.
You be a-tired an' cwold enough, I s'pose;
Zit down an' rest your bwones, an' warm your nose.

JOHN

Why I be nippy: what is there to eat?

WIFE

Your supper's nearly ready. I've a-got
Some teäties here a-doen in the pot;
I wish wi' all my heart I had some meat.
I got a little ceäke too, here, a-beäken o'n
Upon the vier. 'Tis done by this time though.
He's nice an' moist; vor when I wer a-meäken o'n
I stuck some bits ov apple in the dough.

CHILD

Well, father; what d'ye think? The pig got out
This mornen; an' avore we zeed or heärd en,
He run about, an' got out into geärden,
An' routed up the groun' zoo wi' his snout!

JOHN

Now only think o' that! You must contrive
To keep en in, or else he'll never thrive.

CHILD

An' father, what d'ye think? I voun' to-day
The nest where thik wold hen ov our's do lay:
'Twer out in orcha'd hedge, an' had vive aggs.

WIFE

Lo'k there: how wet you got your veet an' lags!
How did ye get in such a pickle, Jahn?

JOHN

I broke my hoss, an' been a-fwo'ced to stan'
All's day in mud an' water vor to dig,
An' meäde myzelf so wetshod as a pig.

CHILD

Father, teäke off your shoes, then come, and I
Will bring your wold woones vor ye, nice an' dry.

WIFE

An' have ye got much hedgen mwore to do?

JOHN

Enough to last vor dree weeks mwore or zoo.

WIFE

An' when y'ave done the job you be about,
D'ye think you'll have another vound ye out?

JOHN

O ees, there'll be some mwore: vor after that,
I got a job o' trenchen to goo at;
An' then zome trees to shroud, an' wood to vell, –
Zoo I do hope to rub on pretty well
Till zummer time; an' then I be to cut
The wood an' do the trenchen by the tut.

CHILD

An' nex' week, father, I'm a-gwaïn to goo
A-picken stwones, d'ye know, vor Farmer True.

WIFE

An' little Jack, you know, 's a-gwaïn to eärn
A penny too, a-keepen birds off corn.

JOHN

O brave! What wages do 'e meän to gi'e?

WIFE

She dreppence vor a day, an' twopence he.

JOHN

Well, Polly; thou must work a little spracker
When thou bist out, or else thou wu'ten pick
A dungpot lwoad o' stwones up very quick.

CHILD

Oh! yes I shall. But Jack do want a clacker:
An' father, wull ye teäke an' cut
A stick or two to meäke his hut?

JOHN

You wench! why you be always up a-baggen.
I be too tired now to-night, I'm sure,
    To zet a-doen any mwore:
Zoo I shall goo up out o' the waÿ o' the waggon.

ECLOGUE: A GHOST
JEM AN' DICK

JEM

This is a darkish evenen; b'ye afeärd
O' zights? Theäse leän's a-haunted, I've a-heärd.

DICK

No, I ben't much afeärd. If vo'k don't strive
To over-reach me while they be alive,
I don't much think the dead wull ha' the will
To come back here to do me any ill.
An' I've a-been about all night, d'ye know,
Vrom candle-lighten till the cock did crow;
But never met wi' nothen bad enough
To be much wo'se than what I be myzuf;
Though I, lik' others, have a-heärd vo'k zay
The girt house is a-haunted, night an' day.

JEM

Aye; I do mind woone winter 'twer a-zaid
The farmer's vo'k could hardly sleep a-bed,
They heärd at night such scuffens an' such jumpens,
Such ugly naîses an' such rottlen thumpens.

DICK

Aye, I do mind I heärd his son, young Sammy,
Tell how the chairs did dance an' doors did slammy;
He stood to it – though zome vo'k woulden heed en –
He didden only hear the ghost, but zeed en;
An', hang me! if I han't a'most a-shook,
To hear en tell what ugly sheäpes it took.
Did zometimes come vull six veet high, or higher,
In white, he zaid, wi' eyes lik' coals o' vier;
An' zometimes, wi' a feäce so peäle as milk,
A smileless leädy, all a-deck'd in silk.
His heäir, he zaid, did use to stand upright,
So stiff's a bunch o' rushes, wi' his fright.

JEM

An' then you know that zome'hat is a-zeed
Down there in leäne, an' over in the meäd,
A-comen zometimes lik' a slinken hound,
Or rollen lik' a vleece along the ground.

An' woonce, when gramfer wi' his wold grey meäre
Wer riden down the leäne vrom Shroton feäir,
It roll'd so big's a pack ov wool across
The road just under en, an' leäm'd his hoss.

DICK

Aye; did ye ever hear – vo'k zaid 'twer true –
O' what bevell Jack Hine zome years agoo?
Woone vrosty night, d'ye know, at Chris'mas tide,
Jack, an' another chap or two bezide,
'D a-been out, zomewhere up at tother end
O' parish, to a naïghbour's house to spend
A merry hour, an' mid a-took a cup
Or two o' eäle a-keepen Chris'mas up;
Zoo I do lot 'twer leäte avore the peärty
'D a-burnt their bron out; I do lot, avore
They thought o' turnen out o' door
'Twer mornen, vor their friendship then wer hearty.
Well; clwose ageän the vootpath that do leäd
Vrom higher parish over withy-meäd,
There's still a hollow, you do know: they tried there,
In former times, to meäke a cattle-pit,
But gi'ed it up, because they coulden get
The water any time to bide there.
Zoo when the merry fellows got
Just overright theäse lwonesome spot,
Jack zeed a girt big house-dog wi' a collar,
A-stannen down in thik there hollor.
Lo'k there, he zaid, there's zome girt dog a-prowlen:
I'll just goo down an' gi'en a goodish lick
Or two wi' theäse here groun'-ash stick,
An' zend the shaggy rascal hwome a-howlen.
Zoo there he run, an' gi'ed en a good whack
Wi' his girt ashen stick athirt his back;
An', all at woonce, his stick split right all down
In vower pieces; an' the pieces vled
Out ov his hand all up above his head,
An' pitch'd in vower corners o' the groun'.
An' then he velt his han' get all so num',
He coulden veel a vinger or a thum;
An' after that his eärm begun to zwell,
An' in the night a-bed he vound

127

The skin o't peelen off all round.
'Twer near a month avore he got it well.

JEM

That wer vor hetten o'n. He should a-let en
Alwone d'ye zee: 'twer wicked vor to het en.

UNCLE OUT O' DEBT AN'
OUT O' DANGER

Ees; uncle had thik small hwomestead,
   The leäzes an' the bits o' meäd,
   Bezides the orcha'd in his prime,
   An' copse-wood vor the winter time.
   His wold black meäre, that draw'd his cart,
   An' he, wer seldom long apeärt;
   Vor he work'd hard an' païd his woy,
   An' zung so litsome as a bwoy,
     As he toss'd an' work'd,
     An' blow'd an' quirk'd,
  'I'm out o' debt an' out o' danger,
  An' I can feäce a friend or stranger;
I've a vist for friends, an' I'll vind a peäir
Vor the vu'st that do meddle wi' me or my meäre.'

   His meäre's long vlexy vetlocks grow'd
   Down roun' her hoofs so black an' brode;
   Her head hung low, her taïl reach'd down
   A-bobben nearly to the groun'.
   The cwoat that uncle mwostly wore
   Wer long behind an' straïght avore,
   An' in his shoes he had girt buckles,
   An' breeches button'd round his huckles;
     An' he zung wi' pride,
     By's wold meäre's zide,
  'I'm out o' debt an' out o' danger,
  An' I can feäce a friend or stranger;
I've a vist for friends, an' I'll vind a peäir
Vor the vu'st that do meddle wi' me or my meäre.'

   An' he would work, – an' lwoad, an' shoot,
   An' spur his heaps o' dung or zoot;
   Or car out haÿ, to sar his vew
   Milch cows in corners dry an' lew;

Or dreve a zyve, or work a pick,
To pitch or meäke his little rick;
Or thatch en up wi' straw or zedge,
Or stop a shard, or gap, in hedge;
    An' he work'd an' flung
    His eärms, an' zung
'I'm out o' debt an' out o' danger,
An' I can feäce a friend or stranger;
I've a vist vor friends, an I'll vind a peäir
Vor the vu'st that do meddle wi' me or my meäre.'

An' when his meäre an' he'd a-done
Their work, an' tired ev'ry bwone,
He zot avore the vire, to spend
His evenen wi' his wife or friend;
An' wi' his lags out-stratch'd vor rest,
An' woone hand in his wes'coat breast,
While burnen sticks did hiss an' crack,
An' fleämes did bleäzy up the back,
    There he zung so proud
    In a bakky cloud,
'I'm out o' debt an' out o' danger,
An' I can feäce a friend or stranger;
I've a vist vor friends, an I'll vind a peäir
Vor the vu'st that do meddle wi' me or my meäre.'

From market how he used to ride,
Wi' pots a-bumpen by his zide
Wi' things a-bought – but not vor trust,
Vor what he had he païd vor vu'st;
An' when he trotted up the yard,
The calves did bleäry to be sar'd,
An' pigs did scoat all drough the muck,
An' geese did hiss, an' hens did cluck;
    An' he zung aloud,
    So pleased an' proud,
'I'm out o' debt an' out o' danger,
An' I can feäce a friend or stranger;
I've a vist vor friends, an I'll vind a peäir
Vor the vu'st that do meddle wi' me or my meäre.'

When he wer joggen hwome woone night
Vrom market, after candle-light,

(He mid a-took a drop o' beer,
Or midden, vor he had noo fear),
Zome ugly, long-lagg'd, herren-ribs,
Jump'd out an' ax'd en vor his dibs;
But he soon gi'ed en such a mawlen,
That there he left en down a-sprawlen,
  While he jogg'd along
  Wi' his own wold zong,
 'I'm out o' debt an' out o' danger,
 An' I can feäce a friend or stranger;
I've a vist vor friends, an' I'll vind a peäir
Vor the vu'st that do meddle wi' me or my meäre.'

THE WOLD WAGGON

The girt wold waggon uncle had,
When I wer up a hardish lad,
Did stand, a-screen'd vrom het an' wet,
In zummer at the barken geäte,
Below the elems' spreaden boughs,
A-rubb'd by all the pigs an' cows.
An' I've a-clom his head an' zides,
A-riggen up or jumpen down
A-plaÿen, or in happy rides
Along the leäne or drough the groun'.
An' many souls be in their greäves,
That rod' together on his reäves;
An' he, an' all the hosses too,
'V a-ben a-done vor years agoo.

Upon his head an' taïl wer pinks,
A-païnted all in tangled links;
His two long zides wer blue, – his bed
Bent slightly upward at the head;
His reäves rose upward in a bow
Above the slow hind-wheels below.
Vour hosses wer a-kept to pull
The girt wold waggon when 'twer vull:
The black meäre *Smiler*, strong enough
To pull a house down by herzuf,
So big, as took my widest strides
To straddle halfway down her zides;

An' champen *Vi'let*, sprack an' light,
That foam'd an' pull'd wi' all her might:
An' *Whitevoot*, leäzy in the treäce,
Wi' cunnen looks an' snow-white feäce;
Bezides a baÿ woone, short-taïl *Jack*,
That wer a treäce-hoss or a hack.

How many lwoads o' vuzz, to scald
The milk, thik waggon have a-haul'd!
An' wood vrom copse, an' poles vor raïls,
An' bavens wi' their bushy taïls;
An' loose-ear'd barley, hangen down
Outside the wheels a'most to groun',
An' lwoads o' haÿ so sweet an' dry,
A-builded straïght, an' long, an' high;
An' haÿ-meäkers, a-zitten roun'
The reäves, a-riden hwome vrom groun',
When Jim gi'ed Jenny's lips a smack,
An' jealous Dicky whipp'd his back,
An' maïdens scream'd to veel the thumps
A-gi'ed by trenches an' by humps.
But he, an' all his hosses too,
'V a-ben a-done vor years agoo.

THE COMMON A-TOOK IN

Oh! no, Poll, no! Since they've a-took
The common in, our lew wold nook
Don't seem a bit as used to look
    When we had runnen room;
Girt banks do shut up ev'ry drong,
An' stratch wi' thorny backs along
Where we did use to run among
    The vuzzen an' the broom.

Ees; while the ragged colts did crop
The nibbled grass, I used to hop
The emmet-buts, vrom top to top,
    So proud o' my spry jumps:
Wi' thee behind or at my zide,
A-skippen on so light an' wide
'S thy little frock would let thee stride,
    Among the vuzzy humps.

131

Ah while the lark up over head
Did twitter, I did search the red
Thick bunch o' broom, or yollow bed
   O' vuzzen vor a nest;
An' thou di'st hunt about, to meet
Wi' strawberries so red an' sweet,
Or clogs, or shoes off hosses' veet,
   Or wild thyme vor thy breast;

Or when the cows did run about
A-stung, in zummer, by the stout,
Or when they plaÿ'd, or when they foüght,
   Di'st stand a-looken on:
An' where white geese, wi' long red bills,
Did veed among the emmet-hills,
There we did goo to vind their quills
   Alongzide o' the pon'.

What fun there wer among us, when
The haÿward come, wi' all his men,
To dreve the common, an' to pen
   Strange cattle in the pound;
The cows did bleäre, the men did shout
An' toss their eärms an' sticks about,
An' vo'ks, to own their stock, come out
   Vrom all the housen round.

THE VAICES THAT BE GONE

When evenen sheädes o' trees do hide
A body by the hedge's zide,
An' twitt'ren birds, wi' plaÿsome flight,
Do vlee to roost at comen night,
Then I do saunter out o' zight
   In orcha'd, where the pleäce woonce rung
   Wi' laughs a-laugh'd an' zongs a-zung
      By vaïces that be gone.

There's still the tree that bore our swing,
An' others where the birds did zing;
But long-leav'd docks do overgrow
The groun' we trampled beäre below,

Wi' merry skippens to an' fro
  Bezide the banks, where Jim did zit
  A-plaÿen o' the clarinit
    To vaïces that be gone.

How mother, when we us'd to stun
Her head wi' all our naïsy fun,
Did wish us all a-gone vrom home:
An' now that zome be dead, an' zome
A-gone, an' all the pleäce is dum',
  How she do wish, wi' useless tears,
  To have ageän about her ears
    The vaïces that be gone.

Vor all the maïdens an' the bwoys
But I, be marri'd off all woys,
Or dead an' gone; but I do bide
At hwome, alwone, at mother's zide,
An' often, at the evenen-tide,
  I still do saunter out, wi' tears,
  Down drough the orcha'd, where my ears
    Do miss the vaïces gone.

AUNT'S TANTRUMS

Why ees, aunt Anne's a little staïd,
But kind an' merry, poor wold maïd!
If we don't cut her heart wi' slights,
She'll zit an' put our things to rights,
Upon a hard day's work, o' nights;
  But zet her up, she's jis' lik' vier,
  An' woe betide the woone that's nigh 'er,
    When she is in her tantrums.

She'll toss her head, a-steppen out
Such strides, an' fling the païls about;
An' slam the doors as she do goo,
An' kick the cat out wi' her shoe,
Enough to het her off in two.
  The bwoys do bundle out o' house,
  A-lassen they should get a towse,
    When aunt is in her tantrums.

She whurr'd, woone day, the wooden bowl
In such a veag at my poor poll;
It brush'd the heäir above my crown,
An' whizz'd on down upon the groun',
An' knock'd the bantam cock right down;
   But up he sprung, a-teäken flight
   Wi' tothers, clucken in a fright,
     Vrom aunt in such a tantrum!

But Dick stole in, an' reach'd en down
The biggest blather to be voun',
An' crope an' put en out o' zight
Avore the vire, an' plimm'd en tight,
An' crack'd en wi' the slice there-right.
   She scream'd, an' bundled out o' house,
   An' got so quiet as a mouse, –
     It frighten'd off her tantrum.

A WITCH

There's thik wold hag, Moll Brown, look zee, jus' past!
I wish the ugly sly wold witch
Would tumble over into ditch;
I woulden pull her out not very vast.
No, no. I don't think she's a bit belied,
No, she's a witch; aye, Molly's evil-eyed.
Vor I do know o' many a withren blight
A-cast on vo'k by Molly's mutter'd spite;
She did, woone time, a dreadvul deäl o' harm
To Farmer Gruff's vo'k, down at Lower Farm.
Vor there, woone day, they happened to offend her,
An' not a little to their sorrow,
Because they woulden gi'e or lend her
Zome'hat she come to bag or borrow;
An' zoo, they soon began to vind
That she'd a-gone an' left behind
Her evil wish, that had such pow'r
That she did meäke their milk an' eäle turn zour,
An' addle all the aggs their vowls did lay;
They coulden vetch the butter in the churn,
An' all the cheese begun to turn

134

All back ageän to curds an' whey;
The little pigs, a-runnen wi' the zow,
Did zicken, zomehow, noobody know'd how,
An' vall, an' turn their snouts toward the sky,
An' only gi'e woone little grunt, an' die;
An' all the little ducks an' chicken
Wer death-struck out in yard a-picken
Their bits o' food, an' vell upon their head,
An' flapp'd their little wings an' drapp'd down dead.
They coulden fat the calves, they woulden thrive;
They coulden seäve their lambs alive;
Their sheep wer all a-coath'd, or gi'ed noo wool;
The hosses vell away to skin an' bwones,
An' got so weak they coulden pull
A half a peck o' stwones:
The dog got dead-alive an' drowsy,
The cat vell zick an' woulden mousy;
An' every time the vo'k went up to bed,
They wer a-hag-rod till they wer half dead.
They us'd to keep her out o' house, 'tis true,
A-naïlen up at door a hosses shoe;
An' I've a-heärd the farmer's wife did try
To dawk a needle or a pin
In drough her wold hard wither'd skin,
An' draw her blood, a-comen by:
But she could never vetch a drap,
For pins would ply an' needles snap
Ageän her skin; an' that, in coo'se,
Did meäke the hag bewitch em woo'se.

ECLOGUE: THE TIMES
JOHN AN' TOM

JOHN

Well, Tom, how be'st? Zoo thou'st a-got thy neäme
Among the leaguers, then, as I've a-heärd.

TOM

Aye John, I have, John; an' I ben't afeärd
To own it. Why, who woulden do the seäme?

135

We shan't goo on lik' this long, I can tell ye.
Bread is so high an' wages be so low,
That, after worken lik' a hoss, you know,
A man can't eärn enough to vill his belly.

Ah! well! Now there, d'ye know, if I wer sure
That theäsem men would gi'e me work to do
All drough the year, an' always paÿ me mwore
Than I'm a-eärnen now, I'd jein em too.
If I wer sure they'd bring down things so cheap,
That what mid buy a pound o' mutton now
Would buy the hinder quarters, or the sheep,
Or what wull buy a pig would buy a cow:
In short, if they could meäke a shillen goo
In market just so vur as two,
Why then, d'ye know, I'd be their man;
But, hang it! I don't think they can.

Why ees they can, though you don't know't,
An' theäsem men can meäke it clear.
Why vu'st they'd zend up members ev'ry year
To Parli'ment, an' ev'ry man would vote;
Vor if a fellow midden be a squier,
He mid be just so fit to vote, an' goo
To meäke the laws at Lon'on, too,
As many that do hold their noses higher.
Why shoulden fellows meäke good laws an' speeches
A-dressed in fusti'n cwoats an' cord'roy breeches?
Or why should hooks an' shovels, zives an' axes,
Keep any man vrom voten o' the taxes?
An' when the poor've a-got a sheäre
In meäken laws, they'll teäke good ceäre
To meäke zome good woones vor the poor.
Do stan' by reason, John; because
The men that be to meäke the laws
Will meäke em vor theirzelves, you mid be sure.

Ees, that they wull. The men that you mid trust
To help you, Tom, would help their own zelves vu'st.

TOM

Aye, aye. But we would have a better plan
O' voten, than the woone we got. A man,
As things be now, d'ye know, can't goo an' vote
Ageän another man, but he must know't.
We'll have a box an' balls, vor voten men
To pop their hands 'ithin, d'ye know; an' then,
If woone don't happen vor to lik' a man,
He'll drop a little black ball vrom his han',
An' zend en hwome ageän. He woon't be led
To choose a man to teäke away his bread.

JOHN

But if a man you midden like to 'front,
Should chance to call upon ye, Tom, zome day,
An' ax ye vor your vote, what could ye zay?
Why if you woulden answer, or should grunt
Or bark, he'd know you'd meän 'I won't.'
To promise woone a vote an' not to gi'e't,
Is but to be a liar an' a cheat.
An' then, bezides, when he did count the balls,
An' vind white promises a-turn'd half black;
Why then he'd think the voters all a pack
O' rogues together, – ev'ry woone o'm false.
An' if he had the power, very soon
Perhaps he'd vall upon em, ev'ry woone.
The times be pinchen me, so well as you,
But I can't tell what ever they can do.

TOM

Why meäke the farmers gi'e their leäbouren men
Mwore wages, – half or twice so much ageän
As what they got.

JOHN

             But, Thomas, you can't meäke
A man paÿ mwore away than he can teäke.
If you do meäke en gi'e, to till a vield,
So much ageän as what the groun' do yield,
He'll shut out farmen – or he'll be a goose –
An' goo an' put his money out to use.
Wages be low because the hands be plenty;
They mid be higher if the hands wer skenty.

137

Leäbour, the seäme's the produce o' the vield,
Do zell at market price – jist what 't 'ill yield.
Thou wouldsten gi'e a zixpence, I do guess,
Vor zix fresh eggs, if zix did zell for less.
If theäsem vo'k could come an' meäke mwore lands,
If they could teäke wold England in their hands
An' stratch it out jist twice so big ageän,
They'd be a–doen zome'hat vor us then.

TOM

But if they wer a–zent to Parli'ment
To meäke the laws, dost know, as I've a-zaid,
They'd knock the corn-laws on the head;
An' then the landlards must let down their rent,
An' we should very soon have cheaper bread:
Farmers would gi'e less money vor their lands.

JOHN

Aye, zoo they mid, an' prices mid be low'r
Vor what their land would yield; an' zoo their hands
Would be jist where they wer avore.
An' if theäse men wer all to hold together,
They coulden meäke new laws to change the weather!
They ben't so mighty as to think o' frightenen
The vrost an' raïn, the thunder an' the lightenen!
An' as vor me, I don't know what to think
O' them there fine, big-talken, cunnen,
Strange men, a–comen down vrom Lon'on.
Why they don't stint theirzelves, but eat an' drink
The best at public-house where they do staÿ;
They don't work gratis, they do get their paÿ.
They woulden pinch theirzelves to do us good,
Nor gi'e their money vor to buy us food.
D'ye think, if we should meet em in the street
Zome day in Lon'on, they would stand a treat?

TOM

They be a–païd because they be a-zent
By corn-law vo'k that be the poor man's friends,
To tell us all how we mid gaïn our ends,
A-zenden peäpers up to Parli'ment.

Ah! teäke ceäre how dost trust em. Dost thou know
The funny feäble o' the pig an' crow?
Woone time a crow begun to strut an' hop
About zome groun' that men 'd a-been a-drillen
Wi' barley or zome wheat, in hopes o' villen
Wi' good fresh corn his empty crop.
But lik' a thief, he didden like the païns
O' worken hard to get en a vew graïns;
Zoo while the sleeky rogue wer there a-hunten,
Wi' little luck, vor corns that mid be vound
A-pecken vor, he heärd a pig a-grunten
Just tother zide o' hedge, in tother ground.
'Ah!' thought the cunnen rogue, an' gi'ed a hop,
'Ah! that's the way vor me to vill my crop;
Aye, that's the plan, if nothen don't defeat it.
If I can get thik pig to bring his snout
In here a bit an' turn the barley out,
Why, hang it! I shall only have to eat it.'
Wi' that he vled up straïght upon a woak,
An' bowen, lik' a man at hustens, spoke:
'My friend,' zaid he, 'that's poorish liven vor ye
In thik there leäze. Why I be very zorry
To zee how they hard-hearted vo'k do sarve ye.
You can't live there. Why! do they meän to starve ye?'
'Ees,' zaid the pig, a-grunten, 'ees;
What wi' the hosses an' the geese,
There's only docks an' thissles here to chaw.
Instead o' liven well on good warm straw,
I got to grub out here, where I can't pick
Enough to meäke me half an ounce o' flick.'
'Well,' zaid the crow, 'd'ye know, if you'll stan' that,
You mussen think, my friend, o' getten fat.
D'ye want some better keep? Vor if you do,
Why, as a friend, I be a-come to tell ye,
That if you'll come an' jus' get drough
Theäse gap up here, why you mid vill your belly.
Why, they've a-been a-drillen corn, d'ye know,
In theäse here piece o' groun' below;
An' if you'll just put in your snout,
An' run en up along a drill,

139

Why, hang it! you mid grub it out,
An' eat, an' eat your vill.
There idden any fear that vo'k mid come,
Vor all the men be jist a-gone in hwome.'
The pig, believen ev'ry single word
That wer a-twold en by the cunnen bird
Wer only vor his good, an' that 'twer true,
Just gi'ed a grunt, an' bundled drough,
An' het his nose, wi' all his might an' maïn,
Right up a drill, a-routen up the grain;
An' as the cunnen crow did gi'e a caw
A-praïsen o'n, oh! he did veel so proud!
An' work'd, an' blow'd, an' toss'd, an' plough'd
The while the cunnen crow did vill his maw.
An' after worken till his bwones
Did eäche, he soon begun to veel
That he should never get a meal,
Unless he dined on dirt an' stwones.
'Well,' zaid the crow, 'why don't ye eat?'
'Eat what, I wonder!' zaid the heäiry plougher,
A-brislen up an' looken rather zour;
'I don't think dirt an' flints be any treat.'
'Well,' zaid the crow, 'why you be blind.
What! don't ye zee how thick the corn do lie
Among the dirt? an' don't ye zee how I
Do pick up all that you do leäve behind?
I'm zorry that your bill should be so snubby.'
'No,' zaid the pig, 'methinks that I do zee
My bill wull do uncommon well vor thee,
Vor thine wull peck, an' mine wull grubby.'
An' just wi' this a-zaid by mister Flick
To mister Crow, wold John the farmer's man
Come up, a-zwingen in his han'
A good long knotty stick,
An' laid it on, wi' all his might,
The poor pig's vlitches, left an' right;
While mister Crow, that talk'd so fine
O' friendship, left the pig behine,
An' vled away upon a distant tree,
Vor pigs can only grub, but crows can vlee.

Aye, thik there teäle mid do vor childern's books;
But you wull vind it hardish for ye
To frighten me, John, wi' a storry
O' silly pigs an' cunnen rooks.
If we be grubben pigs, why then, I s'pose,
The farmers an' the girt woones be the crows.

'Tis very odd there idden any friend
To poor-vo'k hereabout, but men mus' come
To do us good away from tother end
Ov England! Han't we any frien's near hwome?
I mus' zay, Thomas, that 'tis rather odd
That strangers should become so very civil, –
That ouer vo'k be childern o' the Devil,
An' other vo'k be all the vo'k o' God!
If we've a-got a friend at all,
Why who can tell – I'm sure thou cassen –
But that the squier, or the pa'son,
Mid be our friend, Tom, after all?
The times be hard, 'tis true! an' they that got
His blessens, shoulden let theirzelves vorget
How 'tis where vo'k do never zet
A bit o' meat within their rusty pot.
The man a-zitten in his easy chair
To flesh, an' vowl, an' vish, should try to speäre
The poor theäse times, a little vrom his store;
An' if he don't, why sin is at his door.

Ah! we won't look to that; we'll have our right, –
If not by feäir meäns, then we wull by might.
We'll meäke times better vor us; we'll be free
Ov other vo'k an' others' charity.

Ah! I do think you mid as well be quiet;
You'll meäke things wo'se, i'-ma'-be, by a riot.
You'll get into a mess, Tom, I'm afeärd;
You'll goo vor wool, an' then come hwome a-sheär'd.

BLACKMWORE MAIDENS

The primrwose in the sheäde do blow,
The cowslip in the zun,
The thyme upon the down do grow,
The clote where streams do run;
An' where do pretty maïdens grow
An' blow, but where the tow'r
Do rise among the bricken tuns,
In Blackmwore by the Stour.

If you could zee their comely gaït,
An' pretty feäces' smiles,
A-trippen on so light o' waïght,
An' steppen off the stiles;
A-gwaïn to church, as bells do swing
An' ring 'ithin the tow'r,
You'd own the pretty maïdens' pleäce
Is Blackmwore by the Stour.

If you vrom Wimborne took your road,
To Stower or Paladore,
An' all the farmers' housen show'd
Their daughters at the door;
You'd cry to bachelors at hwome –
'Here, come: 'ithin an hour
You'll vind ten maïdens to your mind,
In Blackmwore by the Stour.'

An' if you look'd 'ithin their door,
To zee em in their pleäce,
A-doen housework up avore
Their smilen mother's feäce;
You'd cry – 'Why, if a man would wive
An' thrive, 'ithout a dow'r,
Then let en look en out a wife
In Blackmwore by the Stour.'

As I upon my road did pass
A school-house back in Maÿ,
There out upon the beäten grass
Wer maïdens at their plaÿ;

An' as the pretty souls did tweil
An' smile, I cried, 'The flow'r
O' beauty, then, is still in bud
In Blackmwore by the Stour.'

MY ORCHA'D IN LINDEN LEA

'Ithin the woodlands, flow'ry gleäded,
  By the woak tree's mossy moot,
The sheenen grass-bleädes, timber-sheäded,
  Now do quiver under voot;
An' birds do whissle over head,
An' water's bubblen in its bed,
An' there vor me the apple tree
Do leän down low in Linden Lea.

When leaves that leätely wer a-springen
  Now do feäde 'ithin the copse,
An' painted birds do hush their zingen
  Up upon the timber's tops;
An' brown-leav'd fruit's a-turnen red,
In cloudless zunsheen, over head,
Wi' fruit vor me, the apple tree
Do leän down low in Linden Lea.

Let other vo'k meäke money vaster
  In the aïr o' dark-room'd towns,
I don't dread a peevish meäster;
  Though noo man do heed my frowns,
I be free to goo abrode,
Or teäke ageän my homeward road
To where, vor me, the apple tree
Do leän down low in Linden Lea.

BISHOP'S CAUNDLE

At peace day, who but we should goo
To Caundle vor an' hour or two:
As gaÿ a day as ever broke
Above the heads o' Caundle vo'k,

Vor peace, a-come vor all, did come
To them wi' two new friends at hwome.
Zoo while we kept, wi' nimble peäce,
The wold dun tow'r avore our feäce,
The aïr, at last, begun to come
Wi' drubbens ov a beätèn drum;
An' then we heärd the horn's loud droats
Plaÿ off a tuen's upper notes;
An' then ageän a risèn cheärm
Vrom tongues o' people in a zwarm:
An' zoo, at last, we stood among
The merry feäces o' the drong.
An' there, wi' garlands all a-tied
In wreaths an' bows on every zide,
An' color'd flags, a-fluttren high
An' bright avore the sheenen sky,
The very guide-post wer a-drest
Wi' posies on his eärms an' breast.
At last, the vo'k zwarm'd in by scores
An' hundreds droo the high barn-doors,
To dine on English feäre, in ranks,
A-zot on chairs, or stools, or planks,
By bwoards a-reachen, row an' row,
Wi' cloths so white as driven snow.
An' while they took, wi' merry cheer,
Their pleäces at the meat an' beer,
The band did blow an' beät aloud
Their merry tuens to the crowd;
An' slowly-zwingen flags did spread
Their hangen colors over head.
An' then the vo'k, wi' jaÿ an' pride,
Stood up in stillness, zide by zide,
Wi' downcast heads, the while their friend
Rose up avore the teäble's end,
An' zaid a timely greäce, an' blest
The welcome meat to every guest.
An' then arose a mingled naïse
O' knives an' pleätes, an' cups an' traÿs,
An' tongues wi' merry tongues a-drown'd
Below a deaf'nen storm o' sound.
An' zoo, at last, their worthy host
Stood up to gi'e em all a twoast,

That they did drink, wi' shouts o' glee,
An' whirlen eärms to dree times dree.
An' when the bwoards at last wer beäre
Ov all the cloths an' goodly feäre,
An' froth noo longer rose to zwim
Within the beer-mug's sheenen rim,
The vo'k, a-streamen drough the door,
Went out to geämes they had in store.
An' on the blue-reäv'd waggon's bed,
Above his vower wheels o' red,
Musicians zot in rows, an' plaÿ'd
Their tuens up to chap an' maïd,
That beät, wi' plaÿsome tooes an' heels,
The level ground in nimble reels.
An' zome ageän, a-zet in line,
An' starten at a given sign,
Wi' outreach'd breast, a-breathen quick
Droo op'nen lips, did nearly kick
Their polls, a-runnen sich a peäce,
Wi' streamen heäir, to win the reäce.
An' in the house, an' on the green,
An' in the shrubb'ry's leafy screen,
On ev'ry zide we met sich lots
O' smilen friends in happy knots,
That I do think, that drough the feäst
In Caundle, vor a day at leäst,
You woudden vind a scowlen feäce.
Or dumpy heart in all the pleäce.

DAY'S WORK A-DONE

An' oh! the jaÿ our rest did yield,
    At evenen by the mossy wall,
When we'd a-work'd all day a-vield,
    While zummer zuns did rise an' vall,
        As there a-letten
        Goo all fretten,
An' vorgetten all our tweils,
We zot among our childern's smiles.

An' under skies that glitter'd white,
    The while our smoke, arisèn blue,

145

Did melt in aïr, out o' zight,
  Above the trees that kept us lew,
    Wer birds a-zingen,
    Tongues a-ringen,
Childern springen, vull o' jaÿ,
A-finishen the day in plaÿ.

An' back behind, a-stannen tall,
  The cliff did sheen to western light;
An' while avore the watervall,
  A-rottlen loud, an' foamen white,
    The leaves did quiver,
    Gnots did whiver,
By the river, where the pool,
In evenen aïr did glissen cool.

An' childern there, a-runnen wide,
  Did plaÿ their geämes along the grove,
Vor though to us 'twer jaÿ to bide
  At rest, to them 'twer jaÿ to move,
    The while my smilen
    Jeäne, beguilen
All my tweilen, wi' her ceäre,
Did call me to my evenen feäre.

THE WAGGON A-STOODED

Dree o'm a-ta'ken o't

GEORGE

Well, here we be, then, wi' the vu'st poor lwoad
O' vuzz we brought, a-stooded in the road.

JEAMES

The road, George, no. There's na'r a road. That's wrong.
If we'd a road, we mid ha' got along.

GEORGE

Noo road! Ees 'tis, the road that we do goo.

JEAMES

Do goo, George, no. The pleäce we can't get drough.

146

GEORGE

Well, there, the vu'st lwoad we've a-haul'd to–day
Is here a–stooded in theäse bed o' clay.
Here's rotten groun'! an' how the wheels do cut!
The little woone's a–zunk up to the nut.

WILLIAM

An' yeet this rotten groun' don't reach a lug.

GEORGE

Well, come, then, gi'e the plow another tug.

JEAMES

They meäres wull never pull the waggon out,
A–lwoaded, an' a–stooded in thik rout.

WILLIAM

We'll try. Come, *Smiler*, come! C'up, *Whitevoot*, gee!

JEAMES

White–voot wi' lags all over mud! Hee! Hee!

WILLIAM

'Twoon't wag. We shall but snap our gear,
An' overstraïn the meäres. 'Twoon't wag, 'tis clear.

GEORGE

That's your work, William. No, in coo'se, 'twoon't wag.
Why did ye dreve en into theäse here quag?
The vore–wheels be a–zunk above the nuts.

WILLIAM

What then? I coulden leäve the beäten track,
To turn the waggon over on the back
Ov woone o' theäsem wheel–high emmet–butts.
If you be sich a drever, an' do know't,
You dreve the plow, then; but you'll overdrow't.

GEORGE

I dreve the plow, indeed! Oh! ees, what, now
The wheels woon't wag, then, *I* mid dreve the plow!
We'd better dig away the groun' below
The wheels.

JEAMES

There's na'r a speäde to dig wi'.

GEORGE

An' teäke an' cut a lock o' frith, an' drow
Upon the clay.

JEAMES

Nor hook to cut a twig wi'.

GEORGE

Oh! here's a bwoy a-comen. Here, my lad,
Dost know vor a'r a speäde, that can be had?

BWOY

At father's.

GEORGE

Well, where's that?

BWOY

At Sam'el Riddick's.

GEORGE

Well run, an' ax vor woone. Fling up your heels,
An' mind: a speäde to dig out theäsem wheels,
An' hook to cut a little lock o' widdicks.

WILLIAM

Why, we shall want zix ho'ses, or a dozen,
To pull the waggon out, wi' all theäse vuzzen.

GEORGE

Well, we mus' lighten en; come, Jeämes, then, hop
Upon the lwoad, an' jus' fling off the top.

JEAMES

If I can clim' en; but 'tis my consaït,
That I shall overzet en wi' my waïght.

GEORGE

You overzet en! No, Jeämes, he won't vall,
The lwoad's a-built so firm as any wall.

148

JEAMES

Here! lend a hand or shoulder vor my knee
Or voot. I'll scramble to the top an' zee
What I can do. Well, here I be, among
The fakkets, vor a bit, but not vor long.
Heigh, George! Ha! Ha! Why this wull never stand.
Your firm's a wall, is all so loose as zand;
'Tis all a–come to pieces. Oh! Teäke ceäre!
Ho! I'm a–vallèn, vuzz an' all! Haë! There!

GEORGE

Lo'k there, thik fellor is a–vell lik' lead,
An' half the fuzzen wi'n, heels over head!
There's all the vuzz a–lyen lik' a staddle,
An' he a–deäb'd wi' mud. Oh! Here's a caddle!

WILLIAM

An' zoo you soon got down zome vuzzen, Jimmy.

JEAMES

Ees, I do know 'tis down, I brought it wi' me.

WILLIAM

Your lwoad, George, wer a rather slick–built thing,
But there, 'twer prickly vor the hands! Did sting?

GEORGE

Oh! ees, d'ye teäke me vor a nincompoop?
No, no. The lwoad wer up so firm's a rock,
But two o' theäsem emmet–butts would knock
The tightest barrel nearly out o' hoop.

WILLIAM

Oh! now then, here's the bwoy a–bringen back
The speäde. Well done, my man. That idden slack.

JEAMES

Well done, my lad, sha't have a ho'se to ride
When thou'st a meäre.

BWOY

       Next never's–tide.

WILLIAM

Now let's dig out a spit or two
O' clay, avore the little wheels;
Oh! so's, I can't pull up my heels,
I be a–stogg'd up over shoe.

GEORGE

Come, William, dig away! Why you do spuddle
A'most so weak's a child. How you do muddle!
Gi'e me the speäde a bit. A pig would rout
It out a'most so nimbly wi' his snout.

WILLIAM

Oh! so's, d'ye hear it then. How we can thunder!
How big we be, then George! What next I wonder?

GEORGE

Now, William, gi'e the waggon woone mwore twitch,
The wheels be free, an' 'tis a lighter nitch.

WILLIAM

Come, *Smiler*, gee! C'up *Whitevoot*.

GEORGE

                      That wull do.

JEAMES

Do wag.

GEORGE

    Do goo at last.

WILLIAM

             Well done. 'Tis drough.

GEORGE

Now, William, till you have mwore ho'ses' lags,
Don't dreve the waggon into theäsem quags.

WILLIAM

You build your lwoads up tight enough to ride.

GEORGE

I can't do less, d'ye know, wi' you vor guide.

ELLEN BRINE OV ALLENBURN

Noo soul did hear her lips complaïn,
An' she's a-gone vrom all her païn,
An' others' loss to her is gaïn
Vor she do live in heaven's love;
Vull many a longsome day an' week
She bore her aïlen, still, an' meek;
A-worken while her strangth held on,
An' guiden housework, when 'twer gone.
Vor Ellen Brine ov Allenburn,
Oh! there be souls to murn.

The last time I'd a-cast my zight
Upon her feäce, a-feäded white,
Wer in a zummer's mornen light
In hall avore the smwold'ren vier,
The while the childern beät the vloor,
In plaÿ, wi' tiny shoes they wore,
An' call'd their mother's eyes to view
The feäts their little limbs could do.
Oh! Ellen Brine ov Allenburn,
They childern now mus' murn.

Then woone, a-stoppen vrom his reäce,
Went up, an' on her knee did pleäce
His hand, a-looken in her feäce,
An' wi' a smilen mouth so small,
He zaid, 'You promised us to goo
To Shroton feäir, an teäke us two!'
She heärd it wi' her two white ears,
An' in her eyes there sprung two tears,
Vor Ellen Brine ov Allenburn
Did veel that they mus' murn.

September come, wi' Shroton feäir,
But Ellen Brine wer never there!
A heavy heart wer on the meäre
Their father rod his hwomeward road.
'Tis true he brought zome feäirens back,
Vor them two childern all in black;

But they had now, wi' plaÿthings new,
Noo mother vor to shew em to,
Vor Ellen Brine ov Allenburn
Would never mwore return.

THE MAID O' NEWTON

In zummer, when the knaps wer bright
In cool-aïr'd evenen's western light,
An' haÿ that had a-dried all day,
Did now lie grey, to dewy night;
I went, by happy chance, or doom,
Vrom Broadwoak Hill, athirt to Coomb,
An' met a maïd in all her bloom:
    The feäirest maïd o' Newton.

She bore a basket that did ride
So light, she didden leän azide;
Her feäce wer oval, an' she smil'd
So sweet's a child, but walk'd wi' pride.
I spoke to her, but what I zaid
I didden know; wi' thoughts a-vled,
I spoke by heart, an' not by head,
    Avore the maïd o' Newton.

I call'd her, oh! I don't know who,
'Twer by a neäme she never knew;
An' to the heel she stood upon,
She then brought on her hinder shoe,
An' stopp'd avore me, where we met,
An' wi' a smile woone can't vorget,
She zaid, wi' eyes a-zwimmen wet,
    'No, I be woone o' Newton.'

Then on I rambled to the west,
Below the zunny hangen's breast,
Where, down athirt the little stream,
The brudge's beam did lie at rest:
But all the birds, wi' lively glee,
Did chirp an' hop vrom tree to tree,
As if it wer vrom pride, to zee
    Goo by the maïd o' Newton.

By fancy led, at evenen's glow,
I woonce did goo, a-roven slow,
Down where the elems, stem by stem,
Do stan' to hem the grove below;
But after that, my veet vorzook
The grove, to seek the little brook
At Coomb, where I mid zometimes look,
    To meet the maïd o' Newton.

MEARY'S SMILE

When mornen winds, a-blowen high,
Do zweep the clouds vrom all the sky,
An' laurel-leaves do glitter bright,
The while the newly broken light
Do brighten up, avore our view,
The vields wi' green, an' hills wi' blue;
What then can highten to my eyes
The cheerful feäce ov e'th an' skies,
    But Meäry's smile, o' Morey's Mill,
    My rwose o' Mowy Lea.

An' when, at last, the evenen dews
Do now begin to wet our shoes;
An' night's a-riden to the west,
To stop our work, an' gi'e us rest,
Oh! let the candle's ruddy gleäre
But brighten up her sheenen heäir;
Or else, as she do walk abroad,
Let moonlight show, upon the road,
    My Meäry's smile, o' Morey's Mill,
    My rwose o' Mowy Lea.

An' O! mid never tears come on,
To wash her feäce's blushes wan,
Nor kill her smiles that now do plaÿ
Like sparklen weäves in zunny Maÿ;
But mid she still, vor all she's gone
Vrom souls she now do smile upon,
Show others they can vind woone jaÿ
To turn the hardest work to plaÿ.
    My Meäry's smile, o' Morey's Mill,
    My rwose o' Mowy Lea.

THE WINDOW FREAM'D WI' STWONE

When Pentridge House wer still the nest
O' souls that now ha' better rest,
Avore the vier burnt to ground
His beams an' walls, that then wer sound,
'Ithin a naïl-bestudded door,
An' passage wi' a stwonen vloor,
There spread the hall, where zun-light shone
In drough a window freäm'd wi' stwone.

A clavy-beam o' sheenen woak
Did span the he'th wi' twisten smoke,
Where fleämes did shoot in yollow streaks,
Above the brands, their flashen peaks;
An' aunt did pull, as she did stand
O' tip-tooe, wi' her lifted hand,
A curtain feäded wi' the zun,
Avore the window freäm'd wi' stwone.

When hwome-ground grass, below the moon,
Wer damp wi' evenen dew in June,
An' aunt did call the maïdens in
Vrom walken, wi' their shoes too thin,
They zot to rest their litty veet
Upon the window's woaken seat,
An' chatted there, in light that shone
In drough the window freäm'd wi' stwone.

An' as the seasons, in a ring,
Roll'd slowly roun' vrom Spring to Spring,
An' brought em on zome holy-tide,
When they did cast their tools azide;
How glad it meäde em all to spy
In Stwonylands their friends draw nigh,
As they did know em all by neäme
Out drough the window's stwonen freäme.

O evenen zun, a-riden drough
The sky, vrom Sh'oton Hill o' blue,
To leäve the night a-brooden dark
At Stalbridge, wi' its grey-wall'd park;

Small jaÿ to me the vields do bring,
Vor all their zummer birds do zing,
Since now thy beams noo mwore do fleäme
In drough the window's stwonen freäme.

THE WATER-SPRING IN THE LEANE

Oh! aye! the spring 'ithin the leäne,
A-leäden down to Lyddan Brook;
An' still a-nesslen in his nook,
As weeks do pass, an' moons do weäne.
   Nwone the drier,
   Nwone the higher,
Nwone the nigher to the door
Where we did live so long avore.

An' oh! what vo'k his mossy brim
Ha' gathered in the run o' time!
The wife a-blushen in her prime;
The widow wi' her eyezight dim;
   Maïdens dippen,
   Childern sippen,
Water drippen, at the cool
Dark wallen ov the little pool.

Behind the spring do lie the lands
My father till'd, vrom Spring to Spring,
A-waïten on vor time to bring
The crops to paÿ his weary hands.
   Wheat a-growen,
   Beäns a-blowen,
Grass vor mowen, where the bridge
Do leäd to Ryall's on the ridge.

But who do know when liv'd an' died
The squier o' the mwoldren hall;
That lined en wi' a stwonen wall,
An' steän'd so cleän his wat'ry zide?
   We behind en,
   Now can't vind en,
But do mind en, an' do thank
His meäker vor his little tank.

THE POPLARS

If theäse day's work an' burnen sky
'V' a–zent hwome you so tired as I,
Let's zit an' rest 'ithin the screen
O' my wold bow'r upon the green;
Where I do goo myself an' let
The evenen aïr cool my het,
When dew do wet the grasses bleädes,
A–quiv'ren in the dusky sheädes.

There yonder poplar trees do plaÿ
Soft music, as their heads do swaÿ,
While wind, a–rustlen soft or loud,
Do stream ageän their lofty sh'oud;
An' seem to heal the ranklen zore
My mind do meet wi' out o' door,
When I've a–bore, in downcast mood,
Zome evil where I look'd vor good.

O' they two poplars that do rise
So high avore our naïghbours' eyes,
A–zet by gramfer, hand by hand,
Wi' grammer, in their bit o' land;
The woone upon the western zide
Wer his, an' woone wer grammer's pride,
An' since they died, we all do teäke
Mwore ceäre o'm vor the wold vo'k's seäke.

An' there, wi' stems a–growen tall
Avore the houses mossy wall,
The while the moon ha' slowly past
The leafy window, they've a–cast
Their sheädes 'ithin the window peäne;
While childern have a–grown to men,
An' then ageän ha' left their beds,
To bear their childern's heavy heads.

THE LINDEN ON THE LAWN

No! Jenny, there's noo pleäce to charm
My mind lik' yours at Woakland farm,
A–peärted vrom the busy town,
By longsome miles ov aïry down,

Where woonce the meshy wall did gird
Your flow'ry geärden, an' the bird
Did zing in zummer wind that stirr'd
The spreäden linden on the lawn.

An' now ov all the trees wi' sheädes
A-wheelen round in Blackmwore gleädes,
There's noo tall poplar by the brook,
Nor elem that do rock the rook,
Nor ash upon the shelven ledge,
Nor low-bough'd woak bezide the hedge,
Nor withy up above the zedge,
So dear's thik linden on the lawn.

Vor there, o' zummer nights, below
The wall, we zot when aïr did blow,
An' sheäke the dewy rwose a-tied
Up roun' the window's stwonen zide.
An' while the carter rod' along
A-zingen, down the dusky drong,
There you did zing a sweeter zong
Below the linden on the lawn.

An' while your warbled ditty wound
Drough playsome flights o' mellow sound,
The nightengeäle's sh'ill zong, that broke
The stillness ov the dewy woak,
Rung clear along the grove, an' smote
To sudden stillness ev'ry droat;
As we did zit, an' hear it float
Below the linden on the lawn.

Where dusky light did softly vall
'Ithin the stwonen-window'd hall,
Avore your father's blinken eyes,
His evenen whiff o' smoke did rise,
An' vrom the bedroom window's height
Your little John, a-cloth'd in white,
An' gwaïn to bed, did cry 'good night'
Towards the linden on the lawn.

But now, as *Dobbin*, wi' a nod
Vor ev'ry heavy step he trod,
Did bring me on, to-night, avore
The geäbled house's pworched door,

Noo laughen child, a–cloth'd in white,
Look'd drough the stwonen window's light,
An' noo vaïce zung, in dusky night,
Below the linden on the lawn.

An' zoo, if you should ever vind
My kindness seem to grow less kind,
An' if upon my clouded feäce
My smile should yield a frown its pleäce,
Then, Jenny, only laugh an' call
My mind 'ithin the geärden wall,
Where we did plaÿ at even-fall,
Below the linden on the lawn.

ZUN-ZET

Where the western zun, unclouded,
    Up above the grey hill-tops,
Did sheen drough ashes, lofty sh'ouded,
    On the turf bezide the copse,
        In zummer weather,
        We together,
        Sorrow-slighten, work-vorgetten,
        Gambol'd wi' the zun a-zetten.

There, by flow'ry bows o' bramble,
    Under hedge, in ash-tree sheädes,
The dun-heaïr'd ho'se did slowly ramble
    On the grasses' dewy bleädes,
        Zet free o' lwoads,
        An' stwony rwoads,
        Vorgetvul o' the lashes fretten,
        Grazen wi' the zun a-zetten.

There wer rooks a-beätèn by us
    Drough the aïr, in a vlock,
An' there the lively blackbird, nigh us,
    On the meäple bough did rock,
        Wi' ringen droat,
        Where zunlight smote
        The yellow boughs o' zunny hedges
        Over western hills' blue edges.

158

Waters, drough the meäds a–purlen,
  Glissen'd in the evenen's light,
An' smoke, above the town a–curlen,
  Melted slowly out o' zight;
    An' there, in glooms
    Ov unzunn'd rooms,
    To zome, wi' idle sorrows fretten,
    Zuns did zet avore their zetten.

We were out in geämes and reäces,
  Loud a–laughen, wild in me'th,
Wi' windblown heäir, an' zunbrown'd feäces,
  Leäpen on the high–sky'd e'th,
    Avore the lights
    Wer tin'd o' nights,
    An' while the gossamer's light netten
    Sparkled to the zun a–zetten.

SPRING

    Now the zunny aïr's a–blowen
    Softly over flowers a–growen;
    An' the sparklen light do quiver
    On the ivy–bough an' river;
    Bleäten lambs, wi' woolly feäces,
    Now do plaÿ, a–runnen reäces;
      An' the springen
      Lark's a–zingen,
    Lik' a dot avore the cloud,
    High above the ashes' sh'oud.

    Housen, in the open brightness,
    Now do sheen in spots o' whiteness;
    Here an' there, on upland ledges,
    In among the trees an' hedges,
    Where, along by vlocks o' sparrows,
    Chatt'ren at the ploughman's harrows,
      Dousty rwoaded,
      Errand–lwoaded,
    Jenny, though her cloak is thin,
    Do wish en hwome upon the pin.

Zoo come along, noo longer heedvul
Ov the vier, leätely needvul,
Over grass o' slopen leäzes,
Zingen zongs in zunny breezes;
Out to work in copse, a-mooten,
Where the primrwose is a-shooten,
　　An' in gladness,
　　Free o' sadness,
In the warmth o' Spring vorget
Leafless winter's cwold an' wet.

THE WATER CROWVOOT

O small-feäc'd flow'r that now dost bloom
To stud wi' white the shallow Frome,
An' leäve the clote to spread his flow'r
On darksome pools o' stwoneless Stour,
When sof'ly-rizèn aïrs do cool
The water in the sheenen pool,
Thy beds o' snow-white buds do gleam
So feäir upon the sky-blue stream,
As whitest clouds, a-hangen high
Avore the blueness o' the sky;
An' there, at hand, the thin-heäir'd cows,
In aïry sheädes o' withy boughs,
Or up bezide the mossy raïls,
Do stan' an' zwing their heavy taïls,
The while the ripplen stream do flow
Below the dousty bridge's bow;
An' quiv'ren water-gleams do mock
The weäves, upon the sheäded rock;
An' up athirt the copen stwone
The laïtren bwoy do leän alwone,
A-watchen, wi' a stedvast look,
The vallèn waters in the brook,
The while the zand o' time do run
An' leäve his errand still undone.
An' oh! as long's thy buds would gleam
Above the softly-sliden stream,
While sparklen zummer-brooks do run
Below the lofty-climen zun,

I only wish that thou could'st staÿ
Vor noo man's harm, an' all men's jaÿ.
But no, the waterman 'ull weäde
Thy water wi' his deadly bleäde,
To slaÿ thee even in thy bloom,
Fair small-feäc'd flow'r o' the Frome.

THE LILAC

Dear lilac-tree, a-spreaden wide
Thy purple blooth on ev'ry zide,
As if the hollow sky did shed
Its blue upon thy flow'ry head;
Oh! whether I mid sheäre wi' thee
Thy open aïr, my bloomen tree,
Or zee thy blossoms vrom the gloom,
'Ithin my zunless worken-room,
My heart do leäp, but leäp wi' sighs,
At zight o' thee avore my eyes,
Vor when thy grey-blue head do swaÿ
In cloudless light, 'tis Spring, 'tis Maÿ.

'Tis Spring, 'tis Maÿ, as Maÿ woonce shed
His glowen light above thy head –
When thy green boughs, wi' bloomy tips,
Did sheäde my childern's laughen lips;
A-screenen vrom the noonday gleäre
Their rwosy cheäks an' glossy heäir;
The while their mother's needle sped,
Too quick vor zight, the snow-white thread.
Unless her han, wi' loven ceäre,
Did smooth their little heads o' heäir;
Or wi' a sheäke, tie up anew
Vor zome wild voot, a slippen shoe;
An' I did leän bezide thy mound
Ageän the deäisy-dappled ground,
The while the woaken clock did tick
My hour o' rest away too quick,
An' call me off to work anew,
Wi' slowly-ringen strokes, woone, two.

Zoo let me zee noo darksome cloud
Bedim to–day thy flow'ry sh'oud,
But let en bloom on ev'ry spraÿ,
Drough all the days o' zunny Maÿ.

THE BLACKBIRD

'Twer out at Penley I'd a–past
A zummer day that went too vast,
An' when the zetten zun did spread
On western clouds a vi'ry red;
The elems' leafy limbs wer still
Above the gravel–bedded rill,
An' under en did warble sh'ill,
Avore the dusk, the blackbird.

An' there, in sheädes o' darksome yews,
Did vlee the maïdens on their tooes,
A–laughen sh'ill wi' merry feäce
When we did vind their hiden pleäce,
'Ithin the loose–bough'd ivy's gloom,
Or lofty lilac, vull in bloom,
Or hazzle–wrides that gi'ed em room
Below the zingen blackbird.

Above our heads the rooks did vlee
To reach their nested elem–tree,
An' splashen vish did rise to catch
The wheelen gnots above the hatch;
An' there the miller went along,
A–smilen, up the sheädy drong,
But yeet too deaf to hear the zong
A–zung us by the blackbird.

An' there the sh'illy bubblen brook
Did leäve behind his rocky nook,
To run drough meäds a–chill'd wi' dew,
Vrom hour to hour the whole night drough;
But still his murmers wer a–drown'd
By vaïces that mid never sound
Ageän together on that ground,
Wi' whislens o' the blackbird.

162

LYDLYNCH BELLS

When skies wer peäle wi' twinklen stars,
An' whislen aïr a-risèn keen;
An' birds did leäve the icy bars
To vind, in woods, their mossy screen;
When vrozen grass, so white's a sheet,
Did scrunchy sharp below our veet,
An' water, that did sparkle red
At zunzet, wer a-vrozen dead;
The ringers then did spend an hour
A-ringen changes up in tow'r;
Vor Lydlinch bells be good vor sound,
An' liked by all the naïghbours round.

An' while along the leafless boughs
O' ruslen hedges, win's did pass,
An' orts ov haÿ, a-left by cows,
Did russle on the vrozen grass,
An' maïdens' païls, wi' all their work
A-done, did hang upon their vurk,
An' they, avore the fleämen brand,
Did teäke their needle-work in hand,
The men did cheer their heart an hour
A-ringen changes up in tow'r;
Vor Lydlinch bells be good vor sound,
An' liked by all the naïghbours round.

Their sons did pull the bells that rung
Their mothers' wedden peals avore,
The while their fathers led em young
An' blushen vrom the churches door,
An' still did cheem, wi' happy sound,
As time did bring the Zundays round,
An' call em to the holy pleäce
Vor heav'nly gifts o' peace an' greäce;
An' vo'k did come, a-streamen slow
Along below the trees in row,
While they, in merry peals, did sound
The bells vor all the naïghbours round.

An' when the bells, wi' changen peal,
Did smite their own vo'k's window-peänes,
Their sof'en'd sound did often steal
Wi' west winds drough the Bagber leänes;
Or, as the win' did shift, mid goo
Where woody Stock do nessle lew,
Or where the risèn moon did light
The walls o' Thornhill on the height;
An' zoo, whatever time mid bring
To meäke their vive clear vaïces zing,
Still Lydlinch bells wer good vor sound,
An' liked by all the naïghbours round.

THE STAGE COACH

Ah! when the wold vo'k went abroad
  They thought it vast enough
If vow'r good ho'ses beät the road
  Avore the coach's ruf;
      An' there they zot,
      A-cwold or hot,
An' roll'd along the groun',
    While the whip did smack
    On the ho'ses' back,
An' the wheels went swiftly roun, good so's;
      The wheels went swiftly roun'.

Noo iron raïls did streak the land
  To keep the wheels in track.
The coachman turn'd his vow'r-in-hand,
  Out right, or left, an' back;
      An' he'd stop avore
      A man's own door,
To teäke en up or down:
    While the reïns vell slack
    On the ho'ses' back,
Till the wheels did rottle roun' ageän;
      Till the wheels did rottle roun'.

An' there, when wintry win' did blow,
  Athirt the plaïn an' hill,
An' the zun wer peäle above the snow,
  An' ice did stop the mill,

They did laugh an' joke,
      Wi' cwoat or cloke
So warmly roun' em boun',
      While the whip did crack
      On the ho'ses' back,
An' the wheels did trundle roun', d'ye know;
         The wheels did trundle roun'.

An' when the rumblen coach did pass
   Where hufflen winds did roar,
They'd stop to teäke a warmen glass
   By the sign above the door;
         An' did laugh an' joke
         An' ax the vo'k
The miles they wer vrom town,
      Till the whip did crack
      On the ho'ses' back,
An' the wheels did truckle roun', good vo'k;
         The wheels did truckle roun'.

An' gaïly rod wold age or youth,
   When zummer light did vall
On woods in leaf, or trees in blooth,
   Or girt vo'k's parkzide wall.
         An' they thought they past
         The pleäces vast,
Along the dousty groun',
      When the whip did smack
      On the ho'ses' back,
An' the wheels spun swiftly roun'. Them days
         The wheels spun swiftly roun'.

TREES BE COMPANY

When zummer's burnen het's a-shed
Upon the droopen grasses head,
A–drevèn under sheädy leaves
The workvo'k in their snow-white sleeves,
We then mid yearn to clim' the height,
   Where thorns be white, above the vern;

165

An' aïr do turn the zunsheen's might
  To softer light too weak to burn –
    On woodless downs we mid be free,
    But lowland trees be company.

Though downs mid show a wider view
O' green a-reachen into blue
Than roads a-winden in the glen,
An' ringen wi' the sounds o' men;
The thissle's crown o' red an' blue
  In Fall's cwold dew do wither brown,
An' larks come down 'ithin the lew,
  As storms do brew, an' skies do frown –
    An' though the down do let us free,
    The lowland trees be company.

Where birds do zing, below the zun,
In trees above the blue-smok'd tun,
An' sheädes o' stems do overstratch
The mossy path 'ithin the hatch;
If leaves be bright up over head,
  When Maÿ do shed its glitt'ren light;
Or, in the blight o' Fall, do spread
  A yollow bed avore our zight –
    Whatever season it mid be,
    The trees be always company.

When dusky night do nearly hide
The path along the hedge's zide,
An' daylight's hwomely sounds be still
But sounds o' water at the mill;
Then if noo feäce we long'd to greet
  Could come to meet our lwonesome treäce;
Or if noo peäce o' weary veet,
  However fleet, could reach its pleäce –
    However lwonesome we mid be,
    The trees would still be company.

JESSIE LEE

Above the timber's benden sh'ouds,
  The western wind did softly blow;
An' up avore the knap, the clouds
  Did ride as white as driven snow.

166

Vrom west to east the clouds did zwim
Wi' wind that plied the elem's lim';
Vrom west to east the stream did glide,
A-sheenen wide, wi' winden brim.

How feäir, I thought, avore the sky
    The slowly-zwimmen clouds do look;
How soft the win's a-streamen by;
    How bright do roll the weävy brook:
When there, a-passen on my right,
A-walken slow, an' treaden light,
Young Jessie Lee come by, an' there
Took all my ceäre, an' all my zight.

Vor lovely wer the looks her feäce
    Held up avore the western sky:
An' comely wer the steps her peäce
    Did meäke a-walken slowly by:
But I went east, wi' beätèn breast,
Wi' wind, an' cloud, an' brook, vor rest,
Wi' rest a-lost, vor Jessie gone
So lovely on, toward the west.

Blow on, O winds, athirt the hill;
    Zwim on, O clouds; O waters vall,
Down mæshy rocks, vrom mill to mill;
    I now can overlook ye all.
But roll, O zun, an' bring to me
My day, if such a day there be,
When zome dear path to my abode
Shall be the road o' Jessie Lee.

IVY HALL

If I've a-stream'd below a storm
    An' not a-velt the raïn,
An' if I ever velt me warm,
    In snow upon the plaïn,
'Twer when, as evenen skies wer dim,
An' vields below my eyes wer dim,
I went alwone at evenen-fall,
Athirt the vields to Ivy Hall.

I voun' the wind upon the hill,
   Last night, a-roaren loud,
An' rubben boughs a-creaken sh'ill
   Upon the ashes' sh'oud;
But oh! the reelen copse mid groan,
An' timber's lofty tops mid groan;
The hufflen winds be music all,
Bezide my road to Ivy Hall.

A sheädy grove o' ribbed woaks,
   Is Wootton's shelter'd nest,
An' woaks do keep the winter's strokes
   Vrom Knapton's evenen rest.
An' woaks ageän wi' bossy stems,
An' elems wi' their mossy stems,
Do rise to screen the leafy wall
An' stwonen ruf ov Ivy Hall.

The darksome clouds mid fling their sleet,
   An' vrost mid pinch me blue,
Or snow mid cling below my veet,
   An' hide my road vrom view.
The winter's only jaÿ ov heart,
An' storms do meäke me gaÿ ov heart,
When I do rest, at evenen-fall,
Bezide the he'th ov Ivy Hall.

There leafy stems do clim' around
   The mossy stwonen eaves;
An' there be window-zides a-bound
   Wi' quiv'ren ivy-leaves.
But though the sky is dim 'ithout,
An' feäces mid be grim 'ithout,
Still I ha' smiles when I do call,
At evenen-tide, at Ivy Hall.

THE WIFE A-LOST

Since I noo mwore do zee your feäce,
   Up steäirs or down below,
I'll zit me in the lwonesome pleäce,
   Where flat-bough'd beech do grow;

Below the beeches' bough', my love,
　　Where you did never come,
An' I don't look to meet ye now,
　　As I do look at hwome.

Since you noo mwore be at my zide,
　　In walks in zummer het,
I'll goo alwone where mist do ride,
　　Drough trees a-drippen wet;
Below the raïn-wet bough, my love,
　　Where you did never come,
An' I don't grieve to miss ye now,
　　As I do grieve at hwome.

Since now bezide my dinner-bwoard
　　Your vaïce do never sound,
I'll eat the bit I can avvword,
　　A-yield upon the ground;
Below the darksome bough, my love,
　　Where you did never dine,
An' I don't grieve to miss ye now,
　　As I at hwome do pine.

Since I do miss your vaïce an' feäce
　　In praÿer at eventide,
I'll praÿ wi' woone sad vaïce vor greäce
　　To goo where you do bide;
Above the tree an' bough, my love,
　　Where you be gone avore,
An' be a-waïten vor me now,
　　To come vor evermwore.

HERRENSTON

Zoo then the leädy an' the squier,
　　At Chris'mas, gather'd girt an' small,
Vor me'th, avore their roaren vier,
　　An' roun' their bwoard, 'ithin the hall;
An' there, in glitt'ren rows, between
The roun'-rimm'd pleätes, our knives did sheen,
　　Wi' frothy eäle, an' cup an' can,
　　Vor maïd an' man, at Herrenston.

An' there the jeints o' beef did stand,
  Lik' cliffs o' rock, in goodly row;
Where woone mid quarry till his hand
  Did tire, an' meäke but little show;
An' after we'd a-took our seat,
An' greäce had been a-zaid vor meat,
  We zet to work, an' zoo begun
  Our feäst an' fun at Herrenston.

An' mothers there, bezide the bwoards,
  Wi' little childern in their laps,
Did stoop, wi' loven looks an' words,
  An' veed em up wi' bits an' draps;
An' smilen husbands went in quest
O' what their wives did like the best;
  An' you'd ha' zeed a happy zight,
  Thik merry night, at Herrenston.

An' then the band, wi' each his leaf
  O' notes, above us at the zide,
Play'd up the praïse ov England's beef
  An' vill'd our hearts wi' English pride;
An' leafy chaïns o' garlands hung,
Wi' dazzlen stripes o' flags, that swung
  Above us, in a bleäze o' light,
  Thik happy night, at Herrenston.

An' then the clerk, avore the vier,
  Begun to leäd, wi' smilen feäce,
A carol, wi' the Monkton quire,
  That rung drough all the crowded pleäce.
An' dins o' words an' laughter broke
In merry peals drough clouds o' smoke;
  Vor hardly wer there woone that spoke,
  But pass'd a joke, at Herrenston.

Then man an' maïd stood up by twos,
  In rows, drough passage, out to door,
An' gaïly beät, wi' nimble shoes,
  A dance upon the stwonen vloor.
But who is worthy vor to tell,
If she that then did bear the bell,
  Wer woone o' Monkton, or o' Ceäme,
  Or zome sweet neäme ov Herrenston.

Zoo peace betide the girt vo'k's land,
    When they can stoop, wi' kindly smile,
An' teäke a poor man by the hand,
    An' cheer en in his daily tweil.
An' oh! mid He that's vur above
The highest here, reward their love,
    An' gi'e their happy souls, drough greäce,
    A higher pleäce than Herrenston.

PENTRIDGE BY THE RIVER

Pentridge! – oh! my heart's a-zwellen
Vull o' jaÿ wi' vo'k a-tellen
    Any news o' thik wold pleäce,
An' the boughy hedges round it,
An' the river that do bound it
    Wi' his dark but glis'nen feäce.
Vor there's noo land, on either hand,
To me lik' Pentridge by the river.

Be there any leaves to quiver
On the aspen by the river?
    Doo he sheäde the water still,
Where the rushes be a-growen,
Where the sullen Stour's a-flowen
    Drough the meäds vrom mill to mill?
Vor if a tree wer dear to me,
Oh! 'twer thik aspen by the river.

There, in eegrass new a-shooten,
I did run on even vooten,
    Happy, over new-mow'd land;
Or did zing wi' zingen drushes
While I plaïted, out o' rushes,
    Little baskets vor my hand;
Bezide the clote that there did float,
Wi' yollow blossoms, on the river.

When the western zun's a-vallèn,
What sh'ill vaïce is now a-callen
    Hwome the deäiry to the païls;
Who do dreve em on, a-flingen

Wide-bow'd horns, or slowly zwingen
  Right an' left their tufty taïls?
As they do goo a-huddled drough
The geäte a-leäden up vrom river.

Bleäded grass is now a-shooten
Where the vloor wer woonce our vooten,
  While the hall wer still in pleäce.
Stwones be looser in the wallen;
Hollow trees be nearer vallèn;
  Ev'ry thing ha' chang'd its feäce.
But still the neäme do bide the seäme –
'Tis Pentridge – Pentridge by the river.

THE TURN O' THE DAYS

O the wings o' the rook wer a-glitteren bright,
As he wheel'd on above, in the zun's evenen light,
An' noo snow wer a-left, but in patches o' white,
  On the hill at the turn o' the days.
An' along on the slope wer the beäre-timber'd copse,
Wi' the dry wood a-sheäkèn, wi' red-twigged tops,
Vor the dry-flowen wind, had a-blow'd off the drops
  O' the raïn, at the turn o' the days.

There the stream did run on, in the sheäde o' the hill,
So smooth in his flowen, as if he stood still,
An' bright wi' the skylight, did slide to the mill,
  By the meäds, at the turn o' the days.
An' up by the copse, down along the hill brow,
Wer vurrows a-cut down, by men out at plough,
So straïght as the zunbeams, a-shot drough the bough
  O' the tree at the turn o' the days.

Then the boomen wold clock in the tower did mark
His vive hours, avore the cool evenen wer dark,
An' ivy did glitter a-clung round the bark
  O' the tree, at the turn o' the days.
An' women afraïd o' the road in the night,
Wer a-heästenen on to reach hwome by the light,
A-casten long sheädes on the road, a-dried white,
  Down the hill, at the turn o' the days.

The father an' mother did walk out to view
The moss-bedded snow–drop, a-sprung in the lew,
An' hear if the birds wer a-zingen anew,
  In the boughs, at the turn o' the days.
An' young vo'k a–laughen wi' smooth glossy feäce,
Did hie over vields, wi' a light-vooted peäce,
To friends where the tow'r did betoken a pleäce
  Among trees, at the turn o' the days.

GAMMONY GAY

Oh! thik Gammony Gaÿ is so droll,
That if he's at hwome by the he'th,
Or wi' vo'k out o' door, he's the soul
O' the meeten vor antics an' me'th;
He do cast off the thoughts ov ill luck
As the water's a-shot vrom a duck;
He do zing where his naïghbours would cry –
He do laugh where the rest o's would sigh:
Noo other's so merry o' feäce,
  In the pleäce, as Gammony Gaÿ.

An' o'worken days, Oh! he do wear
Such a funny roun' hat, – you mid know't –
Wi' a brim all a-strout roun' his heäir,
An' his glissenen eyes down below't;
An' a cwoat wi' broad skirts that do vlee
In the wind ov his walk, round his knee;
An' a peäir o' girt pockets lik' bags,
That do swing an' do bob at his lags:
While me'th do walk out drough the pleäce,
  In the feäce o' Gammony Gaÿ.

An' if he do goo over groun'
Wi' noo soul vor to greet wi' his words,
The feäce o'n do look up an' down,
An' round en so quick as a bird's;
An' if he do vall in wi' vo'k,
Why, tidden vor want ov a joke,
If he don't zend em on vrom the pleäce
Wi' a smile or a grin on their feäce:
An' the young wi' the wold have a-heärd
A kind word vrom Gammony Gaÿ.

An' when he do whissel or hum,
'Ithout thinken o' what he's a–doen,
He'll beät his own lags vor a drum,
An' bob his gaÿ head to the tuen;
An' then you mid zee, 'etween whiles,
His feäce all alive wi' his smiles,
An' his gaÿ-breathen bozom do rise,
An' his me'th do sheen out ov his eyes:
An' at last to have praïse or have bleäme,
Is the seäme to Gammony Gaÿ.

When he drove his wold cart out, an' broke
The nut o' the wheel at a butt,
There wer 'woo'se things,' he cried, wi' a joke,
'To grieve at than cracken a nut.'
An' when he tipp'd over a lwoad
Ov his reed-sheaves woone day on the rwoad,
Then he spet in his han's, out o' sleeves,
An' whissel'd, an' flung up his sheaves,
As very vew others can wag,
Eärm or lag, but Gammony Gaÿ.

He wer wi' us woone night when the band
Wer a–come vor to gi'e us a hop,
An' he pull'd Grammer out by the hand
All down drough the dance vrom the top;
An' Grammer did hobble an' squall,
Wi' Gammon a-leädèn the ball;
While Gammon did sheäke up his knee
An' his voot, an' zing 'Diddle-ee-dee!'
An' we laugh'd ourzelves all out o' breath
At the me'th o' Gammony Gaÿ.

When our tun wer o' vier he rod
Out to help us, an' meäde us sich fun,
Vor he clomb up to dreve in a wad
O' wet thorns, to the he'th, vrom the tun;
An' there he did stamp wi' his voot,
To push down the thorns an' the zoot,
Till at last down the chimney's black wall
Went the wad, an' poor Gammon an' all:
An' seäfe on the he'th, wi' a grin
On his chin, pitch'd Gammony Gaÿ.

All the house-dogs do waggle their taïls,
If they do but catch zight ov his feäce;
An' the ho'ses do look over raïls,
An' do whicker to zee'n at the pleäce;
An' he'll always bestow a good word
On a cat or a whisselen bird;
An' even if culvers do coo,
Or an owl is a-cryen 'Hoo, hoo,'
Where he is, there's always a joke
To be spoke, by Gammony Gaÿ.

LEEBURN MILL

Ov all the meäds wi' shoals an' pools,
Where streams did sheäke the limber zedge,
An' milken vo'k did teäke their stools,
In evenen zun-light under hedge:
Ov all the weirs the brook did vill,
Or all the hatches where a sheet
O' foam did leäp below woone's veet,
The pleäce vor me wer Leeburn Mill.

An' while below the mossy wheel
All day the foamen stream did roar,
An' up in mill the floaten meal
Did pitch upon the sheäkèn vloor,
We then could vind but vew han's still,
Or veet a-resten off the ground,
An' seldom hear the merry sound
O' geämes a-plaÿ'd at Leeburn Mill.

But when they let the stream goo free,
Bezide the drippen wheel at rest,
An' leaves upon the poplar-tree
Wer dark avore the glowen west;
An' when the clock, a-ringen sh'ill,
Did slowly beät zome evenen hour,
Oh! then 'ithin the leafy bow'r
Our tongues did run at Leeburn Mill.

An' when November's win' did blow,
Wi' hufflen storms along the plaïn,
An' blacken'd leaves did lie below
The neäked tree, a-zoak'd wi' raïn,

175

I werden at a loss to vill
The darkest hour o' raïny skies,
If I did vind avore my eyes
The feäces down at Leeburn Mill.

WOONE SMILE MWORE

O! Meäry, when the zun went down,
    Woone night in Spring, wi' vi'ry rim,
Behind the knap wi' woody crown,
    An' left your smilen feäce so dim;
Your little sister there, inside,
    Wi' bellows on her little knee,
Did blow the vier, a-gleären wide
    Drough window-peänes, that I could zee, –
As you did stan' wi' me, avore
The house, a-peärten, – woone smile mwore.

The chatt'ren birds, a-risèn high,
    An' zinken low, did swiftly vlee
Vrom shrinken moss, a-growen dry,
    Upon the leänen apple tree.
An' there the dog, a-whippen wide
    His heäiry taïl, an' comen near,
Did fondly lay ageän your zide
    His coal-black nose an' russet ear:
To win what I'd a-won avore,
Vrom your gaÿ feäce, his woone smile mwore.

An' while your mother bustled sprack,
    A-getten supper out in hall,
An' cast her sheäde, a-whiv'ren black
    Avore the vier, upon the wall,
Your brother come, wi' easy peäce,
    In drough the slammen geäte, along
The path, wi' healthy-bloomen feäce,
    A-whis'len shrill his last new zong;
An' when he come avore the door,
He met vrom you his woone smile mwore.

Now you that wer the daughter there,
　　Be mother on a husband's vloor,
An' mid ye meet wi' less o' ceäre
　　Than what your hearty mother bore;
An' if abroad I have to rue
　　The bitter tongue, or wrongvul deed,
Mid I come hwome to sheäre wi' you
　　What's needvul free o' pinchen need:
An' vind that you ha' still in store,
My evenen meal, an' woone smile mwore.

WOAK HILL

When sycamore leaves wer a-spreaden,
　　Green-ruddy, in hedges,
Bezide the red doust o' the ridges,
　　A-dried at Woak Hill;

I packed up my goods all a-sheenen
　　Wi' long years o' handlen,
On dousty red wheels ov a waggon,
　　To ride at Woak Hill.

The brown thatchen ruf o' the dwellen
　　I then wer a-leäven,
Had shelter'd the sleek head o' Meäry,
　　My bride at Woak Hill.

But now vor zome years, her light voot-vall
　　'S a-lost vrom the vlooren.
Too soon vor my jaÿ an' my childern,
　　She died at Woak Hill.

But still I do think that, in soul,
　　She do hover about us;
To ho vor her motherless childern,
　　Her pride at Woak Hill.

Zoo – lest she should tell me hereafter
　　I stole off 'ithout her,
An' left her, uncall'd at house-ridden,
　　To bide at Woak Hill –

I call'd her so fondly, wi' lippens
    All soundless to others,
An' took her wi' aïr-reachen hand,
    To my zide at Woak Hill.

On the road I did look round, a-talken
    To light at my shoulder,
An' then led her in at the door-way,
    Miles wide vrom Woak Hill.

An' that's why vo'k thought, vor a season,
    My mind wer a-wandren
Wi' sorrow, when I wer so sorely
    A-tried at Woak Hill.

But no; that my Meäry mid never
    Behold herzelf slighted,
I wanted to think that I guided
    My guide vrom Woak Hill.

THE HEDGER

Upon the hedge theäse bank did bear,
    Wi' lwonesome thought untwold in words,
I woonce did work, wi' noo sound there
    But my own strokes, an' chirpen birds;
As down the west the zun went wan,
An' days brought on our Zunday's rest,
When sounds o' cheemen bells did vill
The aïr, an' hook an' axe wer still.

Along the wold town-path vo'k went,
    An' met unknown, or friend wi' friend,
The maïd her busy mother zent,
    The mother wi' noo maïd to zend;
An' in the light the gleäzier's glass,
As he did pass, wer dazzlen bright,
Or woone went by wi' down-cast head,
A-wrapp'd in blackness vor the dead.

An' then the bank, wi' risèn back,
    That's now a'most a-trodden down,
Bore thorns wi' rind o' sheeny black,
    An' meäple stems o' ribby brown;

An' in the lewth o' theäse tree heads,
Wer primrwose beds a-sprung in blooth,
An' here a geäte, a-slammen to,
Did let the slow-wheel'd plough roll drough.

Ov all that then went by, but vew
    Be now a-left behine', to beät
The mornen flow'rs or evenen dew,
    Or slam the woaken vive-bar'd geäte;
But woone, my wife, so litty-stepp'd,
That have a-kept my path o' life,
Wi' her vew errands on the road,
Where woonce she bore a mother's lwoad.

THE FLOOD IN SPRING

Last night below the elem in the lew
    Bright the sky did gleam
On water blue, while aïr did softly blow
    On the flowen stream,
An' there wer gil'cups' buds untwold,
An deäisies that begun to vwold
Their low-stemm'd blossoms vrom my zight
Ageän the night, an' evenen's cwold.

But, oh! so cwold below the darksome cloud
    Soon the night-wind roar'd,
Wi' raïny storms that zent the zwollen streams
    Over ev'ry vword.
The while the drippen tow'r did tell
The hour, wi' storm-be-smother'd bell,
An' over ev'ry flower's bud
Roll'd on the flood, 'ithin the dell.

But when the zun arose, an lik' a rwose
    Shone the mornen sky;
An' roun' the woak, the wind a-blowen weak,
    Softly whiver'd by;
Though drown'd wer still the deäisy bed
Below the flood, its feäce instead
O' flow'ry groun', below our shoes
Show'd feäirest views o' skies o'er head.

179

An' zoo to try if all our faïth is true
　　Jaÿ mid end in tears,
An' hope, woonce feäir, mid sadden into fear,
　　Here in e'thly years.
But He that tried our soul do know
To meäke us good amends, an' show
Instead o' things a-took awaÿ,
Some higher jaÿ that He'll bestow.

COMEN HWOME

As clouds did ride wi' heästy flight,
An' woods did swaÿ upon the height,
An' bleädes o' grass did sheäke, below
The hedge-row bremble's swingen bow,
I come back hwome where winds did zwell,
　　In whirls along the woody gleädes,
　　On primrwose beds, in windy sheädes,
To Burnley's dark-tree'd dell.

There hills do screen the timber's bough,
The trees do screen the leäze's brow,
The timber-sheäded leäze do bear
A beäten path that we do wear.
The path do stripe the leäze's zide,
　　To willows at the river's edge,
　　Where hufflen winds did sheäke the zedge,
An' sparklen weäves did glide.

An' where the river, bend by bend,
Do draïn our meäd, an' mark its end,
The hangen leäze do teäke our cows,
An' trees do sheäde em wi' their boughs,
An' I the quicker beät the road,
　　To zee a-comen into view,
　　Still greener vrom the sky-line's blue,
Wold Burnley our abode.

EARLY PLAYMEATE

After many long years had a-run,
  The while I wer a-gone vrom the pleäce,
I come back to the vields, where the zun
  Ov her childhood did show me her feäce.
There her father, years wolder, did stoop,
  An' her brother, wer now a-grow'd staïd,
An' the apple tree lower did droop,
  Out in orcha'd where we had a-plaÿ'd.
There wer zome things a-seemen the seäme,
  But Meäry's a-married awaÿ.

There wer two little childern a-zent,
  Wi' a message to me, oh! so feäir
As the mother that they did zoo ment,
  When in childhood she plaÿ'd wi' me there.
Zoo they twold me that if I would come
  Down to Coomb, I should zee a wold friend,
Vor a plaÿmeäte o' mine wer at hwome,
  An' would staÿ till another week's end.
At the dear pworched door, could I dare
  To zee Meäry a-married awaÿ!

On the flower-not, now all a-trod
  Stwony hard, the green grass wer a-spread,
An' the long-slighted woodbine did nod
  Vrom the wall, wi' a loose-hangen head.
An' the martin's clay nest wer a-hung
  Up below the brown oves, in the dry,
An' the rooks had a-rock'd broods o' young
  On the elems below the Maÿ sky;
But the bud on the bed, coulden bide,
  Wi' young Meäry a-married awaÿ.

There the copse-wood, a-grow'd to a height,
  Wer a-vell'd, an' the primrwose in blooth,
Among chips on the ground a-turn'd white,
  Wer a-quiv'ren, all beäre ov his lewth.
The green moss wer a-spread on the thatch,
  That I left yollow reed, an' avore

The small green, there did swing a new hatch,
   Vor to let me walk into the door.
Oh! the rook did still rock o'er the rick,
   But wi' Meäry a-married awaÿ.

PICKEN O' SCROFF

Oh! the wood wer a-vell'd in the copse,
   An' the moss-bedded primrwose did blow;
An' vrom tall-stemmed trees' leafless tops,
   There did lie but slight sheädes down below.
An' the sky wer a-showen, in drough
By the tree-stems, the deepest o' blue,
Wi' a light that did vall on an' off
The dry ground, a-strew'd over wi' scroff.

There the hedge that wer leätely so high,
   Wer a-plush'd, an' along by the zide,
Where the waggon 'd a-haul'd the wood by,
   There did reach the deep wheelrouts, a-dried.
An' the groun' wi' the sticks wer bespread,
Zome a-cut off alive, an' zome dead,
An' vor burnen, well wo'th reäken off,
By the childern a-picken o' scroff.

In the tree-studded leäze, where the woak
   Wer a-spreaden his head out around,
There the scrags that the wind had a-broke,
   Wer a-lyen about on the ground,
Or the childern, wi' little red hands,
Wer a-tyen em up in their bands;
Vor noo squier or farmer turn'd off
Little childern a-picken o' scroff.

There wer woone bloomen child wi' a cloak
   On her shoulders, as green as the ground;
An' another, as gray as the woak,
   Wi' a bwoy in a brown frock, a-brown'd.
An' woone got up, in plaÿ, vor to taït,
On a woak-limb, a-growen out straïght.
But she soon wer a-taïted down off,
By her meätes out a-picken o' scroff.

When they childern do grow to staïd vo'k,
  An' goo out in the worold, all wide
Vrom the copse, an' the zummerleäze woak,
  Where at last all their elders ha' died,
They wull then vind it touchen to bring,
To their minds, the sweet springs o' their spring,
Back avore the new vo'k did turn off
The poor childern a-picken o' scroff.

GOOD NIGHT

While down the meäds wound slow,
  Water vor green-wheel'd mills,
Over the stream's bright bow,
  Win' come vrom dark-back'd hills.
Birds on the wing shot along down steep
Slopes, wi' a swift-swung zweep.
Dim weän'd the red streak'd west.
Lim'-weary souls 'Good rest.'

Up on the plough'd hill brow,
  Still wer the zull's wheel'd beam,
Still wer the red-wheel'd plough,
  Free o' the strong limb'd team,
Still wer the shop that the smith meäde ring,
Dark where the sparks did spring;
Low shot the zun's last beams.
Lim'-weary souls 'Good dreams.'

Where I vrom dark bank-sheädes
  Turn'd up the west hill road,
Where all the green grass bleädes
  Under the zunlight glow'd,
Startled I met, as the zunbeams plaÿ'd
Light, wi' a zunsmote maïd,
Come vor my day's last zight.
Zun-brighten'd maïd 'Good night.'

WENT HWOME

Upon the slope, the hedge did bound
The vield wi' blossom-whited zide,
An' charlock patches, yollow-dyed,
Did reach along the white-soil'd ground;

An' vo'k, a–comen up vrom meäd,
    Brought gil'cup meal upon the shoe;
Or went on where the road did leäd,
    Wi' smeechy doust vrom heel to tooe,
As noon did smite, wi' burnen light,
The road so white, to Meldonley.

An' I did tramp the zun–dried ground,
By hedge–climb'd hills, a–spread wi' flow'rs,
An' watershooten dells, an' tow'rs,
By elem–trees a–hemm'd all round,
To zee a vew wold friends, about
    Wold Meldon, where I still ha' zome,
That bid me speed as I come out,
    An' now ha' bid me welcome hwome,
As I did goo, while skies wer blue,
Vrom view to view, to Meldonley.

An' there wer timber'd knaps, that show'd
Cool sheädes, vor rest, on grassy ground,
An' thatch–brow'd windows, flower-bound,
Where I could wish wer my abode.
I pass'd the maïd avore the spring,
    An' shepherd by the thornen tree;
An' heärd the merry drever zing,
    But met noo kith or kin to me,
Till I come down, vrom Meldon's crown
To rufs o' brown, at Meldonley.

CHILDERN'S CHILDERN

Oh! if my ling'ren life should run,
    Drough years a–reckon'd ten by ten,
Below the never–tiren zun,
    Till beäbes ageän be wives an' men;
An' stillest deafness should ha' bound
My ears, at last, vrom ev'ry sound;
Though still my eyes in that sweet light,
Should have the zight o' sky an' ground:
        Would then my steäte
        In time so leäte,
Be jaÿ or païn, be païn or jaÿ?

When Zunday then, a-weänen dim,
　As theäse that now's a-clwosen still,
Mid lose the zun's down-zinken rim,
　In light behind the vier-bound hill;
An' when the bells' last peal's a-rung,
An' I mid zee the wold an' young
A-vlocken by, but shoulden hear,
However near, a voot or tongue:
　　　Mid zuch a zight,
　　　In that soft light
Be jaÿ or païn, be païn or jaÿ?

If I should zee among em all,
　In merry youth, a-gliden by,
My son's bwold son, a-grown man-tall,
　Or daughter's daughter, woman-high;
An' she mid smile wi' your good feäce,
Or she mid walk your comely peäce,
But seem, although a-chatten loud,
So dumb's a cloud, in that bright pleäce:
　　　Would youth so feäir,
　　　A-passen there,
Be jaÿ or païn, be païn or jaÿ?

'Tis seldom strangth or comeliness
　Do leäve us long. The house do show
Men's sons wi' mwore, as they ha' less,
　An' daughters brisk, vor mothers slow.
A dawn do clear the night's dim sky,
Woone star do zink, an' woone goo high,
An' liven gifts o' youth do vall,
Vrom girt to small, but never die:
　　　An' should I view,
　　　What God mid do,
Wi' jaÿ or païn, wi' païn or jaÿ?

THE RWOSE IN THE DARK

In zummer, leäte at evenen tide,
　I zot to spend a moonless hour
'Ithin the window, wi' the zide
　A-bound wi' rwoses out in flow'r,
Bezide the bow'r, vorsook o' birds,
An' listen'd to my true-love's words.

185

A-risèn to her comely height,
   She push'd the swingen ceäsement round;
And I could hear, beyond my zight,
   The win'-blow'd beech-tree softly sound,
On higher ground, a-swaÿen slow,
On drough my happy hour below.

An' tho' the darkness then did hide
   The dewy rwose's blushen bloom,
He still did cast sweet aïr inside
   To Jeäne, a-chatten in the room;
An' though the gloom did hide her feäce,
Her words did bind me to the pleäce.

An' there, while she, wi' runnen tongue,
   Did talk unzeen 'ithin the hall,
I thought her like the rwose that flung
   His sweetness vrom his darken'd ball,
'Ithout the wall, an' sweet's the zight
Ov her bright feäce by mornen light.

ZUMMER WINDS

Let me work, but mid noo tie
Hold me vrom the open sky,
When zummer winds, in plaÿsome flight,
Do blow on vields in noon-day light,
Or ruslen trees, in twilight night.
   Sweet's a stroll,
By flow'ry knowl, or blue-feäced pool
That zummer win's do ruffle cool.

When the moon's broad light do vill
Plaïns, a-sheenen down the hill,
A-glitteren on window glass,
O then, while zummer win's do pass
The rippled brook, an' swaÿen grass,
   Sweet's a walk,
Where we do talk, wi' feäces bright,
In whispers in the peacevul night.

When the swaÿen men do mow
Flow'ry grass, wi' zweepen blow,
In het a'most enough to dry
The flat-spread clote-leaf that do lie
Upon the stream a-stealen by,
    Sweet's their rest,
Upon the breast o' knap or mound
Out where the goocoo's vaïce do sound.

Where the sleek-heäir'd maïd do zit
Out o' door to zew or knit,
Below the elem where the spring
'S a-runnen, an' the road do bring
The people by to hear her zing,
    On the green,
Where she's a-zeen, an' she can zee,
O gaÿ is she below the tree.

Come, O zummer wind, an' bring
Sounds o' birds as they do zing,
An' bring the smell o' bloomen maÿ,
An' bring the smell o' new mow'd haÿ;
Come fan my feäce as I do straÿ,
    Fan the heäir
O' Jessie feäir; fan her cool,
By the weäves o' stream or pool.

ZUMMER STREAM

Ah! then the grassy-meäded Maÿ
Did warm the passen year, an' gleam
Upon the yollow-grounded stream,
That still by beech-tree sheädes do straÿ.
The light o' weäves, a-runnen there,
    Did plaÿ on leaves up over head,
An' vishes sceäly zides did gleäre,
    A-darten on the shallow bed,
An' like the stream a-sliden on,
My zun out-measur'd time's a-gone.

187

There by the path, in grass knee-high,
Wer buttervlees in giddy flight,
All white above the deäisies white,
Or blue below the deep blue sky.
Then glowen warm wer ev'ry brow,
  O' maïd, or man, in zummer het,
  An' warm did glow the cheäks I met
That time, noo mwore to meet em now.
As brooks, a-sliden on their bed,
My season-measur'd time's a-vled.

Vrom yonder window, in the thatch,
Did sound the maïdens' merry words,
As I did stand, by zingen birds,
Bezide the elem-sheäded hatch.
'Tis good to come back to the pleäce,
  Back to the time, to goo noo mwore;
'Tis good to meet the younger feäce
  A-menten others here avore.
As streams do glide by green meäd-grass,
My zummer-brighten'd years do pass.

LINDENORE

At Lindenore upon the steep,
  Bezide the trees a-reachen high,
The while their lower limbs do zweep
  The river-stream a-flowen by;
By grægle bells in beds o' blue,
Below the tree-stems in the lew,
Calm aïr do vind the rwose-bound door,
Ov Ellen Dare o' Lindenore.

An' there noo foam do hiss avore
  Swift bwoats, wi' water-plowen keels,
An' there noo broad high-road's a-wore
  By vur-brought trav'lers' cracklen wheels;
Noo crowd's a-passen to an' fro,
Upon the bridge's high-sprung bow:
An' vew but I do seek the door
Ov Ellen Dare o' Lindenore.

Vor there the town, wi' zun-bright walls,
  Do sheen vur off, by hills o' grey,
An' town-vo'k ha' but seldom calls
  O' business there, vrom day to day;
But Ellen didden leäve her ruf
To be admir'd, an' that's enough –
Vor I've a-vound 'ithin her door,
Feäir Ellen Dare o' Lindenore.

THE LOVE CHILD

Where the bridge out at Woodley did stride,
  Wi' his wide arches' cool sheäded bow,
Up above the clear brook that did slide
  By the poppies, befoam'd white as snow:
As the gil'cups did quiver among
  The white deäisies, a-spread in a sheet,
There a quick-trippen maïd come along, –
  Aye, a girl wi' her light-steppen veet.

An' she cried 'I do praÿ, is the road
  Out to Lincham on here, by the meäd?'
An' 'oh! ees,' I meäde answer, an' show'd
  Her the way it would turn an' would leäd:
'Goo along by the beech in the nook,
  Where the childern do plaÿ in the cool,
To the steppen stwones over the brook, –
  Aye, the grey blocks o' rock at the pool.'

'Then you don't seem a-born an' a-bred,'
  I spoke up, 'at a place here about;'
An' she answer'd wi' cheäks up so red
  As a pi'ny but leäte a-come out,
'No, I liv'd wi' my uncle that died
  Back in Eäpril, an' now I'm a-come
Here to Ham, to my mother, to bide, –
  Aye, to her house to vind a new hwome.'

I'm asheämed that I wanted to know
  Any mwore ov her childhood or life,
But then, why should so feäir a child grow
  Where noo father did bide wi' his wife;

Then wi' blushes ov zunrisèn morn,
    She replied that 'it midden be known,
Oh! they zent me away to be born, –
    Aye, they hid me when zome would be shown.'

Oh! it meäde me a'most teary-ey'd,
    An' I vound I a'most could ha' groan'd –
What! so winnen, an' still cast azide –
    What! so lovely, an' not to be own'd;
Oh! a God-gift a-treated wi' scorn,
    Oh! a child that a squier should own;
An' to zend her away to be born! –
    Aye, to hide her where others be shown!

TIMES O' YEAR

Here did swaÿ the eltrot flow'rs,
When the hours o' night wer vew,
An' the zun, wi' eärly beams
Brighten'd streams, an' dried the dew,
An' the goocoo there did greet
Passers by wi' dousty veet.

There the milkmaïd hung her brow
By the cow, a-sheenen red;
An' the dog, wi' upward looks,
Watch'd the rooks above his head,
An' the brook, vrom bow to bow,
Here went swift, an' there wer slow.

Now the cwolder-blowen blast,
Here do cast vrom elems' heads
Feäded leaves, a-whirlen round,
Down to ground, in yollow beds,
Ruslen under milkers' shoes,
When the day do dry the dews.

Soon shall grass, a-vrosted bright,
Glisten white instead o' green,
An' the wind shall smite the cows,
Where the boughs be now their screen.
Things do change as years do vlee;
What ha' years in store vor me?

ZUMMER AN' WINTER

When I led by zummer streams
   The pride o' Lea, as naïghbours thought her,
While the zun, wi' evenen beams,
   Did cast our sheädes athirt the water;
     Winds a-blowen,
     Streams a-flowen,
     Skies a-glowen,
Tokens ov my jaÿ zoo fleeten,
Heighten'd it, that happy meeten.

Then, when maïd an' man took pleäces,
   Gaÿ in winter's Chris'mas dances,
Showen in their merry feäces
   Kindly smiles an' glisnen glances;
     Stars a-winken,
     Days a-shrinken,
     Sheädes a-zinken,
Brought anew the happy meeten,
That did meäke the night too fleeten.

TO ME

At night, as drough the meäd I took my waÿ,
In aïr a-sweeten'd by the new-meäde haÿ,
A stream a-vallèn down a rock did sound,
   Though out o' zight wer foam an' stwone to me.

Behind the knap, above the gloomy copse,
The wind did russle in the trees' high tops,
Though evenen darkness, an' the risèn hill,
   Kept all the quiv'ren leaves unshown to me.

Within the copse, below the zunless sky,
I heärd a nightengeäle, a-warblen high
Her lwoansome zong, a-hidden vrom my zight,
   An' showen nothen but her mwoan to me.

An' by a house, where rwoses hung avore
The thatch-brow'd window, an' the open door,
I heärd the merry words, an' hearty laugh
   O' zome feäir maïd, as eet unknown to me.

High over head the white-rimm'd clouds went on,
Wi' woone a-comen up, vor woone a-gone;
An' feäir they floated in their sky-back'd flight,
But still they never meäde a sound to me.

An' there the miller, down the stream did float
Wi' all his childern, in his white-saïl'd bwoat,
Vur off, beyond the stragglen cows in meäd,
But zent noo vaïce, athirt the ground, to me.

An' then a buttervlee, in zultry light,
A-wheelen on about me, vier-bright,
Did show the gaÿest colors to my eye,
But still did bring noo vaïce around to me.

I met the merry laugher on the down,
Bezide her mother, on the path to town,
An' oh! her sheäpe wer comely to the zight,
But wordless then wer she a-vound to me.

Zoo, sweet ov unzeen things mid be the sound,
An' feäir to zight mid soundless things be vound,
But I've the laugh to hear, an' feäce to zee,
Vor they be now my own, a-bound to me.

TOKENS

Green mwold on zummer bars do show
   That they've a-dripp'd in Winter wet;
The hoof-worn ring o' groun' below
   The tree, do tell o' storms or het;
The trees in rank along a ledge
Do show where woonce did bloom a hedge;
An' where the vurrow-marks do stripe
The down, the wheat woonce rustled ripe.
Each mark ov things a-gone vrom view –
To eyezight's woone, to soulzight two.

The grass ageän the mwoldren door
   'S a token sad o' vo'k a-gone,
An' where the house, bwoth wall an' vloor,
   'S a-lost, the well mid linger on.
What tokens, then, could Meäry gi'e

That she'd a–liv'd, an' liv'd vor me,
But things a–done vor thought an' view?
Good things that nwone ageän can do,
An' every work her love ha' wrought,
To eyezight's woone, but two to thought.

TWEIL

The rick ov our last zummer's haulen
  Now vrom grey's a–feäded dark,
An' off the barken raïl's a–vallèn,
  Day by day, the rottèn bark. –
But short's the time our works do stand,
So feäir's we put em out ov hand.
Vor time a–passen, wet an' dry,
Do spweil em wi' his changen sky,
The while wi' strivèn hope, we men,
  Though a–ruen time's undoen,
Still do tweil an' tweil ageän.

In wall–zide sheädes, by leafy bowers,
  Underneath the swaÿen tree,
O' leäte as round the bloomen flowers,
  Lowly humm'd the giddy bee,
My childern's small left voot did smite
Their tiny speäde, the while the right
Did trample on a deäisy head,
Bezide the flower's dousty bed,
An' though their work wer idle then,
  They a–smilen, an' a–tweilen,
Still did work an' work ageän.

Now their little limbs be stronger,
  Deeper now their vaïce do sound;
An' their little veet be longer,
  An' do tread on other ground;
An' rust is on the little bleädes
Ov all the broken–hafted speädes,
An' flow'rs that wer my hope an' pride
Ha' long agoo a–bloom'd an' died,
But still as I did leäbor then
  Vor love ov all them childern small,
Zoo now I'll tweil an' tweil ageän.

193

When the smokeless tun's a-growen
  Cwold as dew below the stars,
An' when the vier noo mwore's a-glowen
  Red between the window bars,
We then do lay our weary heads
In peace upon their nightly beds,
An' gi'e woone sock, wi' heaven breast,
An' then breathe soft the breath o' rest,
Till day do call the sons o' men
  Vrom night-sleep's blackness, vull o' sprackness,
Out abroad to tweil ageän.

Where the vaïce o' winds is mildest,
  In the plaïn, their stroke is keen;
Where their dreatnen vaïce is wildest,
  In the grove, the grove's our screen.
An' where the worold in their strife
Do dreaten mwost our tweilsome life,
Why there Almighty ceäre mid cast
A better screen ageän the blast.
Zoo I woon't live in fear o' men,
  But, man-neglected, God-directed,
Still wull tweil an' tweil ageän.

EVENEN LIGHT

The while I took my bit o' rest,
  Below my house's eastern sheäde,
  The things that stood in vield an' gleäde
Wer bright in zunsheen vrom the west.
  There bright wer eastward mound an' wall,
  An' bright wer trees, a-risèn tall,
An' bright did break 'ithin the brook,
  Down rocks, the watervall.

There deep 'ithin my pworches bow
  Did hang my heavy woaken door,
  An' in beyond en, on the vloor,
The evenen dusk did gather slow;
  But bright did gleäre the twinklen spwokes
  O' runnen carriage wheels, as vo'ks
Out east did ride along the road,
  Bezide the low-bough'd woaks.

An' I'd a-lost the zun vrom view,
    Until ageän his feäce mid rise,
    A-sheenen vrom the eastern skies
To brighten up the rwose-borne dew;
    But still his lingren light did gi'e
    My heart a touchen jaÿ, to zee
His beams a-shed, wi' stratchen sheäde,
    On eastward wall an' tree.

When jaÿ, a-zent me vrom above,
    Vrom my sad heart is now a-gone,
    An' others be a-walken on,
Amid the light ov Heaven's love,
    Oh! then vor loven-kindness seäke,
    Mid I rejaïce that zome to teäke
My hopes a-gone, until ageän
    My happy dawn do breäk.

VIELDS BY WATERVALLS

When our downcast looks be smileless,
    Under others' wrongs an' slightens,
When our daily deeds be guileless,
    An' do meet unkind requitens,
You can meäke us zome amends
Vor wrongs o' foes, an' slights o' friends; –
O flow'ry-gleäded, timber-sheäded
Vields by flowen watervalls!

Here be softest aïrs a-blowen
    Drough the boughs, wi' zingen drushes,
Up above the streams, a-flowen
    Under willows, on by rushes.
Here below the bright-zunn'd sky
The dew-bespangled flow'rs do dry,
In woody-zided, stream-divided
Vields by flowen watervalls.

Waters, wi' their giddy rollens,
    Breezes wi' their plaÿsome wooens,
Here do heal, in soft consolens,
    Hearts a-wrung wi' man's wrong doens.

Day do come to us as gaÿ
As to a king of widest swaÿ,
In deäisy-whiten'd, gil'cup-brighten'd
Vields by flowen watervalls.

Zome feäir buds mid outlive blightens,
    Zome sweet hopes mid outlive sorrow;
After days ov wrongs an' slightens
    There mid break a happy morrow.
We mid have noo e'thly love;
But God's love-tokens vrom above
Here mid meet us, here mid greet us,
In the vields by watervalls.

FALL TIME

The gather'd clouds, a-hangen low,
    Do meäke the woody ridge look dim;
An' raïn-vill'd streams do brisker flow,
    A-risèn higher to their brim.
In the tree, vrom lim' to lim',
    Leaves do drop
Vrom the top, all slowly down,
Yollow, to the gloomy groun'.

The rick's a-tipp'd an' weather-brown'd,
    An' thatch'd wi' zedge a-dried an' dead;
An' orcha'd apples, red half round,
    Have all a-happer'd down, a-shed
Underneath the trees' wide head.
    Ladders long,
Rong by rong, to clim' the tall
Trees, be hung upon the wall.

The crumpled leaves be now a-shed
    In mornen winds a-blowen keen;
When they wer green the moss wer dead,
    Now they be dead the moss is green.
Low the evenen zun do sheen
    By the boughs,
Where the cows do swing their taïls
Over merry milkers' païls.

THE ZILVER-WEED

The zilver-weed upon the green,
   Out where my sons an' daughters plaÿ'd,
Had never time to bloom between
   The litty steps o' bwoy an' maïd.
But rwose-trees down along the wall,
   That then wer all the maïdens' ceäre,
An' all a-trimm'd an' traïn'd, did bear
   Their bloomen buds vrom Spring to Fall.

But now the zilver leaves do show
   To zummer day their goolden crown,
Wi' noo swift shoe-zoles' litty blow,
   In merry plaÿ to beät em down.
An' where vor years zome busy hand
   Did traïn the rwoses wide an' high;
Now woone by woone the trees do die,
   An' vew of all the row do stand.

THE FANCY FEAIR AT MAIDEN
NEWTON

The Frome, wi' ever-water'd brink,
Do run where shelven hills do zink
Wi' housen all a-cluster'd roun'
The parish tow'rs below the down.
An' now, vor woonce, at leäst, ov all
The pleäcen where the stream do vall,
There's woone that zome to-day mid vind,
Wi' things a-suited to their mind,
   An' that's out where the Fancy Feäir
   Is on at Maïden Newton.

An' vo'k, a-smarten'd up, wull hop
Out here, as ev'ry traïn do stop,
Vrom up the line, a longish ride,
An' down along the river-zide.
An' zome do beät, wi' heels an' tooes,
The leänes an' paths, in nimble shoes,

An' bring, bezides, a biggish knot,
Ov all their childern that can trot,
  A-vlocken where the Fancy Feäir
  Is here at Maïden Newton.

If you should go, to–day, avore
A Chilfrome house or Downfrome door,
Or Frampton's park-zide row, or look
Drough quiet Wraxall's slopy nook,
Or elbow-streeted Catt'stock, down
By Castlehill's cwold-winded crown,
An' zee if vo'k be all at hwome,
You'd vind em out – they be a–come
  Out hither, where the Fancy Feäir
  Is on at Maïden Newton.

Come, young men, come, an' here you'll vind
A gift to please a maïden's mind;
Come, husbands, here be gifts to please
Your wives, an' meäke em smile vor days;
Come, so's, an' buy at Fancy Feäir
A keepseäke vor your friends elsewhere;
You can't but stop an' spend a cwein
Wi' leädies that ha' goods so fine;
  An' all to meäke, vor childern's seäke,
  The School at Maïden Newton.

I'M OUT O' DOOR

I'm out, when, in the Winter's blast,
  The zun, a-runnen lowly round,
Do mark the sheädes the hedge do cast
  At noon, in hoarvrost, on the ground.
I'm out when snow's a-lyen white
  In keen-aïr'd vields that I do pass,
An' moonbeams, vrom above, do smite
  On ice an' sleeper's window-glass.
    I'm out o' door,
    When win' do zweep,
    By hangen steep,
    Or hollow deep,
      At Lindenore.

198

O welcome is the lewth a–vound
  By rustlen copse, or ivied bank,
Or by the haÿ–rick, weather–brown'd
  By barken–grass, a–springen rank;
Or where the waggon, vrom the team
  A–freed, is well a–housed vrom wet,
An' on the dousty cart–house beam
  Do hang the cobweb's white–lin'd net;
    While storms do roar,
    An' win' do zweep,
    By hangen steep,
    Or hollow deep,
      At Lindenore.

An' when a good day's work 's a–done
  An' I do rest, the while a squall
Do rumble in the hollow tun,
  An' ivy–stems do whip the wall,
Then in the house do sound about
  My ears, dear vaïces vull or thin,
A–praÿen vor the souls vur out
  At sea, an' cry wi' bibb'ren chin –
    Oh! shut the door.
    What soul can sleep,
    Upon the deep,
    When storms do zweep
      At Lindenore.

SLIDEN

  When wind wer keen,
  Where ivy green
  Did clwosely wind
  Roun' woak–tree rind,
    An' ice shone bright,
An' meäds wer white, wi' thin–spread snow,
  Then on the pond, a–spreaden wide,
  We bwoys did zweep along the slide,
A–striken on in merry row.

199

There ruddy-feäced,
In busy heäste,
We all did wag
A spanken lag,
To win good speed,
When we, straïght-knee'd, wi' voreright tooes,
  Should shoot along the slipp'ry track,
  Wi' grinden sound, a-getten slack,
The slower went our clumpen shoes.

Vor zome slow chap,
Did teäke mishap,
As he did veel
His hinder heel
A-het a thump,
Wi' zome big lump, o' voot an' shoe.
  Down vell the voremost wi' a squall,
  An' down the next went wi' a sprawl,
An' down went all the laughen crew.

As to an' fro,
In merry row,
We all went round
On ice, on ground,
The maïdens nigh,
A-stannen shy, did zee us slide,
  An' in their eäprons small, did vwold
  Their little hands, a-got red-cwold,
Or slide on ice o' two veet wide.

By leafless copse,
An' beäre tree-tops,
An' zun's low beams,
An' ice-boun' streams,
An' vrost-boun' mill,
A-stannen still, come wind, blow on,
  An' gi'e the bwoys, this Chris'mas tide,
  The glitt'ren ice to meäke a slide,
As we had our slide, years agone.

THE HUMSTRUM

Why woonce, at Chris'mas-tide, avore
The wold year wer a-reckon'd out,
The humstrums here did come about,
A-sounden up at ev'ry door.
But now a bow do never screäpe
   A humstrum, any where all round,
An' zome can't tell a humstrum's sheäpe,
   An' never heärd his jinglen sound,
As *ing-an-ing* did ring the string,
As *ang-an-ang* the wires did clang.

The strings a-tighten'd lik' to crack
Athirt the canister's tin zide,
Did reach, a-glitt'ren, zide by zide,
Above the humstrum's hollow back.
An' there the bwoy, wi' bended stick,
   A-strung wi' heäir, to meäke a bow,
Did dreve his elbow, light'nen quick,
   Athirt the strings vrom high to low,
As *ing-an-ing* did ring the string,
As *ang-an-ang* the wires did clang.

The mother there did stan' an' hush
Her child, to hear the jinglen sound,
The merry maïd, a-scrubben round
Her white-steäv'd païl, did stop her brush.
The mis'ess there, vor wold time's seäke,
   Had gifts to gi'e, and smiles to show,
An' meäster, too, did stan' an' sheäke
   His two broad zides, a-chucklen low,
While *ing-an-ing* did ring the string,
While *ang-an-ang* the wires did clang.

The plaÿers' pockets wer a-strout,
Wi' wold brown pence, a-rottlen in,
Their zwangen bags did soon begin,
Wi' brocks an' scraps, to plim well out.

The childern all did run an' poke
　　Their heads vrom hatch or door, an' shout
A-runnen back to wolder vo'k,
　　'Why, here! the humstrums be about!'
As *ing-an-ing* did ring the string,
As *ang-an-ang* the wires did clang.

SHAFTESBURY FEAIR

When hillborne Paladore did show
So bright to me down miles below,
As woonce the zun, a-rollen west,
Did brighten up his hill's high breast,
Wi' walls a-looken dazzlen white,
Or yollow, on the grey-topp'd height
Ov Paladore, as peäle day wore
　　　Away so feäir;
Oh! how I wish'd that I wer there.

The pleäce wer too vur off to spy
The liven vo'k a-passen by;
The vo'k too vur vor aïr to bring
The words that they did speak or zing.
All dum' to me wer each abode,
An' empty wer the down-hill road
Vrom Paladore, as peäle day wore
　　　Away so feäir,
But how I wish'd that I wer there.

But when I clomb the lofty ground
Where liven veet an' tongues did sound,
At feäir, bezide your bloomen feäce,
The pertiest in all the pleäce,
As you did look, wi' eyes as blue
As yonder southern hills in view,
Vrom Paladore – O Polly dear,
　　　Wi' you up there,
How merry then wer I at feäir.

Since vu'st I trod thik steep hill-zide
My grieven soul 'v a-been a-tried
Wi' païn, an' loss o' worldly gear,
An' souls a-gone I wanted near;

But you be here to goo up still,
An' look to Blackmwore vrom the hill
O' Paladore. Zoo, Polly dear,
     We'll goo up there,
An' spend an hour or two at feäir.

The wold brown meäre's a–brought vrom grass,
An' rubb'd an' cwomb'd so bright as glass;
An' now we'll hitch her in, an' start
To feäir upon the new green cart,
An' teäke our little Poll between
Our zides, as proud's a little queen,
To Paladore. Aye, Poll a dear,
     Vor now 'tis feäir,
An' she's a–longen to goo there.

While Paladore, on watch, do straïn
Her eyes to Blackmwore's blue-hill'd plaïn,
While Duncliffe is the traveller's mark,
Or cloty Stour's a–rollen dark;
Or while our bells do call, vor greäce,
The vo'k avore their Seävior's feäce,
Mid Paladore, an' Poll a dear,
     Vor ever know
O' peace and plenty down below.

DANIEL DWITHEN, THE WISE CHAP

Dan Dwithen wer the chap to show
His naïghbours mwore than they did know,
Vor he could zee, wi' half a thought,
What zome could hardly be a–taught;
     An' he had never any doubt
Whatever 'twer, but he did know't,
An' had a–reach'd the bottom o't,
     Or soon could meäke it out.

Wi' narrow feäce, an' nose so thin
That light a'most shone drough the skin,
As he did talk, wi' his red peäir
O' lips, an' his vull eyes did steäre,

203

What nippy looks friend Daniel wore,
An' how he smiled as he did bring
Such reasons vor to clear a thing,
   As dather'd vo'k the mwore!

When woonce there come along the road
At night, zome show-vo'k, wi' a lwoad
Ov half the wild outlandish things
That crawl'd, or went wi' veet, or wings,
   Their elephant, to stratch his knees,
Walk'd up the road-zide turf, an' left
His tracks a-zunk wi' all his heft
   As big's a vinny cheese.

An' zoo next mornen zome vo'k vound
The girt round tracks upon the ground,
An' view'd em all wi' stedvast eyes,
An' wi' their vingers spann'd their size,
   An' took their depth below the brink:
An' whether they mid be the tracks
O' things wi' witches on their backs,
   Or what, they coulden think.

At last friend Dan come up, an' brought
His wit to help their dizzy thought,
An' looken on an' off the e'th
He cried, a-drawen a vull breath,
   Why, I do know; what, can't ye zee't?
I'll bet a shillen 'twer a deer
Broke out o' park, an' sprung on here,
   Wi' quoits upon his veet.

JOHN BLOOM IN LONDON
(All true)

John Bloom he wer a jolly soul,
   A grinder o' the best o' meal,
Bezide a river that did roll,
   Vrom week to week, to push his wheel.
His flour wer all a-meäde o' wheat;
An' fit for bread that vo'k mid eat;
Vor he would starve avore he'd cheat.

''Tis pure,' woone woman cried;
'Aye, sure,' woone mwore replied;
'You'll vind it nice. Buy woonce, buy twice,'
Cried worthy Bloom the miller.

Athirt the chest he wer so wide
   As two or dree ov me or you,
An' wider still vrom zide to zide,
   An' I do think still thicker drough.
Vall down, he coulden, he did lie
When he wer up on zide so high
As up on end or perty nigh.
'Meäke room,' woone naïghbour cried;
''Tis Bloom,' woone mwore replied;
'Good morn t'ye all, bwoth girt an' small,'
Cried worthy Bloom the miller.

Noo stings o' conscience ever broke
   His rest, a-twiten o'n wi' wrong,
Zoo he did sleep till mornen broke,
   An' birds did call en wi' their zong.
But he did love a harmless joke,
An' love his evenen whiff o' smoke,
A-zitten in his cheäir o' woak.
'Your cup,' his daughter cried;
'Vill'd up,' his wife replied;
'Aye, aye; a drap avore my nap,'
Cried worthy Bloom the miller.

When Lon'on vo'k did meäke a show
   O' their girt glassen house woone year,
An' people went, bwoth high an' low,
   To zee the zight, vrom vur an' near,
'O well,' cried Bloom, 'why I've a right
So well's the rest to zee the zight;
I'll goo, an' teäke the raïl outright.'
'Your feäre,' the booker cried;
'There, there,' good Bloom replied;
'Why this June het do meäke woone zweat,'
Cried worthy Bloom the miller.

Then up the guard did whissle sh'ill,
    An' then the engine pank'd a blast,
An' rottled on so loud's a mill,
    Avore the traïn, vrom slow to vast.
An' oh! at last how they did spank
By cutten deep, an' high-cast bank
The while their iron ho'se did pank.
'Do whizzy,' woone o'm cried;
'I'm dizzy,' woone replied;
'Aye, here's the road to hawl a lwoad,'
Cried worthy Bloom the miller.

In Lon'on John zent out to call
    A tidy trap, that he mid ride
To zee the glassen house, an' all
    The lot o' things a-stow'd inside.
'Here, Boots, come here,' cried he, 'I'll dab
A zixpence in your han' to nab
Down street a tidy little cab.'
'A feäre,' the boots then cried;
'I'm there,' the man replied;
'The glassen pleäce, your quickest peäce,'
Cried worthy Bloom the miller.

The steps went down wi' rottlen slap,
    The swingen door went open wide:
Wide? no; vor when the worthy chap
    Stepp'd up to teäke his pleäce inside,
Breast-voremost, he wer twice too wide
Vor thik there door. An' then he tried
To edge in woone an' tother zide.
''Twon't do,' the drever cried;
'Can't goo,' good Bloom replied;
'That you should bring theäse vooty thing!'
Cried worthy Bloom the miller.

'Come,' cried the drever, 'pay your feäre;
    You'll teäke up all my time, good man.'
'Well,' answer'd Bloom, 'to meäke that square,
    You teäke up me, then, if you can.'
'I come at call,' the man did nod.
'What then?' cried Bloom, 'I han't a-rod,
An' can't in thik there hodmadod.'

206

'Girt lump,' the drever cried;
'Small stump,' good Bloom replied;
'A little mite, to meäke so light,
O' jolly Bloom the miller.'

'You'd best be off now perty quick,'
    Cried Bloom, 'an' vind a lighter lwoad,
Or else I'll vetch my voot, an' kick
    The vooty thing athirt the road.'
'Who is the man?' they cried, 'meäke room,'
A halfstarv'd Do'set man,' cried Bloom;
'You be?' another cried;
'Hee! Hee!' woone mwore replied.
'Aye, shrunk so thin, to bwone an' skin,'
Cried worthy Bloom the miller.

SHOP O' MEAT-WEARE
WI' CHILDERN AN' OTHER VO'KS IN HOUSE

A-zellen meat-weäre I shall get noo meat,
I mussen keep a shop o' weäres to eat.
I have zome goods, but I do hardly think
They be a-zwold so vast as they do shrink.
I have zome goods, but zomehow all my stocks
Do weäste away lik' camphor in a box.
Hand after han' do come, and slily clips
A bit an' bit to veed zome peäir o' lips.
You vo'k in house don't waït vor gaïn o' treäde,
But teäke the store avore the gaïn's a-meäde.
I had zome aggs, an' I do miss zome aggs,
An' I don't think they went 'ithout zome lags.
I had zome aggs, an' zome ha' left my store,
But I don't think they travell'd out o' door.
I ha'n't a-got zome aggs that oonce wer mine,
But I don't think they brought me any cwein.
I bought zome aggs, as I do know vull well;
I bought zome aggs, but now ha' nwone to zell.

THE KNOWL

Oh hwome, vo'k do tell us, is hwome
    be it never so hwomely,
An' Meldon's the hwome where my elders
    do sleep by the knowl.

An' there they've a-left me a liven
　　o' land, where, in zummer,
The haÿ, a-dried grey, is a-stannen
　　in heap by the knowl.

An' there, in the bright-bleäded eegrass,
　　or bennets, in Fall-time
My cows do lie down where the river
　　do creep by the knowl.

An' up on the slope o' the hangen,
　　by white-rinded ash-trees,
Be linches o' grass an' o' thyme-beds,
　　wi' sheep by the knowl.

An' down on the west o' my house
　　is a rook'ry, a-rocken
In trees that be lewth vrom the wind
　　that do zweep by the knowl.

An' there I have windows a-looken
　　to viersky'd zunzet,
An' others a-zet where the mornen
　　do peep by the knowl.

An' though there is noo pleäce but heaven
　　without any sorrow,
An' I, like my naïghbours, in trial
　　mid weep by the knowl,

Still, while I mid vill, like an hirelen,
　　the day ov my leäbour,
I'd wish, if my wish idden wicked,
　　to keep by the knowl.

Zoo if you do vind a day empty
　　o' work, wi' fine weather,
An' don't mind the leäbour o' climmen
　　the steep by the knowl,

Come up, an' we'll meäke ourzelves merry
　　vor woonce all together;
You'll vind that your bed an' your bwoard
　　shall be cheap by the knowl.

AT THE DOOR

The stream do roll,
　　A–bubblen by the shoal,
Or leäp the rock, a-foamen in a bow;
The win' do vlee,
　　A-playen roun' the tree,
Along the grove o' woaks, in double row,
Where love do seek the maïdens' evenen vloor,
Wi' stip–step light, an tip-tap slight,
　　　Ageän the door.

Wi' iron bound,
　　The wheels, a–rollen round,
Do crunch the cracklen vlint below their lwoad;
The stwones a-trod
　　By horses iron-shod
Do shockle shrill along the trotted road,
Where chaps do come to seek, in our wold pleäce,
Wi' stip–step light, an' tip-tap slight,
　　　The maïdens' feäce.

And oh! how sweet
　　'S the time a lover's veet
Do come avore the door to vind a bride,
As he do stand,
　　An' knock wi' litty hand,
An' leän to catch the sweetest vaïce inside;
While there a heart do leäp to hear woonce mwore
Wi' stip–step light, an' tip-tap slight,
　　　Ageän the door.

How sweet's the time,
　　When we be in our prime,
An' childern be our hope and aye our jaÿ;
An' child by child
　　Do come, a-skippen wild,
Back hwome vrom daily school, or vrom their plaÿ,
So small upon the doorstwone, well a-wore,
Wi' stip–step light, an' tip-tap slight,
　　　Ageän the door.

Be my abode
    Bezide zome uphill road,
Where vo'k mid pass, but not vor ever bide;
An' not a pleäce
    Where day do bring noo feäce
Wi' kindly smiles, as lwonesome hours do glide;
But let me hear zome friend a-known avore,
Wi' stip-step light, an' tip-tap slight,
        Ageän the door.

HILL OR DELL

At John's, up on Zand-hill, 'tis healthy an' dry,
Though I midden like it, i'-may-be, not I.
Where vir-trees do spindle, wi' teäperen tops,
Vrom leafy-leav'd vern, in the cwold-stunted copse,
An' under sharp vuzzen, all yollow in blooth,
The sky-lark's brown nest is a-hid in the lewth;
An' high on the cliff, where noo voot ever wore
A path to the drashold, 's the zandmartin's door,
On waterless heights, where the wind do stream by,
A-sighen by ivy, avore the blue sky.

I do think I could teäke vor the best o' the two
My timber-screen'd hwome, here below in the lew;
Where rooks be a-builden in high elem boughs
An' broadheaded woaks be a-sheäde vor the cows;
Where greyheaded withies do leän by the feäce
O' greylighted waters, a-slackenen their peäce,
An' only the maïdens an' swans be in white,
Like snow on grey moss in the mid-winter's light,
An' wind do dreve on, wi' a low-russlen sound,
By weäves on the water, an' grass on the ground.

FELLOWSHIP

Well! here we be, woonce mwore at leäst,
A-come along, wi' blinken zight,
By smeechy doust a-vlee-en white
Up off the road, to Lincham feäst,

Bwoth maïd an' man, in dousty shoes,
Wi' trudgen steps o' trampen tooes,
Though we, that mussen hope to ride,
Vor ease or pride, have fellowship.

Poor father always tried to show
Our vo'k, wi' hands o' right or left
A-pull'd by zome big errand's heft,
An' veet a-trudgen to an' fro,
That rich vo'k be but woone in ten,
A-reckon'd out wi' worken men,
An' zoo have less, the while the poor
Ha' ten times mwore o' fellowship.

An' he did think, whatever peärt
We have to plaÿ, we all do vind
That fellowship o' kind wi' kind
Do keep us better up in heart;
An' why should worken vo'k be shy
O' work, wi' all a-worken by,
While kings do live in lwonesome steätes,
Wi' nwone vor meätes in fellowship?

Tall tuns above the high-flown larks,
On houses, lugs in length, an' zights
O' windows, that do gleäre in lights
A-shot up slopes ov woodbound parks,
Be vur an' wide, an' not so thick
As poor men's little hwomes o' brick,
By twos or drees, or else in row
So small an' low, in fellowship.

But we, wherever we do come,
Ha' fellowship o' hands wi' lwoads,
An' fellowship o' veet on roads;
An' lowliness ov house an' hwome;
An' fellowship in hwomely feäre,
An' hwomely clothes vor daily wear;
An' zoo mid Heaven bless the mwore
The worken poor wi' fellowship.

AIR AN' LIGHT

Ah! look an' zee how widely free
To all the land the win' do goo;
If here a tree do swaÿ, a tree
On yon'er hill's a-swaÿen too.
How wide the light do bring to zight
The pleäce an' liven feäce o' man;
How vur the stream do run vor lip
To drink, or hand to sink and dip!

But oone mid be a-smote wi' woe
That midden pass, in wider flight,
To other souls, a-droopen low,
An' hush'd like birds at vall o' night.
But zome be sad wi' others glad;
In turn we all mid murn our lot,
An' many a day that have a-broke
Oone heart is jaÿ to other vo'k.

The mornen zun do cast abroad
His light on drops o' dewy wet,
An' down below his noontide road
The streams do gleäre below his het;
His evenen light do sparkle bright
Across the quiv'ren gossamer;
But I, though fair he still mid glow,
Do miss a zight he cannot show.

MELDON HILL

I took the road wi' dousty vloor
So well a-wore, at Meldon Hill,
Along the knap wi' woody crown
A-slopen down, at Meldon Hill;
While zunlight overshot the copse
Ov underwood wi' brown-twigg'd tops,
By sky-belighted stream an' pool
A-whirlen cool, by Meldon Hill.

An' down below wer many zights
O' yollow lights, by Meldon Hill;
The trees above the brindled cows,
Wi' budden boughs, by Meldon Hill;
An' bridged roads an' watervalls,
An' house by house wi' zunny walls,
An' oone where zomebody mid come
To my own hwome, vrom Meldon Hill.

Whenever I do come to clim'
The hill's high rim, to Meldon Hill,
By elems over twisten smoke,
Or lwonesome woak, to Meldon Hill,
How much I have to tell about;
An' soon mid this good news come out:
That I've a house vor Jeäne to guide,
A-meäde my bride, vrom Meldon Hill.

BLACK AN' WHITE

By the wall o' the geärden, a-stannen chalk white
In the light o' the moon, back in Maÿ,
There wer you all in black at my zide, a-come round
On the ground where the cypress did swaÿ:
Oh! the white an' the black! Which wer feäirest to view?
Why the black, a-meäde feäirest on you.

By the water, a-vallèn in many a bow
White as snow, down the rock's peaky steep,
There your own petted cow wer a-showen her back
O' deep black, a-laid down vor her sleep:
Ah! the white an' the black! Which wer feäirest to view?
Why the black, a-meäde feäirest on you.

When you stroll'd down the village, a-walken bedight
All in white, at the leäte evenen tide,
The while *Towsy*, your own loven dog, wi' his back
Sleeky black, did walk on at your zide:
Ah! the black an' the white! Which wer feäirest to view?
Why the white, a-meäde feäirest on you.

At the end o' the barken the granary stood,
O' black wood, wi' white geese at his zide,
An' the white-winged swans, on the quick-runnen weäve,
By the cave o' black darkness did glide:
Ah! the black an' the white! Which wer feäirest to view?
Why the white, a-meäde feäirest on you.

CLOUDS

A-riden slow, at lofty height,
  Wer clouds, a-blown along the sky,
O' purple-blue, an' pink, an' white,
  In pack an' pile, a-reachen high,
A-shiften off, as they did goo,
  Their sheapes vrom new ageän to new.

An' zome like rocks an' tow'rs o' stwone,
  Or hills or woods, a-reachen wide;
An' zome like roads, wi' doust a-blown,
  A-glitt'ren white up off their zide,
A-comen bright, ageän to feäde
  In sheäpes a-meäde to be unmeäde.

Zoo things do come, but never stand,
  In life. It mid be smiles or tears,
A jaÿ in hope, an' one in hand,
  Zome grounds o' grief, an' zome o' fears;
It mid be good, or mid be ill,
  But never long a-standen still.

THE WIND A-PLAYEN ROUND

How gaïly feäir the flow'ry land
In gleäre o' zummer light did look,
While roamen cows did stalk by meäds
Or brows o' leäzes by the brook;
An' wind did whirl an' curl,
An' zweep by streeches roun' our head
A smeech at ev'ry blast, a peck
At once, or spring wi' haÿ in meäd,
An' fling it up on Jenny's neck,
A-playen round the zummer ground.

As water flow'd below our veet
An' show'd our sheädes in line an' hue,
A gust awoke in sudden flight
An' broke em up away vrom view,
In playsome whirl an' curl.
An' while, wi' darksome sheäde, the zun
Did mark our sheäpe within the gleäde,
The wind brought by a sheäden cloud
On high, an' hid em, sheäde wi' sheäde,
A-streamen soft, wi' clouds aloft.

O winds to roll the thistledown
By knowl or meäd, in zummer light,
Or else to blow, in winter days,
The snow ageän my blinded zight,
Wi' many a whirl an' curl;
Or under rock or smooth-wall'd tow'r
To mock my zong, or ment my call,
Or sway drough hours o' lwonesome night
My flow'rs in bloom, by ground or wall;
Come but soft, an' then come oft.

THE PARRICK

Within the parrick in the lew,
By high-shot elem-trees a-bound,
Where wind drough upper boughs did goo
But hardly zweep so low's the ground,
    By bough, by cow,
Wi' païl an' stool, when wind wer cool,
    We zot in parrick in the lew.

An' there as evenen sheädes did vall
Vrom elems in the western rank,
Or else as moonlight vrom the tall
Stemm'd trees did reach the eastern bank,
    By ledge, by hedge,
We then did walk, or zit in talk,
    Within the parrick in the lew.

Where bright by day the grass do look,
Where cool the sheäde do veel at noon,
Where dark is still our sheädy nook,
Where peäles the groun' below the moon,
    By brook, or nook,
Why I could do wi' only two
  Within the parrick in the lew.

BY THE MILL IN SPRING

The win' did blow, the water flow,
Did flow along the gravel stwone,
The weäves wer bright, the cliffs wer white,
Wer white avore the zetten zun,
Where sheäkèn zedge did softly sigh
As you, wi' windblown locks, went by.

The lambs did swing their taïls an' spring,
Did spring about the groun', chalk white,
The smoke wer blue above the yew,
The yew bezide your house in zight;
An' win' did zing wi' sullen sound
Ageän the trees upon the mound.

Where down at mill the wheel wer still,
Wer still an' dripp'd wi' glitt'ren tears,
Wi' dousty poll, up leäne did stroll
The miller's man wi' mill-stunn'd ears;
Where weakly waïlen win' did zwim
By ground wi' ivy'd elems dim.

My work an' way mid faïl or fay,
Or fay as days do vreeze or glow;
I'll try to bear my tweil or ceäre,
Or ceäre along wi' friend or foe,
If, after all, the evenen tide
Do bring me peace where I do bide.

SHELLBROOK

Then out at Shellbrook, roun' by stile an' tree,
Wi' longer days an' zunny hours a-come,
Wi' spring an' all the zunny show'rs a-come,
Wi' Maÿ an' all its sheenen flow'rs a-come,
How sweet vor young wi' young to meet in glee.

An' there how we in merry talk did goo
By foam below the river baÿ, all white,
By blossom on the green-leaved Maÿ, all white,
By chalk bezide the dousty waÿ, all white,
Where glitt'ren waters match'd the sky wi' blue.

Or else in winden paths by vield or drong,
We over knaps a-slopen steep did wind,
Or down the dells a-zinken deep did wind,
Or where the benden brook did zweep did wind,
All young wi' young in merry laugh or zong.

But now the winter-vrozen churchyard wall do keep
The plot o' tower-sheäded ground all white,
Where friends can vind the vrosted mound, all white,
Wi' turf a-zwellen up so round, all white,
Wi' young a-sunder'd vrom the young in sleep.

RINGS

A veäiry ring so round's the zun
    In summer leäze did show his rim,
An' near, at hand, the weäves did run
    Athirt the pond wi' rounded brim:
An' there by round built ricks ov haÿ,
    By het a-burn'd, by zuns a-brown'd,
We all in merry ring did plaÿ,
    A-springen on, a-wheelen round.

As there a stwone that we did fling
    Did zweep, in flight, a lofty bow,
An' vell in water, ring by ring
    O' weäves bespread the pool below,
Bezide the bridge's arch, that sprung
    Between the banks, within the brims,
Where swung the lowly benden swing,
    On elem boughs, on mossy limbs.

MOTHER O' MOTHERS

By zummer an' fall, an' by tide upon tide,
The apple-tree stem do leän lower azide,
An' the loosenen bricks out in orcha'd do vall
On the tree-begloom'd grass vrom the long-zided wall,

An' the bank-zweepen water, wi' shock upon shock,
Do wash down the tongue o' dry ground at the rock;
    An' wold vo'k oonce gaÿ,
      An' litty o' limb,
      Wi' eyes a-wore dim,
    Do now stoop on their waÿ.

There's a stwone that do leän in the churchyard, bespread
Wi' sceäles o' grey mesh up above a green bed,
Wi' the neäme ov a mother that vew, or that nwone
Now alive did behold by the light o' the zun;
Aye, a mother o' mothers, vrom wolder to young,
To the mother that worded my own little tongue,
    An' vound the wall sound,
      An' apple trees trim,
      An' plaÿ'd by the brim
Now a-wash'd vrom the ground.

Oh! now could she come, as we all be a-twold
She walked in her time, o' the comeliest mwold,
An' show us as what we do zee in a dream,
Her looks an' her smiles by the twilighted stream,
Where stars be a-twinklen drough leaves o' the woak,
An' tell us the teäles o' vorgotten wold vo'k
    That woonce did live on,
      In jaÿ or in woe,
      Vrom sprackness to slowness,
    Vrom bloomen to wan.

What maïd wer a-lov'd or what woman wer bride,
Who drooped in their grief or did straïghten wi' pride,
Who praÿ'd in their worship, wi' head bezide head,
Who stood to the beäbes or did murn vor the dead,
Who zot down a-milken in long-sheäded light,
Who knelt up a-thatchen the rick's peäked height,
    What mower wer strong
      Or what haÿmeäker spry,
      Whose waggon roll'd by
Down the woak-sheäded drong.

THE GEATE A-VALLEN TO

In the zunsheen ov our zummers
   Wi' the haÿ time now a–come,
How busy wer we out a–vield
   Wi' vew a–left at hwome,
When waggons rumbled out ov yard
   Red wheeled, wi' body blue,
As back behind 'em loudly slamm'd
   The geäte a–vallèn to.

Drough daysheen ov how many years
   The geäte ha' now a–swung
Behind the veet o' vull–grown men
   An' vootsteps ov the young.
Drough years o' days it swung to us
   Behind each little shoe,
As we tripped lightly on avore
   The geäte a–vallen to.

In evenen time o' starry night
   How mother zot at hwome,
An' kept her bleäzen vire bright
   Till father should ha' come,
An' how she quicken'd up an' smiled
   An' stirred her vire anew,
To hear the trampen ho'ses' steps
   An' geäte a–vallèn to.

There's moon–sheen now in nights o' fall
   When leaves be brown vrom green,
When, to the slammen o' the geäte,
   Our Jenny's ears be keen,
When the wold dog do wag his taïl,
   An' Jeäne could tell to who,
As he do come in drough the geäte,
   The geäte a–vallèn to.

An' oft do come a saddened hour
   When there must goo away
One well–beloved to our heart's core,
   Vor long, perhaps vor aye:

An' oh! it is a touchen thing
The loven heart must rue,
To hear behind his last farewell
The geäte a–vallèn to.

PART III
SELECTIONS FROM BARNES'
WRITINGS

Introduction

William Barnes wrote many articles in the form of letters to the editor of *The Dorset County Chronicle and Somersetshire Gazette*, between 1827 and 1834. The earlier ones, headed "Linguiana", were initialled "W.B." and gave the address Chantry House, Mere; later he used the pen name "Dilettante".

As *The Oxford English Dictionary* records of this word, "in later use generally applied more or less depreciatively to one who interests himself in an art or science merely as a pastime and without serious aim or study ('a mere dilettante')". In adopting this as his pen name Barnes was being both descriptive and defensive; defensive as a self taught man displaying his learning to the mostly well-to-do gentlemen who subscribed to *The Dorset Chronicle*.

In the case of his "Linguiana" pieces in the *Dorset County Chronicle* they ended after one in which he suggested a means of classifying language according to its sources. A gentleman, who lived in Basingstoke and used the pen name "Qui-Quondam" wrote to the editor.

I have been at various times amused and instructed by your Correspondent, who signs himself Linguiana, but although his various examples are extremely pretty, yet they prove nothing, and are little better than truisms. That the English is a compound of various languages every person knows – nor is it in the least remarkable that Latin words occur in our language. Commerce and conquest will at all times introduce new words, and it would be a greater matter of surprise if the Latin did not form the basis of our language. By the same rule, the Greek became blended with the Latin, and hence we find Greek words which have outlived the wreck of languages, and are used even in the present day.

He then supplied "a few instances of the closest similarity existing between Sanscrit and Latin". (*Dorset County Chronicle*, 10 April 1828). Barnes responded to this with further observations on linguistic roots, and the correspondence ended with Qui-Quondam writing more on the subject and also observing, very patronisingly, "If any remarks of mine may have given pain to his modest worth, I frankly acknowledge my regrets".

The "Linguiana" letters reprinted here give early expression of

223

Barnes' wish that English words could be devised to avoid further introduction of foreign words into the language.

Barnes' Dilettante letters to the *Dorset County Chronicle* covered a wide range of subject, from describing the activities of a local inventor ("The Village Genius", 12 November 1829), reflecting on "Burial" (2 July 1829), praising church pews (15 April 1830, 17 September 1829 and 20 August 1829), advising the editor on the probable origins of mumming (3 April 1828) and on the rise to prominence of Antwerp (27 December 1832). He even provided an "Arithmetical Problem" to the newspaper (12 May 1828). As a group they comprise a mixed bag of random erudition, moralising, and mild eccentricity. The tone is much more conservative than in some of his later writings, indeed whilst vividly depicting the poverty of the farm labourer he could become very reactionary (following Richard Oastler, the conservative factory reformer) on the lot of convicted criminals.

. . . he is sent to a palace, compared with his own hut; he is shielded from the cold by sound walls and fire; he has enough of food and clothing; if he is ill he has a medical attendant sent to him; the magistrates come to assure themselves that he is attended to, that his habitation is kept neat, and that no severity is used towards him by his keeper. Perhaps he works at the tread mill; that is not harder work than many kinds of field labour (2 September 1830).

These letters to *The Dorset County Chronicle* have received less attention than most of his other writings. The selections reprinted here are the more interesting ones, pieces which throw more light on topics and attitudes expressed in his poetry of that period.

AUCTIONS

Dilettante Letter, *Dorset County Chronicle*, 24 September 1829

Na almoeda tem a barba queda   Portuguese Proverb

At a sale keep your beard still.

What a seducing thing to the idle is a sale in a village! How gratifying to guess our neighbour's plan in bidding for this or that article; to discover what young woman is near matrimony, from her buying "something towards housekeeping": how pleasant to hear the witty sayings of the auctioneer, that one may relate them to one's next tea party; and, above all, to sit in continual expectation that fortune may throw "a good bargain" into one's hands. To vary the quiet sameness of a village existence, I lately went to one of these animated scenes, where I found that the auctioneer's jest and jug had put the company into such a good humour, that the wise admonition of my proverb seemed quite disregarded. Another proverb – a good comment on mine – says, that what we do not want, is dear at any price; and believing in the truth of the assertion, I could not help smiling at some of my neighbour's "good bargains". The roasting-jack was knocked down to the poor widow, with whom it was likely to make as many revolutions in a year as the earth does, and a few less than her spinning wheel: a cradle became the property of a grey patriarch, whose offspring had long ago reached the height of the military standard: and half a dozen chairs "went off" to a recruiting sergeant.

In one part of the room the matron was examining her china; in another the promised damsel inspected her chest of drawers, blushing with the idea of depositing in it, ere long, her wedding dress, and other acquisitions of her industry and expected prosperity; while a wicked little girl behind was pinning the village schoolmaster's black coat (in which he had ruled two generations of scholars) to the blacksmith's fustian jacket.

When the last lot had been knocked down, I went home, and sitting down by the fire-side, fell into the following train of thought – How different are the circumstances in which men expose their property to public sale: sometimes the individual is about to "change his residence"; then his mind is busy with thoughts of a fresh habitation, new connextions, and different amusements, and he is delighted with the foretaste of prosperity, or agitated by the fear of the reverse. Sometimes he is "retiring from business", then he is happy in the hope of leaving the bustle of the world, and gliding through a smoother existence; he fore-enjoys the genteel cottage in the pretty village, the morning drive in the neat little vehicle, the armchair by the fire-side, and the snug tea party of kind and genteel neighbours. Sometimes his goods are seized by the sheriff for rent. Alas! a sale is generally followed by a change of circumstance, and that is a thing which at best fills the mind with solicitude; but the feelings of an honest man in the last case are horrible. The thought of coming poverty makes him sad – the necessary dispersion of his children chills his heart, he trembles with agony when he thinks of the sorrows and sufferings of his wife, and the villany of men who have cheated and deserted him excites him to madness; but he reflects on the former goodness of God, and remembers his own sins, and weeps.

A sale of the last mentioned kind of an uncle's stock, and which I saw when a boy, made on my mind a strong impression. My uncle was a farmer in the West of England, but became insolvent from the depression of the agricultural interest after the end of the French war. My aunt had a numerous family, and her long exercised solicitude as a mother, and her continual struggles against misfortunes, had nearly brought her with sorrow to the grave – she was calm, and it was only when either of her daughters passed her, that a tear rolled down her sallow cheek. The young men were in that severe and reckless mood in which men are frequently thrown when assailed by misfortunes, which they can still resist. The girls were bewildered and scarcely knew what happened around them: then were driven away the cows under which the weeping milkmaid had so often sung the simple songs of the country; then went the waggon in which the merry haymakers had so many times rode in to the feast of harvest home; and in short then everything that was dear from familiarity was taken away, and my uncle as he looked on the fields he had so long cultivated with hope, and of which he had taken the produce in grateful joy, sighed and dropped a tear as if he had said, "*Dulcia linquimus arva*".

GARDENING

Dilettante Letter, *Dorset County Chronicle*, 19 November 1829

"Nihil est agricultura melieu, nihil dulciat"   Cicero

There is nothing better or more delightful than agriculture.

I had been working in my garden. The sun was just below the horizon, and the dew was already on the smooth green walks, bordered by sweet-smelling roses and carnations. The stillness of the evening was broken only by the whistling of the blackbird, and the splashing of the water, when the trout sprung after the lively insects that floated in wild mazes over the ponds. I sat down on a rude seat I had formed beneath some old trees that darkened the twilight of the evening into an awful gloom, and as the smell of the bean-blossoms was wafted along on the cool air and I thought on the fruit and plants that were ripening around me, I exclaimed to myself, "*O fortunatos, sua si bena norint, Agricolas!*" How happy, if they know their bliss, are they who till the ground.

Gardening is one of the sweetest amusements that an unambitious man, who lives far from the din of cities, can find; and it is so different from many pleasures which, besides being short, are followed by listlessness or remorse, that it gives one a long and pleasing anticipation of crops, and an increasing gratification while they are growing; and, instead of being expensive, rewards a man for every hour he spends in it. Gardening is an occupation pleasing in itself, because it gives one those cheerful feelings of high health, which always arise from exercise; and because one has always the satisfaction of finding the plot, the path, or the border, visibly bettered by the shorter labour; and the growth of plants, the unfolding of blossoms, and the keeping of fruit, all our own, give us a lasting gratification, which is varied and increased as they assume their shape and colour in growing to perfection: and there is such a numerous succession of flowers and vegetables, from the snow drop that blooms and dies in the cold winds of February, to the gigantic rosemallow of August; and from the fair young potato – the untimely fruit of the spring – to the scarlet blossomed tendril of the late French bean; that the attention is never weary, and the appetite never cloyed. But there are other gratifications in this pleasing occupation. For though the gardener knows that the smallest blade of grass is nothing less than a stupendous work of omnipotence, he yet finds that the growth of plants is regulated and perfected by his skill and attention; so that when he receives the fruits of the soil he has tilled, he proudly identifies his labour in the creation of them. And how much sweeter do things seem when they are the long-known productions of one's own soil, than when we buy them from strange hands! and how pleasing it is to know that, whether one prefers the red and juicy radish, or the cucumber that stretches its tough and bulky body on the warm earth, or whether one wishes for the crooked pear or the yellow apricot; all are within one's reach! and all one's own!

Considering the pleasure and profits of gardening, what a pity it is that the excellent practice of letting out portions of ground to the poor to till in their leisure hours is not more common. The labourer, with his bit of ground, toils for his future wants when he would, without it, be wasting his time spending his little money, and losing his good habits in drinking. And if he is thrown for a week out of work his little farm gives him a profitable occupation, and enables him to live without that paralysing and demoralising help, parish pay. There can be no doubt that the poor man, who knows that he can gain additional good by extra labour, will work very hard and suffer many wants before he will give up his independence of spirit to the overseer. I have known one who was toiling in the field, not only in the twilight of morning, but when the moon shone from on high over the cottage, in which his wife and little offspring had long been sunk into deep sleep.

ASSOCIATIONS

Dilettante Letter, *Dorset County Chronicle* (Part)   24 December 1829

Man, who is naturally and singly one of the most defenceless of
animals, becomes so mighty by intelligence and union that he
governs the whole creation with perfect ease.

[The friendly Societies and the contributary Asylum .... in a district or
in a state.] They are the finest fortresses against the inroads of want and
misery that man ever erected: and I am proud in expecting that through
the fine example of a good gentleman, the latter will soon be, as the
former is already, found in my native and ever-beloved county, Dorset.
Friendly Societies better the moral character of their members, as well as
their state in affliction; for they must be industrious and prudent to save
their contributions; and so far are they from losing their independent
spirit in receiving the club allowance, as in living by parish relief, that
they claim it with pride, as the earning of their own labours.

These ideas were conceived in seeing the yearly meeting of a Friendly
Society in my own parish, when they went to the church to hear an
appropriate discourse from the pulpit, and afterwards dined together.
This "club-walking", of course, made a general holiday and every body
went to see the procession, which moved with becoming dignity. First
went a band of wind-instruments, playing "Auld Lang Syne", and then
the flag, on which were printed "the bee-hive" and "joined hands", with
other emblems of industry and friendship; next to this were the honorary
members, or gentlemen whose contributions were gratuitous, and lastly
walked the Friends, two by two, and each bearing the badge of the
society, a knot of ribbon, in his hat. On each side was a motley crowd of
spectators, and among them, lots of noisy young urchins, whose dim and
ragged garments, dangling in tatters about their naked legs, shewed, by
a melancholy contrast with the glossy coats of the club men, that their
fathers were not among them. These were so eager and so thick that they
trod on each other's heels, but as their nether extremities were in primeval
nakedness, they were not kept back by the teazing necessity of adjusting
the shoe. In another part were seen the ruddy young women of the
village, pointing out, or nodding to, their brothers and friends in the
procession: and even the old women, who spent fifty Sundays of the year
in squalid indolence by the glowing embers of the cottage hearth, took
the staff that supported the almost forgotten form of her grandmother,
and tottered to church.

It is doubtful whether these yearly meetings are beneficial or hurtful to
Friendly Societies, and perhaps something may be said of and against
them. The pomp of the procession, in which the gentlemen constituting
the honorary members, walk with the clubmen; the joyous feast in which
the gentlemen sit down with them, and other distinctions of the day,
perhaps, bring into the society men who might not otherwise join it, and
the only evils in it seem to be those of excess in drinking and its common

effect in low life, quarrelling, through which the "friends" sometimes realize the Irish song –

"They meet with a friend and for love knock him down".

Though the calculations upon which these parish societies are grounded may be wrong, and though the county societies may excel them, they still deserve our respect as the good invention of which the others are an improvement.

THE CHURCH AND CULTURE

Dilettante Letter, dated 29 March 1834,
Dorset County Chronicle, 3 April 1834

While pondering on the origin, or revival, and progress in Europe of the fine arts, architecture, sculpture, painting and music, I have naturally wished to answer myself the question – What has had the greatest influence in advancing them? I think a state religion or episcopal church has done so. I will not dwell on the architecture and statuary of Greece; the geometical harmony and stateliness of the former make it a system of absolute perfection; and the latter, if it has been equalled, has not been, and perhaps cannot be, excelled: but I mean to confine myself chiefly to the arts as they have advanced under Christianity. It was decidedly an episcopal church that introduced and perfected that fine style of architecture of which we have such admirable examples in our cathedrals and collegiate churches: a style in which delicacy of enrichment is so blended with strength of structure, and lightness and stateliness, that we can hardly conceive it capable of improvement: but we may fairly infer that only an episcopal establishment, or something like it, would have perfected that style, because no one among a community of little congregations; that is, no particular parish, would perhaps be found with the means of executing a great and rich design; and consequently, the talents of great architects would not have been brought into action; and the demand for architectural enrichments would not have been great enough to bring the art of working them to a state of perfection.

The church, it is true, did not bring sculpture in this part of Europe to what it was anciently in Greece; but nearly all that was done in advancing it, the church did; and that fine system of carving – the flowing tracery introduced as the enrichment of the pointed arch – originated wholly in the church; and, as is shown by our screens, seats, windows, and panelling, was carried to a high pitch of excellence. Nor must we deny that the altar tomb in its many modifications, an object more stately and not less elegant than the Greek Sacrophagus, has the same origin as church architecture, or forget that some of the figures upon them must be considered, even now, fine productions of the chisel.

It was the influence of the episcopal church of Rome that revived and perfected painting in Italy; for as there was in that church a continual demand for masterly altar pieces, and scripture paintings for the great churches, that sublime school of painting called the Florentine or Italian was under her influence carried to the highest pitch of perfection; since the painter was not only sure to sell his production, but to get any price that might be justified by its excellence; and thus, Da Vinci, Angelo, Raphael, Romano and other great masters, studied with zeal, and worked with enthusiasm, seeing that wealth and immortality might be the rewards of their diligence; and if the English are inferior to the Italians in historical painting, and to the Grecians in sculpture, it is perhaps because they have not, like the former, a great demand for church pictures; or, like the latter, for marble deities. They perhaps excel in animal and portrait painting, because portraits of gentlemen and ladies, and fine horses, and dogs, are much called for.

The same church must also be looked to as the cause of the restoration of music, and the perfection of the doctrine of harmony. The church perfected that noble, though complicated instrument, the organ, by which, as a good composing instrument were soon detected the laws of counterpoint and modulation: laws well understood by the old composers of sacred harmony, as they have shown by some of their noble services and chants; their fine anthems, and the best of those peculiar and difficult compositions the ancient Canons, an example of which we have in *"Non nobis Domine"*. It was to write such compositions as these for the singers in the church service that Argtzne made his great invention of that alphabet of melody the stave and notes. Germany, which can send us such men as Mozart and Handel, has numerous schools of music in the chapels of her princes. The arrangment and action of the keys on the finger board of the church organ having once accomplished, they were easily transferred to Spit - ets, Harp - mithords, Pianofortes and Ealophons. These things (the arrangement and action of the keys) at their first invention, must have been some of the greatest difficulties.

HUMAN PROGRESSION

Dilettante Letter, *Dorset County Chronicle* (Part) 16 July 1829

L'Homme, des lois et des arts l'inventeur admirable
Aveugie pour lui seul, ne peut il discerner,
Quand il n'est question que de se gouverner
La faux bien du bien veritable."

Madam Deseoulieres

Man, the admirable inventor of laws and arts,
blind only to his own ways, when he is
required to govern himself, can he not distinguish the good from the evil?

A great distinction between man and the beasts that perish is that he is
a progressive animal; in one age he covers himself with the skins of
quadrupeds, and shelters himself in caves; in another he is "clad in purple
and fine linen", and dwells in "cloud-capped towers and gorgeous
palaces..."

Progression is not only the distinction of the species, but is the great
promoter of activity with its single members. The man of science always
follows his studies with diligence when he finds himself *advancing* in
wisdom and fame. The trader is unceasingly active where he finds himself advancing towards independence. The labourer works with an
unwearied vigour when he finds that his toil betters his state. But obviate
the progress of these diligent beings; let it be impossible for them to
advance themselves in society by their exertions; their activity ceases; or
perhaps, they begin a course of vice, and become progressive in wicked-
ness: for the mind of man is like a river; if it be turned out of its proper
channel, in which it is a blessing to the world, it will proceed in an
improper course, and become a curse...

With this idea of human progression, how watchful should we be over
our children, and pupils, and our own lives. We should habituate
ourselves to a course of industry and virtue, and shun indulgences of
idleness and vice as the greatest dangers. It is not because children are
taught to read and write at the charity schools, that those establishments
are so beneficial to a state; but because they "train up a child in the way he
should go", and consequently, obviate his progress in a wrong course.

From the consideration of the progressive habits of man, we find the
demoralising tendency of very low wages, and the plan of paying the
poor a *fixed sum* per man out of parish funds; for when a man knows that
he cannot better his condition by exertion, his exertion ceases. And if his
daily wants should leave an odd shilling in his pocket, he spends it in the
alehouse, and becomes "progressive" in sloth. I know a venerable old
man who is not only wealthy himself, but is the patriarch of an industrious and prosperous offspring; when he was young it was possible for
an agricultural labourer, by great industry and frugality, to become

a little farmer himself. He was a labourer, and became a farmer by the exercise of those virtues, and he prospered; but when business became monopolised, and wages are very low, the labourer has no longer a possibility of advancing himself in society by his exertions, and therefore he no longer strives to do it. The only way to keep up the industrious and independent spirit of the poor man, is to reward him according to his labour, and to respect him for his virtues, instead of despising him for his poverty.

LINGUIANA

(1) Letter, *Dorset County Chronicle*, 7 February 1828

When national improvement, by introducing new objects and new ideas, brings in also a necessity for new words, it is better to borrow them from a foreign language, as we have done to a singular extent, or to frame them from one's own as the Grecians and others did, and the Germans &c., have done more recently. The question has often occurred to my mind, and if I were not a little biassed by the practice of the country, I should certainly advocate for the latter plan for several reasons, which I will state to you in due order.

The first is, that such borrowed words, (particularly French), coming from a language the genius of which is different from that of our own, disorder our orthoepy, and are mispronounced by very many because they are not certain whether they should be pronounced as foreign words or not.

I know that it is customary with you editorial gentlemen to distinguish these aliens, for some time after their arrival, by a particular dress (italics); but we get no rules of pronunciation from this laudable practice, Sir; for the word "Corps" and many others have long had this distinction, and yet, were a person to read, in company, that a certain officer's "Corps" had been cut to pieces in some engagement, it would, perhaps, be remarked that it was quite diabolical to carry revenge so far as to mangle the dead; though, at the same time, were he to pronounce the word "Messieurs" in the French manner, he would be sneered at for his affectation.

I think you "Messieurs" Editors, who are men of known influence in the literary world, would issue a decree to the effect that when foreign words should be first brought on trial into the British service, they should be used only by the learned, the only competent judges of their merit; and that when their term of probation (which you should state) should be accomplished, you would clothe them in your uniform to signify that they might be then treated with the familiarity used towards other English subjects. In this case you would, of course, keep a register, (which might be called a register of aliens, in which you would write the epoch of their entering our service; and, if no objection should be made to their naturalization at the proper time, they could be struck off your list and transferred to the dictionary.

(Gives examples of French words used in speech) . . .

I do not dislike the French language, Sir, on the contrary, I am very fond of that as well as the other pretty daughters of the Latin, and have taken, and intend to take, much trouble to make myself acquainted with them; but at the same time I admire the *expressive* features of my native tongue, and do not like to see her bedaubed with French Rou-. Sir, I was just going to shew a practice at variance with my professions by saying *Rouge*; but as it is a French word signifying *red*, I shall call the cosmetic *Redding*, an epithet which will sufficiently distinguish it from the red article for marking sheep, &c., carried about on asses, or donkeys, or neddies, (remark, Sir, the copiousness of our language, need we borrow words?) that commodity being called *Reddie*.

Next week, if you please, I will state my second objection to the practice of borrowing from the French, &c., and if you would have a corner for me in your "vehicle" of knowledge, I shall frequently become one of your passengers.

The following, Sir, is a pretty faithful specimen of modern English:

"The dramatic 'Corps' of the A＿＿＿＿ Theatre have had a valuable accession in Miss B＿＿＿＿, who made her 'Debut' last night with great 'Eclat'; she is a fine young lady, though perhaps a little too 'enbonpoint'.

Now, Sir, how oddly this would read in French with English words, where French are now inserted:

"Le 'Body' dramatique due Theatre d'A＿＿＿＿ a reçu une accession importante en Madlle. B＿＿＿＿, qui fit son 'Essay' la soirée passée avec beaucoup de 'Brillancy'; elle est une belle Damoiselle quoique elle soit, peuthée, un peu trop 'plump'."

LINGUIANA

(2) Letter, *Dorset County Chronicle*, 14 February 1828

My second objection to the adoption of so many French and other foreign words, is, that their critical meaning is not so easily acquired or remembered as that of words formed from our own language, and, consequently, that they are liable to a sort of misapplication, of which the following are examples.

One individual, on being asked if certain people carry on their manufacture by *manual* labour, answers that they do not; *women* only being employed about it. A second expresses himself flattered when he is told that he is a man of great NE*science*, and remarks that same friend of his possesses great *magnanimity* (great *mind*edness) of *mind*. A third observes that the bees build a *super*structure (building above) *downwards*; and it is frequently said that a person has a great aversion (a turning *from*) *to* a thing.

If an English Newspaper, Sir, should be styled in plain English, the "Common News", every body would know what sort of information might be expected from it; but if it should bear the German title of "Allegemeine Zeitung" there would be very many readers to whom the title would not discover the character; and if we adopt a thousand words which want an explanation, instead of the like number which do not, we at least render our language more difficult to be acquired, if we do not place it above common intelligence.

The following compound words from the German shew how easily words may be formed from existing primitives, and that they may be sufficiently expressive.

German	Literal meaning	English equivalents generally borrowed for:
Baumwolle	Tree wool	Cotton
Reisse-sack	Riding-bag	Portmanteau
Herrlickheit	Lordliness	Magnificence
Bildhauer	Image-carver	Sculptor
Menschwerdung	Man-becoming	Incarnation
Christliche Liebe	Christlike-love	Charity
Wundarzt	Wound-artist	Surgeon
Handschuhe	Hand-shoes	Gloves
Widerwille	Contrary will	Antipathy
Kindlickeit	Child-likeness	Innocence
Ausnahme	Out-taking	Exception
RedeKunst	Speaking art	Rhetoric
Vorrede	Fore speech	Preface
Grossmuth	Great mind	Magnanimity
Uneinigkeit	Un–one–ness	Discord
Beschluss.	Lock-up	Conclusion

In the same manner, though the French have adopted our Steam Boat, they have framed an epithet for it from their own language "Bateau de Vapeur"; but we have introduced their "tout ensemble" and their "belles assemble", their "coups" from the "Coup de Grace" down to their "Coup de Pié" or "Coup of *dis*grace" with their "Double entendre", *double meaning*, which John Bull frequently "N'entend pas" does not know the *meaning* of at all; and in short, to rehearse them after the well-known poetical orders of Paddy Carey's admirer;

Their *dejeuné à la fourchette*,

And dinner of *etiquette*;

Their *"beau monde"*

Of *Brunette* and *blonde"*

With *bon mots*

So *apropos*

And their *On dit*

What is going to be

Their *"soi disant"*

And *ci devant*

With *sang froid*

And "je ne scais quoi   de plus, Mr. L'Editeur

But the foregoing are some of those that do not carry their own meaning to a bare English Scholar, nor can their signification be ascertained from an English Dictionary which does not give them place.

LINGUIANA

(3) Letter, *Dorset County Chronicle*, 21 February 1828

My last reason for disliking the adoption of so much continental phraseology is, that being of a different character from that of our own language, it does not coalesce with it. It is like substituting a wire for the string of a violin, and destroys that general consistency of sound observable in all languages which have not vitiated their characters by admitting sounds incompatible with them.

Observe, Sir, the consistent power of the following specimen of German, a language which in nervous force is certainly unrivalled in Europe.

Und	*die*	*Erde*	*war*	*wneste*		*und leer;*	*und*	*es*
And	the	Earth	was	without form	and void;		and	it

war	*finster*	*auf*	*der*	*Erde;*	*und*	*der*	*Geist*	*Gottes*
was	dark	upon	the	Earth;	and	the	spirit of	God

schwebete	*auf*	*dem*	*wasser.*
moved	upon	the	water.

Now to substitute Italian words for some of the foregoing would be like endeavouring to incorporate the characteristics of a dandy with those of a noble British sailor.

Unde die "Terra" war wusta und "vota" und es war "tenebrosa"
auf die "terra" und der "spirito" Gottes schwebete auf dem "acqua".

The German is remarkable for *strength*, the Italian for *sweetness*, and these languages therefore, are as incompatible as the muscular strength of a warrior with the tender beauties of a pretty woman, and such I conceive is the case with the English and the French.

PART IV
GLOSSARY OF DORSET WORDS

A LIST OF
SOME DORSET WORDS

Anewst,)
Anightst,) very near, or nearly.
A'r a, ever a, as.
A'r a dog, ever a dog.
Amper, pus.
A'r'n, e'er a one.
A-stooded (as a waggon), with wheels sunk fast into rotten ground.
A-stogged,) with feet stuck fast in
A-stocked,) clay.
A-strout, stiff stretched.
A-thirt, athwart (*th* soft).
A-vore, afore, before.
Ax, ask.
Axan, ashes.
A-zew, dry, milkless.

Backbran' (brand), (A block of wood
Backbron' (brond), (put on the back of (the fire.
Ballywrag, scold.
Bandy, a long stick with a bent end to beat abroad cow-dung.
Barken,) a stack-yard or cow-yard.
Barton,)
Bavèn, a faggot of long brushwood.
Beä'nhan', bear in hand, uphold or maintain, as an opinion or otherwise.
Beät up, to beat one's way up.
Bennets, flower-stalks of grass.
Be'th, birth.
Bibber, to shake with cold.
Bittle, a beetle.
Blatch, black stuff; smut.
Blather, a bladder.
Bleäre, to low as a cow.
Blind-buck o' Davy, blindman's buff.
Bloodywarrior, the ruddy Stock gilliflower.
Blooèns, blossoms.
Blooth, blossom in the main.
Bluevinny, blue mouldy.
Brack, a breach.

Bran', a brand.
Brantèn, brazen-faced.
Bring-gwaïn (bring-going), to bring one on his way.
Brocks, broken pieces (as of food).
Bron', a brand.
Bruckly, Bruckle, brittle.
Bundle, to bound off; go away quickly.
Bu'st, burst.

Caddle, a muddle.
Car, to carry.
Cassen, casn, canst not.
Chanker, a wide chink.
Charm, a noise as of many voices.
Choor, a chare, a (weekly) job of house work.
Clack,) a bird-clacker;
Clacker,) a bird-boy's clacking tool, to fray away birds; also the tongue.
Clavy,)
Clavy-bwoard,) the mantel-shelf.
Clèden, cleavers, goosegrass.
Clips, to clasp.
Clitty, clingy.
Clocks, ornaments on the ankles of stockings.
Clom', clomb, climbed.
Clote, the yellow water-lily.
Clout, a blow with the flat hand.
Clum, to handle clumsily.
Cluster o' vive (cluster of five), the fist or hand with its five fingers; wording taken from a cluster of nuts.
Cockle, cuckle, the bur of the burdock.
Cockleshell, snail shell.
Colepexy, to glean the few apples left on the tree after picking.
Coll, to embrace.
Conker, the hip, or hep; the fruit of the briar.
Cothe, coath (*th* soft), a disease of sheep.

Cou'den, could not.
Coussen,) *coosn*, couldest not.
Coossen,)
Craze, to crack a little.
Critch, a big pitcher.
Crock, an iron cooking-pot.
Croodle, to crow softly.
Croop,   ) to bend the body; to
Croopy-down,) stoop.
Crope, crept.
Crowshell, shell of the fresh–water
    mussel, as taken out of the river for
    food by crows.
Cubby-hole,   ) between the father's
Cubby-house,) knees.
Culver, the wood pigeon.
Cweïn,) coin.
Cwoïn,)
Cwoffer, a coffer.

Dadder, dather, dudder, to maze or
    bewilder.
Dag, childag, a chilblain.
Dake, to ding or push forth.
Daps, the very likeness, as that of
    a cast from the same mould.
Dent, a dint.
Dewberry, a big kind of blackberry.
Dibs, coins; the small, knee bones
    of a sheep used in the game of
    Dibs.
Didden (didn), did not.
Dod, a dump.
Don, to put on.
Doust, dust.
Drashel, threshold.
Dreaten, threaten.
Dree, three.
Droat, throat.
Drong, throng; also a narrow
    way.
Drough, through.
Drow, throw.
Drub, throb.
Drush, thrush.
Drust, thrust.
Drean, Drène, to drawl.
Drève, drive.
Duck, a darkening, dusk.
Dumbledore, the bee.
Dummet, dusk.

Dunch, dull of hearing, or
    mind.
Dunch-nettle, the dead nettle.
Dunch-pudden, pudding of bare
    dough.
Dungpot, a dungcart.
Dunt, to blunten as an edge or pain.
Durns, the side posts of a door.

Eegrass, aftermath.
Eltrot, cowparsley.
Emmet, an ant.
Emmetbut, an anthill.
En, him.
Eve, to become wet as a cold stone
    floor.
Evet, eft, newt.
Exe, an axle.

Fakket, a faggot.
Fall, autumn; to fall down is
    vall.
Faÿ, to speed, succeed.
Feäst, a village wake or festival.
Flag, a water plant.
Flinders, flying pieces of a body
    smashed; "Hit it all to flinders."
Flounce, a flying fall as into
    water.
Flout, a flinging, or blow of one.
Flush, fledged.
Footy, unhandily little.

Gally, to frighten, fray.
Gee, jee, to go, fit, speed.
Giddygander, the meadow orchis.
Gil'cup, gilt cup, the buttercup.
Girt, great.
Glēne, to smile sneeringly.
Glutch, to swallow.
Gnang, to mock one with jaw
    waggings, and noisy sounds.
Gnot, a gnat.
Goo, go.
Goodnow, good neighbour; my good
    friend.
Goolden chain, the laburnum.
Gout, an underground gutter.
Grægle,) the wild hyacinth.
Greygle,)
Gramfer, grandfather.

Ground-ash, an ash stick that springs from the ground, and so is tough.

Gwoad, a goad.

Hacker, a hoe.

Hagrod, hagridden in sleep, if not under the nightmare.

Haïn, to fence in ground or shut up a field for mowing.

Ha'me, see *Hau'm.*

Hangèn, sloping ground.

Hansel,)
Handsel,) a hand gift.

Hansel,) to use a new thing for
Handsel,) the first time.

Happer, to hop up as hailstones or rain-drops

Haps, a hasp.

Ha'skim, halfskim cheese of milk skimmed only once.

Hassen, hast not.

Haum,) the hollow stalks of plants.
Haulm,) Teätie haum, potatoe
Hulm,) stalks.

Hatch, a low wicket or half door.

Haÿmeäkèn, haymaking.

Hazen, to forebode.

Hazzle, hazel.

Heal, hide, to cover.

Heän, a haft, handle.

Heft, weight.

Herence, hence.

Here right, here on the spot, etc.

Het, heat, also a heat in running.

Het, to hit.

Heth, a hearth, a heath.

Hick, to hop on one leg.

Hidelock,)
Hidlock,) a hiding place.

Hidybuck, hide-and-seek, the game.

Hile of Sheaves, ten, a ridge, and 1 at each end.

Ho, to feel misgiving care.

Holm, ho'me, holly.

Hook, to gore as a cow.

Honeyzuck, honeysuckle.

Ho'se-tinger, the dragonfly.

Hud, a pod, a hood-like thing.

Ho'se, hoss, a board on which a ditcher may stand in a wet ditch.

Hull, a pod, a hollow thing.

Humbuz, a notched strip of lath, swung round on a string, and humming or buzzing.

Humstrum, a rude, home-made musical instrument, now given up.

Jack-o'-lent, a man-like scarecrow.

Jist, just.

Jut, to nudge or jog quickly.

Kag, a keg.

Kapple cow, a cow with a white muzzle.

Kern, to grow into fruit.

Ketch,) to thicken or harden, as
Katch,) melted fat.

Kecks,) a stem of the hemlock or
Kex,) cowparsley.

Keys, the seed vessels of the sycamore.

Kid, a pod, as of the pea.

Kittyboots, low laced boots.

Knap, a hillock, or knob.

Laïter, one run of laying of a hen.

Leän, to lean.

Leäne, a lane.

Leäse, to glean.

Leäse,)
Leäze,) an unmown field.

Leer, Leery, empty.

Lence, a loan, a lending.

Levers, Livers, the corn flag.

Lew, sheltered from cold wind.

Lewth, lewness.

Libbets, loose-hanging rags.

Limber, limp.

Linch, Linchet, a ledge on a hillside.

Litsome, lightsome, gay.

Litty, light and brisk of body.

Lo't, loft, an upper floor.

Lowl, to loll loosely.

Lumper, a loose step.

Maesh,) moss, also a hole or run of
Mesh,) a hare, fox, or other wild animal.

Mammet, an image, scarecrow.

Marrels,) The game of nine men's
Merrels,) morris.

Mawn, mãn, a kind of basket.

Meäden, stinking chamomile.
Ment, to imitate, be like.
Mēsh, moss.
Mid, might.
Miff, a slight feud, a tiff.
Min, observe. You must know.
Mither ho, come hither. A call to
    a horse on the road.
Moot, the bottom and roots of a felled
    tree.
More, a root, taproot.

Na'r a, never a (man).
Nar'n, never a one.
N'eet, not yet.
Nēsh, soft.
Nesthooden, a hooding over a bird's
    nest, as a wren's.
Never'stide, never at all.
Nicky, a very small fagot of sticks.
Nïppy, hungry, catchy.
Nitch, a big fagot of wood; a load.
Not (hnot or knot), hornless.
Nother, neither (adverb).
Nunch, a nog or knob of food.
Nut (of a wheel), the stock or nave.

O', of.
O'm, of em, them.
O'n, of him.
O's, of us.
Orts, leavings of hay put out in little
    heaps in the fields for the cows.
Over-right, opposite.
Oves, eaves.

Paladore, a traditional name of
    Shaftesbury, the British *Caer Paladr*.
Pank, pant.
Par, to shut up close; confine.
Parrick, a small enclosed field; a
    paddock – but paddock was an old
    word for a toad or frog.
Pa'sels, parcels.
Peärt, pert; lively.
Peaze, Peeze, to ooze.
Peewit, the lapwing.
Plesh, Plush (a hedge), to lay it.
Plim, to swell up.
Plock, a hard block of wood.
Plow, a waggon.

Plounce, a strong plunge.
Pluffy, plump.
Popple, a pebble.
Praïse, prize, to tell others of a pain or
    ailment.
Pummy, pomice.

Quaer, queer.
Quag, a quaking bog.
Quar, a quarry.
Quarrel, a square window pane.
Quid, a cud.
Quirk, to grunt with the breath
    without the voice.

Raft, to rouse, excite.
Rake, to reek.
Ram, Rammish, rank of smell.
Rammil, raw milk (cheese), of
    unskimmed milk.
Ramsclaws, the creeping crowfoot.
Randy, a merry uproar or meeting.
Rangle, to range or reach about.
Rathe, early; whence rather.
Ratch, to stretch.
Readship, criterion, counsel.
Reämes, skeleton, frame.
Reän, to reach in greedily in eating.
Reäves, a frame of little rongs on the
    side of a waggon.
Reed, wheat hulm drawn for
    thatching.
Reely, to dance a reel.
Reem, to stretch, broaden.
Rick, a stack.
Rig, to climb about.
Rivel, shrivel; to wrinkle up.
Robin Hood, the red campion.
Rottlepenny, the yellow rattle.
Rouet, a rough tuft of grass.

Sammy, soft, a soft head; simpleton.
Sar, to serve or give food to (cattle).
Sarch, to search.
Scrag, a crooked branch of a tree.
Scram, distorted, awry.
Scroff, bits of small wood or chips.
Scroop, to skreak lowly as new shoes
    or a gate hinge.
Scote, to shoot along fast in running.
Scud, a sudden shower.

Scwo'ce, chop or exchange.
Shard, a small gap in a hedge.
Sharps, shafts of a waggon.
Shatten, shalt not.
Shroud (trees), to cut off branches.
Sheeted cow, with a broad white band round her body.
Shoulden (Shoodn), should not.
Shrow,)
Sh'ow,) the shrew mouse.
Sh'ow-crop,)
Skim,)
Skimmy,) grass; to cut off rank tuffs.
Slent, a tear in clothes.
Slidder, to slide about.
Slim, sly.
Sloo, sloe.
Slooworm, the slow-worm.
Smame, to smear.
Smeech, a cloud of dust.
Smert, to smart; pain.
Snabble, to snap up quickly.
Snags, small sloes, also stumps.
Sneäd, a scythe stem.
Snoatch, to breathe loudly through the nose.
Snoff, a snuff of a candle.
Sock, a short loud sigh.
Spur (dung), to cast it abroad.
Squaïl, to fling something at a bird or ought else.
Squot, to flatten by a blow.
Sowel,)
Zowel,) a hurdle stake.
Sparbill,)
Sparrabill,) a kind of shoe nail.
Speäker, a long spike of wood to bear the hedger's nitch on his shoulder.
Spears,)
Speers,) the stalks of reed grass.
Spik, spike, lavender.
Sprack, active.
Sprethe, to chap as of the skin, from cold.
Staddle, a bed or frame for ricks.
Staïd, steady, oldish.
Stannens, stalls in a fair or market.
Steän (a road), to lay it in stone.
Steärt, a tail or outsticking thing.
Stitch (of corn), a conical pile of sheaves.

Strawmote, a straw or stalk.
Strent, a long tear.
Stubbard, a kind of apple.
Stunpoll, stone head, blockhead; also an old tree almost dead.

Tack, a shelf on a wall.
Taffle, to tangle, as grass or corn beaten down by storms.
Taït, to play at see-saw.
Tamy, tammy, tough.
Teäve, to reach about strongly as in work or a struggle.
Teery, Tewly, weak of growth.
Tewly, weakly.
Theäse, this or these.
Theasum, these.
Tidden (tidn), it is not.
Tilty, touchy, irritable.
Timmersome, restless.
Tine, to kindle, also to fence in ground.
Tistytosty, a toss ball of cowslip blooms.
To-year, this year (as to-day.)
Tranter, a common carrier.
Trendel, a shallow tub.
Tump, a little mound.
Tun, the top of the chimney above the roof ridge.
Tut (work), piecework.
Tutty, a nosegay.
Tweil, toil.

Unheal, uncover, unroof.

Veag, Vēg, a strong fit of anger.
Vern, fern.
Ve'se, vess, a verse.
Vinny cheese, cheese with a blue-mould.
Vitty, nice in appearance.
Vlanker, a flake of fire.
Vlee, fly.
Vo'k, folk.
Vooty, unhandily little.
Vuz, Vuzzen, furze, gorse.

Wag, to stir.
Wagwanton, quaking grass.

Weäse, a pad or wreath for the head under a milkpail.
Weäle, a ridge of dried hay.
Welshnut, a walnut.
Werden, were not or was not.
Wevet, a spider's web.
Whindlèn, weakly, small of growth.
Whicker, to neigh.
Whiver, to hover, quiver.
Whog, g̈o off; to a horse.
Whur, to fling overhanded.
Wi', with.
Widdicks, small brushwood.
Wink, a winch; crank of a well.
Withwind, the bindweed.
Wont, a mole.
Wops, wasp.
Wotshed,) wet-footed.
Wetshod,)

Wride, to spread out in growth.
Wride, the set of stems or stalks from one root or grain of corn.
Writh, a small wreath of touch wands, to link hurdles to the sowels (stakes).
Wrix, wreathed or wattle work, as a fence.

Yop, yelp.

Zand, sand.
Zennit,) seven night; "This day
Zennight,) zennit."
Zew, azew, milkless.
Zoo, so.
Zive, a scythe.
Zull, a plough to plough ground.
Zwath, a swath.